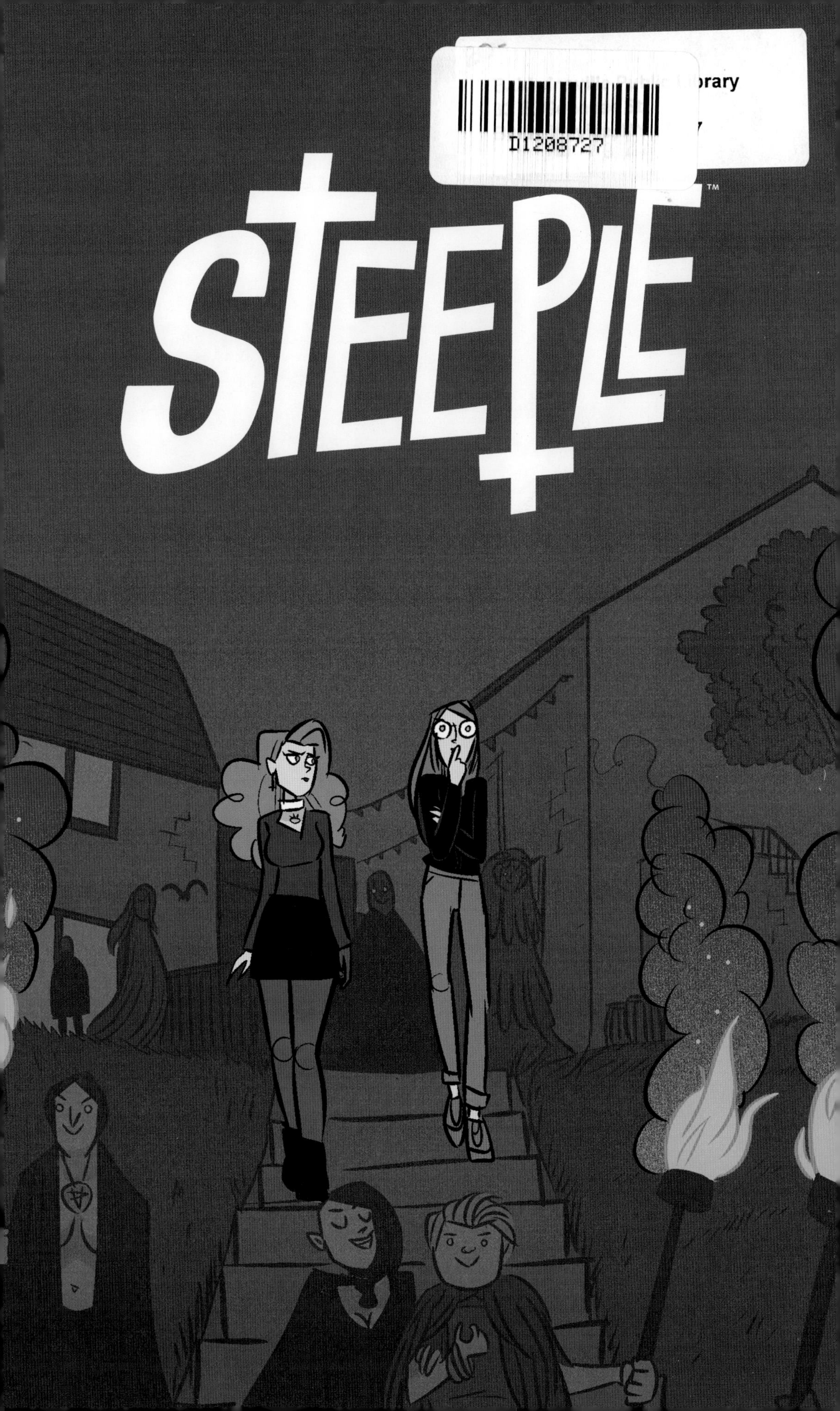
STEEPLE™

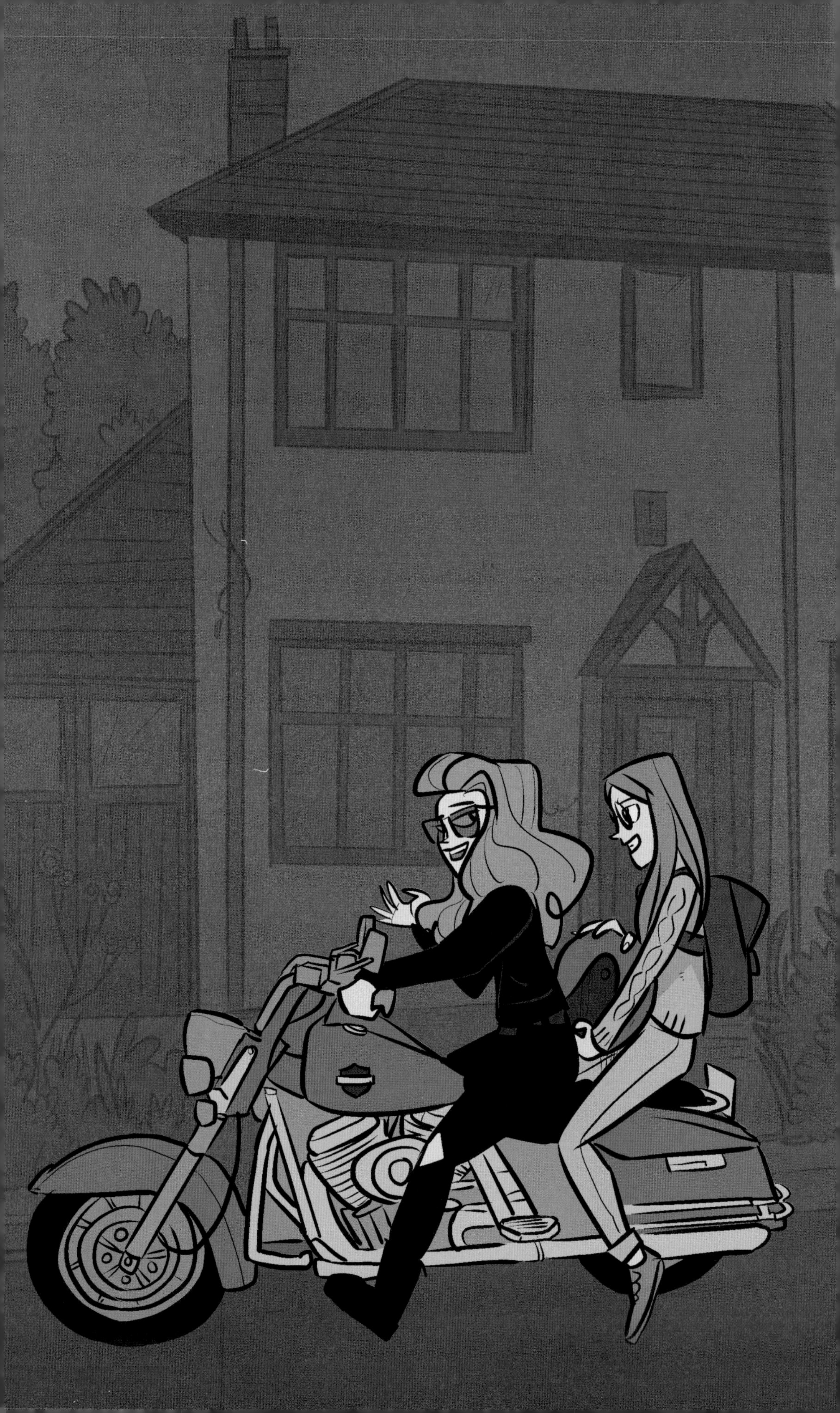

STEEPLE ™

SCRIPT AND ART:
JOHN ALLISON

COLORIST
SARAH STERN

LETTERER
JIM CAMPBELL

CHAPTER BREAKS
JOHN ALLISON WITH SARAH STERN

EPILOGUE SCRIPT, ART, AND COLORS
JOHN ALLISON

COVER BY
JOHN ALLISON

STEEPLE CREATED BY
JOHN ALLISON

DARK HORSE BOOKS

President & Publisher **MIKE RICHARDSON**

Editor **DANIEL CHABON**

Assistant Editor **CHUCK HOWITT**

Graphic Designer **SCOTT ERWERT**

Digital Art Technician **ALLYSON HALLER**

Collects issues #1–#5 of the Dark Horse Comics series *Steeple*.

Library of Congress Cataloging-in-Publication Data

Names: Allison, John, 1976- author, artist. | Stern, Sarah (Colorist),
    colourist. | Campbell, Jim (Letterer), letterer.
Title: Steeple / script and art, John Allison ; colorist, Sarah Stern ;
    letterer, Jim Campbell.
Description: First edition. | Milwaukie, OR : Dark Horse Comics, 2020. |
    "Collects issues #1-#5 of the Dark Horse Comics series Steeple."
Identifiers: LCCN 2019054975 | ISBN 9781506713496 (trade paperback) | ISBN
    9781506713502 (ebook other)
Subjects: LCSH: Comic books, strips, etc.
Classification: LCC PN6728.S7434 A69 2020 | DDC 741.5/973--dc23
LC record available at https://lccn.loc.gov/2019054975

Published by Dark Horse Books | A division of Dark Horse Comics LLC | 10956 SE Main Street, Milwaukie, OR 97222

DarkHorse.com
To find a comics shop in your area, visit comicshoplocator.com
First edition: May 2020
978-1-50671-349-6

1 3 5 7 9 10 8 6 4 2
Printed in China

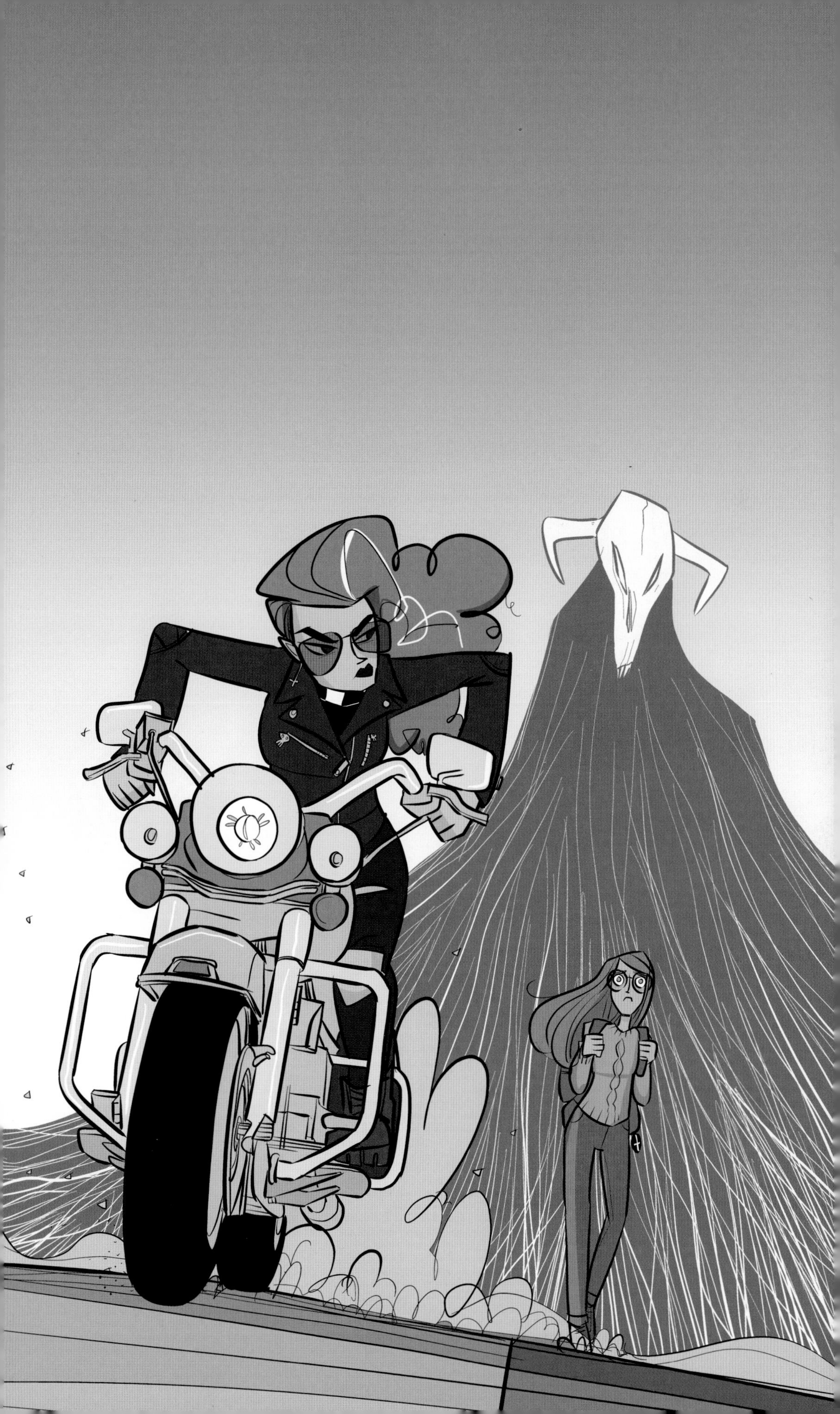

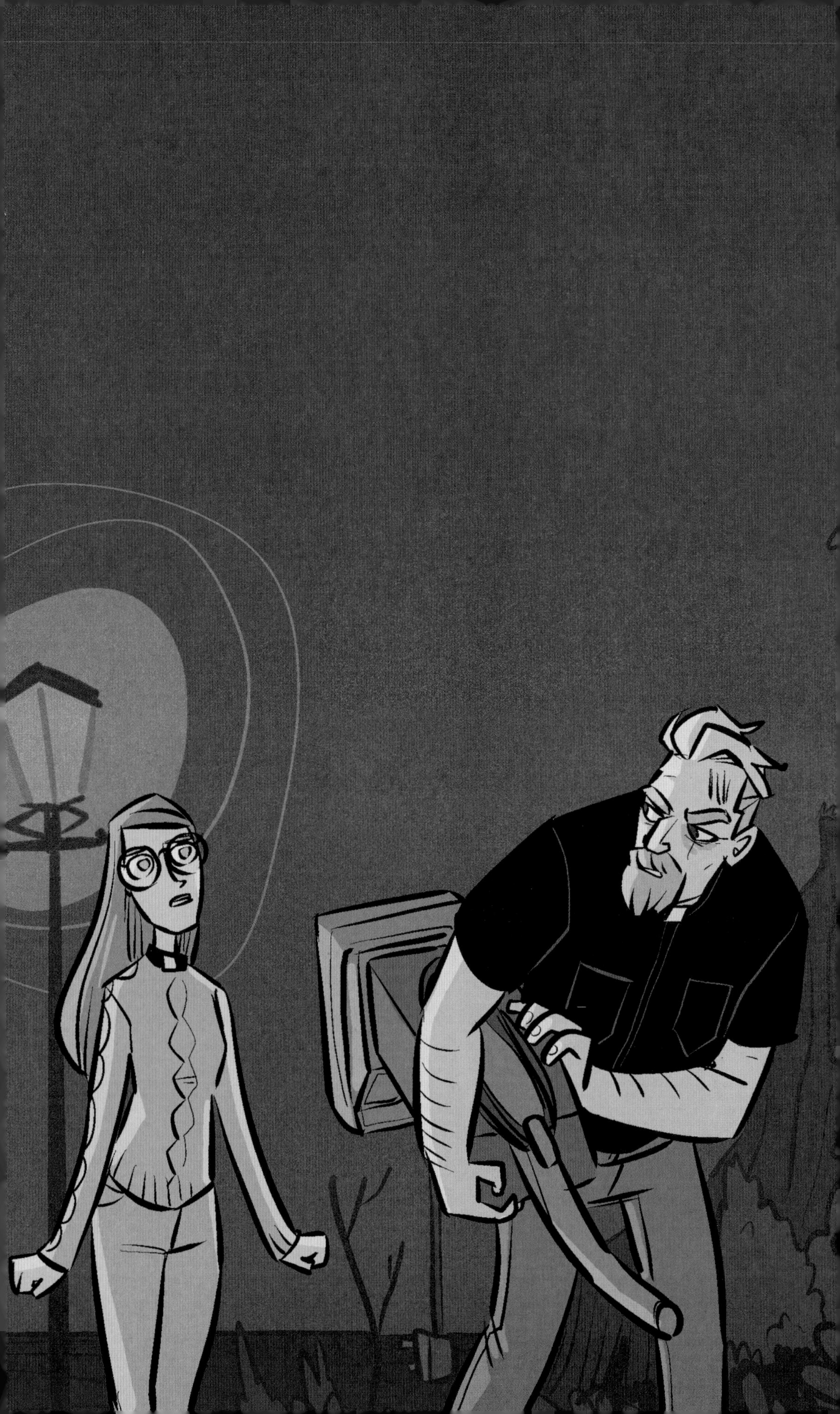

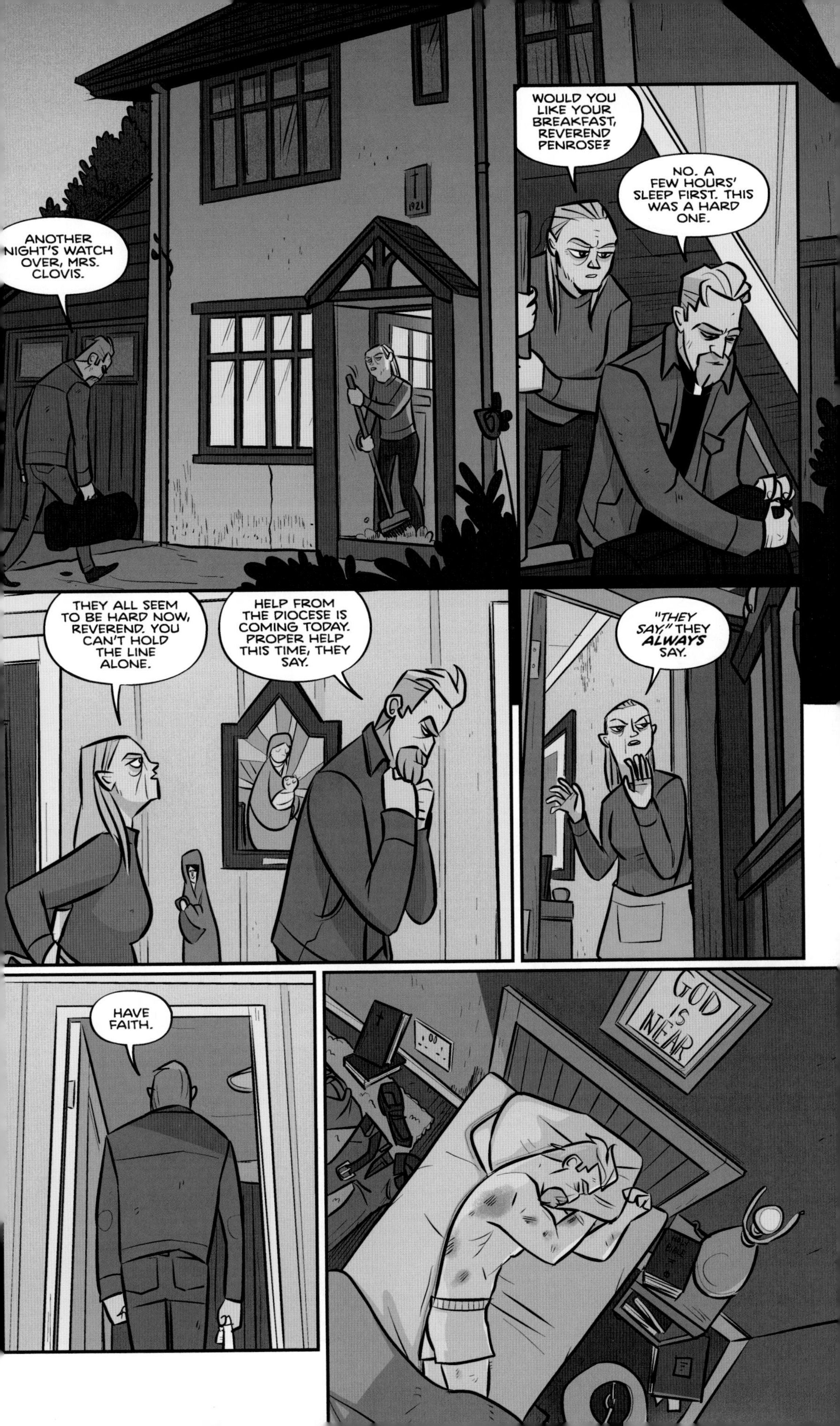

ANOTHER NIGHT'S WATCH OVER, MRS. CLOVIS.
WOULD YOU LIKE YOUR BREAKFAST, REVEREND PENROSE?
NO. A FEW HOURS' SLEEP FIRST. THIS WAS A HARD ONE.
THEY ALL SEEM TO BE HARD NOW, REVEREND. YOU CAN'T HOLD THE LINE ALONE.
HELP FROM THE DIOCESE IS COMING TODAY. PROPER HELP THIS TIME, THEY SAY.
"THEY SAY," THEY ***ALWAYS*** SAY.
HAVE FAITH.
GOD IS NEAR

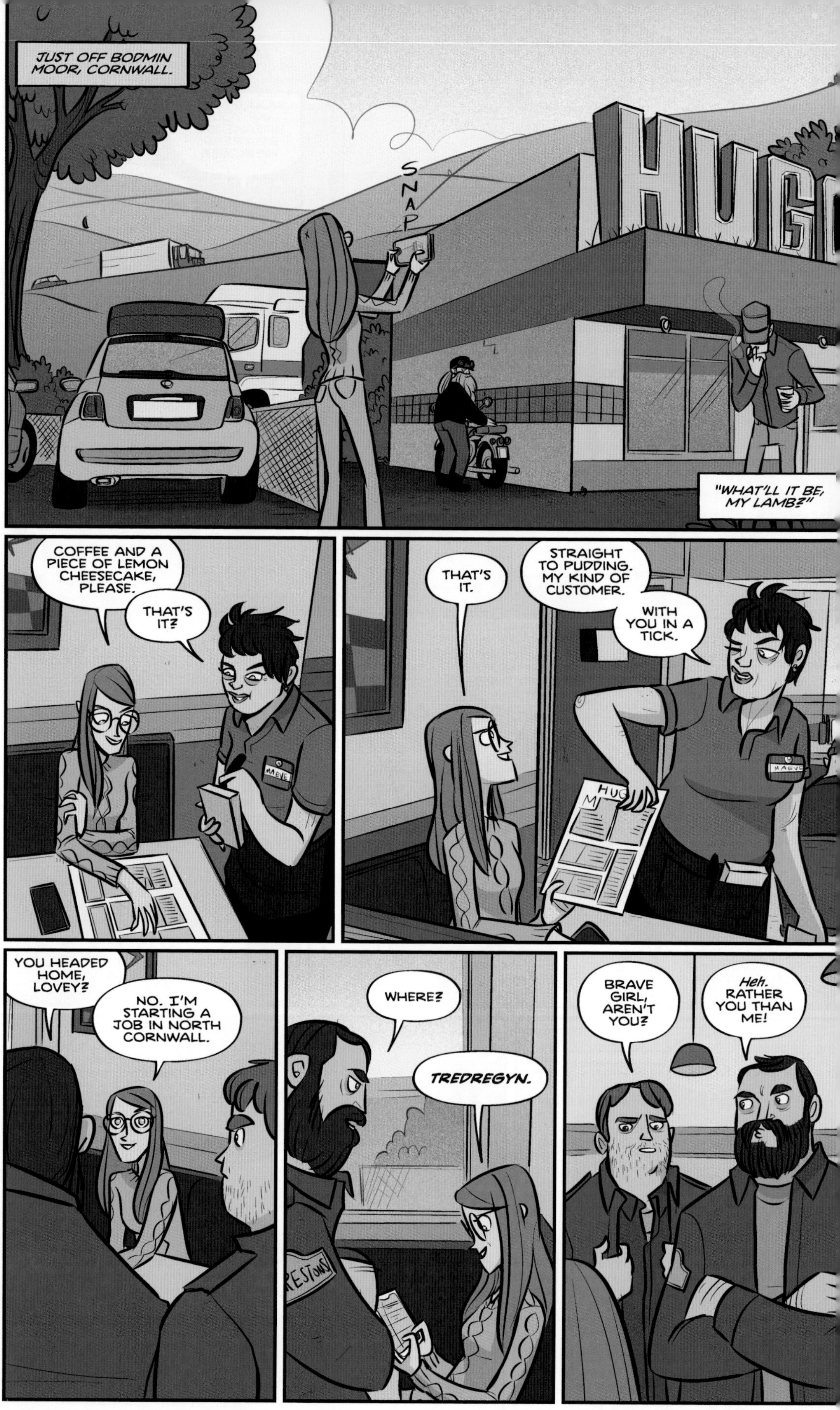
JUST OFF BODMIN MOOR, CORNWALL.
SNAP
HUGO
"WHAT'LL IT BE, MY LAMB?"
COFFEE AND A PIECE OF LEMON CHEESECAKE, PLEASE.
THAT'S IT?
THAT'S IT.
STRAIGHT TO PUDDING. MY KIND OF CUSTOMER.
WITH YOU IN A TICK.
YOU HEADED HOME, LOVEY?
NO. I'M STARTING A JOB IN NORTH CORNWALL.
WHERE?
TREDREGYN.
BRAVE GIRL, AREN'T YOU?
Heh. RATHER YOU THAN ME!

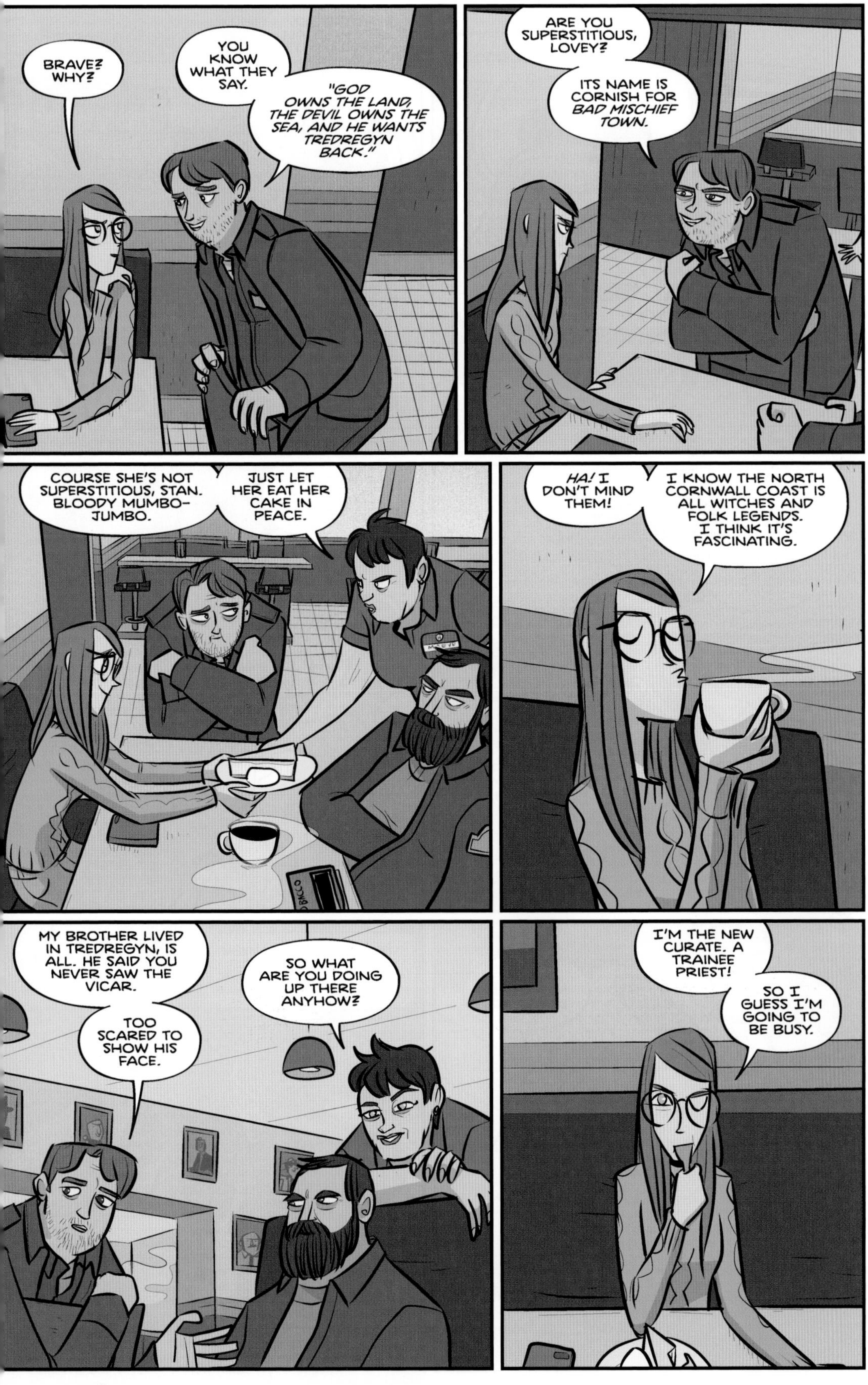
BRAVE? WHY?
YOU KNOW WHAT THEY SAY.
"GOD OWNS THE LAND, THE DEVIL OWNS THE SEA, AND HE WANTS TREDREGYN BACK."
ARE YOU SUPERSTITIOUS, LOVEY?
ITS NAME IS CORNISH FOR *BAD MISCHIEF TOWN.*
COURSE SHE'S NOT SUPERSTITIOUS, STAN. BLOODY MUMBO-JUMBO.
JUST LET HER EAT HER CAKE IN PEACE.
HA! I DON'T MIND THEM!
I KNOW THE NORTH CORNWALL COAST IS ALL WITCHES AND FOLK LEGENDS. I THINK IT'S FASCINATING.
MY BROTHER LIVED IN TREDREGYN, IS ALL. HE SAID YOU NEVER SAW THE VICAR.
TOO SCARED TO SHOW HIS FACE.
SO WHAT ARE YOU DOING UP THERE ANYHOW?
I'M THE NEW CURATE. A TRAINEE PRIEST!
SO I GUESS I'M GOING TO BE BUSY.

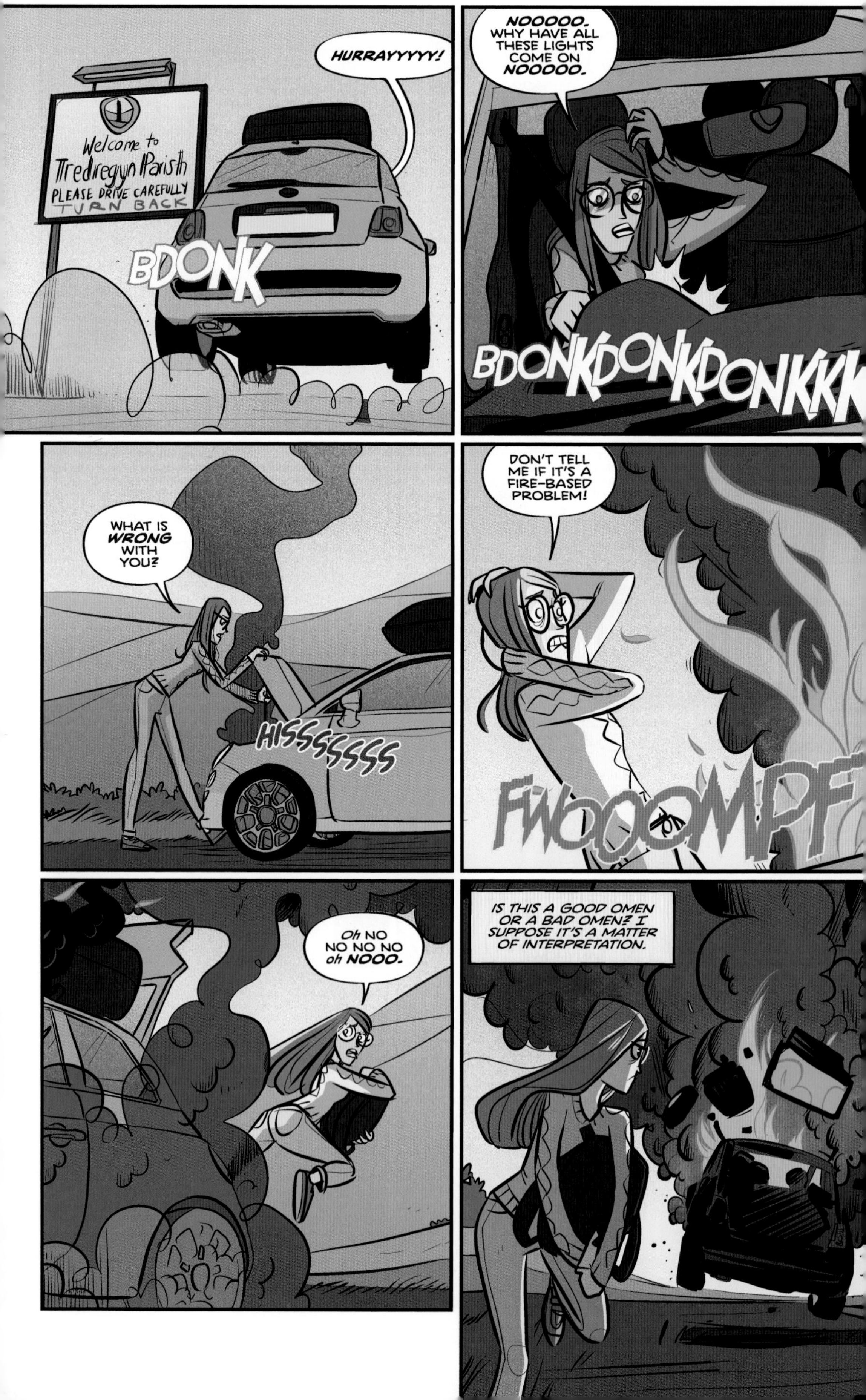
HURRAYYYYY!
Welcome to Tredregyn Parish PLEASE DRIVE CAREFULLY TURN BACK
BDONK
NOOOOO. WHY HAVE ALL THESE LIGHTS COME ON NOOOOO.
BDONKDONKDONKKK
WHAT IS WRONG WITH YOU?
HISSSSSSS
DON'T TELL ME IF IT'S A FIRE-BASED PROBLEM!
FWOOOMPF
Oh NO NO NO NO oh NOOO.
IS THIS A GOOD OMEN OR A BAD OMEN? I SUPPOSE IT'S A MATTER OF INTERPRETATION.

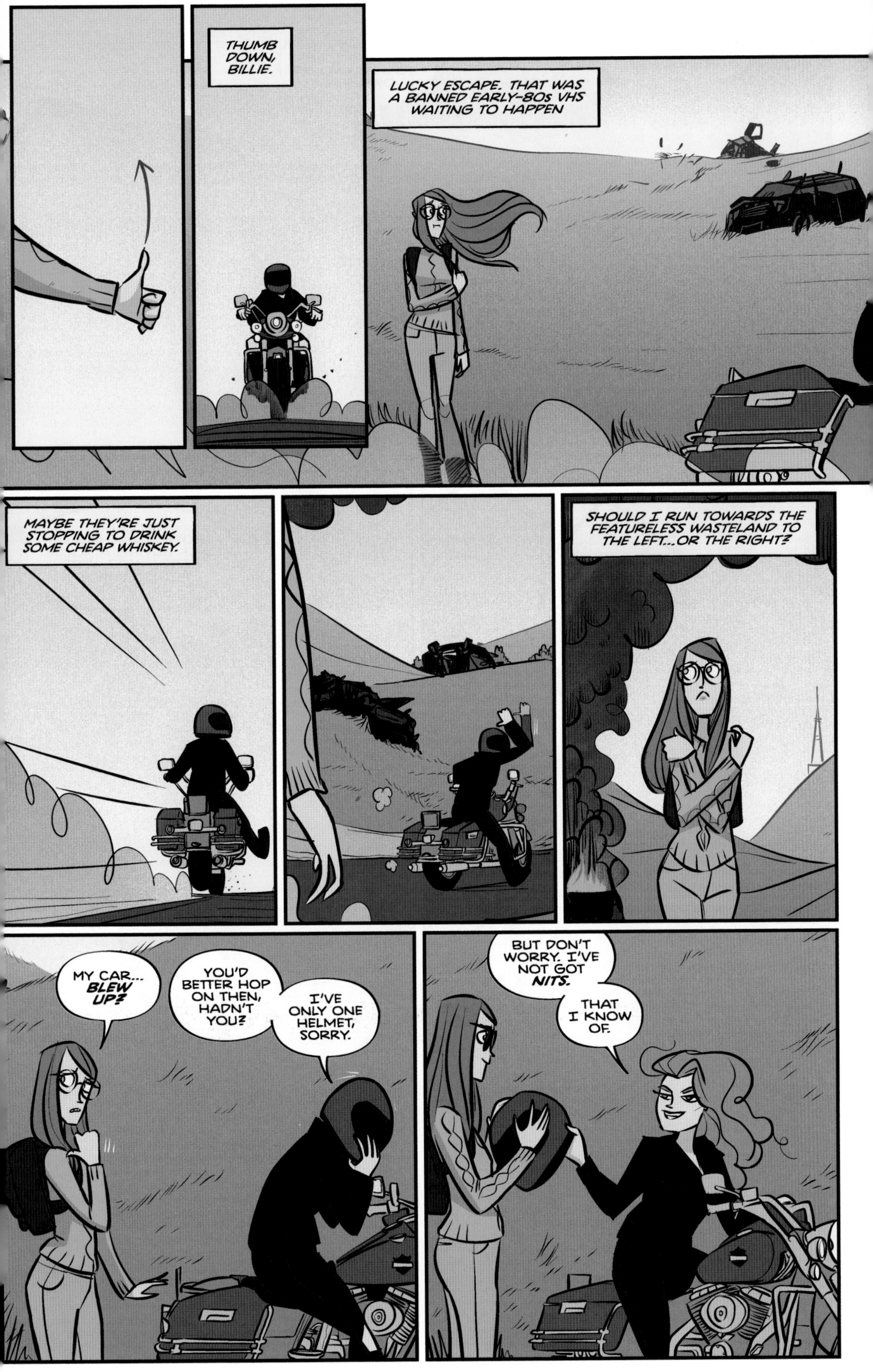
THUMB DOWN, BILLIE.
LUCKY ESCAPE. THAT WAS A BANNED EARLY-80s VHS WAITING TO HAPPEN
MAYBE THEY'RE JUST STOPPING TO DRINK SOME CHEAP WHISKEY.
SHOULD I RUN TOWARDS THE FEATURELESS WASTELAND TO THE LEFT...OR THE RIGHT?
MY CAR... BLEW UP?
YOU'D BETTER HOP ON THEN, HADN'T YOU?
I'VE ONLY ONE HELMET, SORRY.
BUT DON'T WORRY. I'VE NOT GOT NITS.
THAT I KNOW OF.

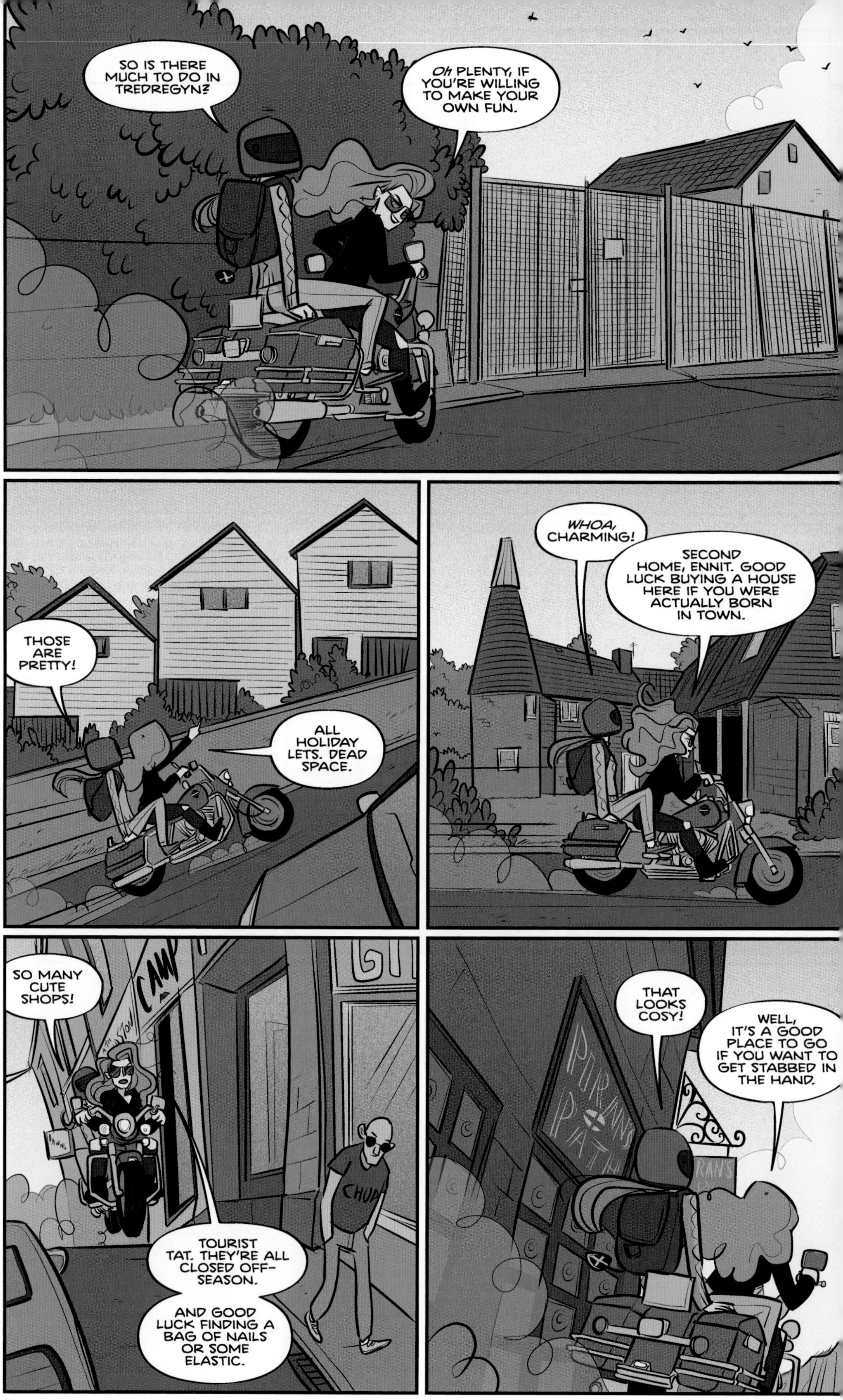
SO IS THERE MUCH TO DO IN TREDREGYN?
Oh PLENTY, IF YOU'RE WILLING TO MAKE YOUR OWN FUN.
THOSE ARE PRETTY!
ALL HOLIDAY LETS. DEAD SPACE.
WHOA, CHARMING!
SECOND HOME, ENNIT. GOOD LUCK BUYING A HOUSE HERE IF YOU WERE ACTUALLY BORN IN TOWN.
SO MANY CUTE SHOPS!
TOURIST TAT. THEY'RE ALL CLOSED OFF-SEASON.
AND GOOD LUCK FINDING A BAG OF NAILS OR SOME ELASTIC.
THAT LOOKS COSY!
WELL, IT'S A GOOD PLACE TO GO IF YOU WANT TO GET STABBED IN THE HAND.

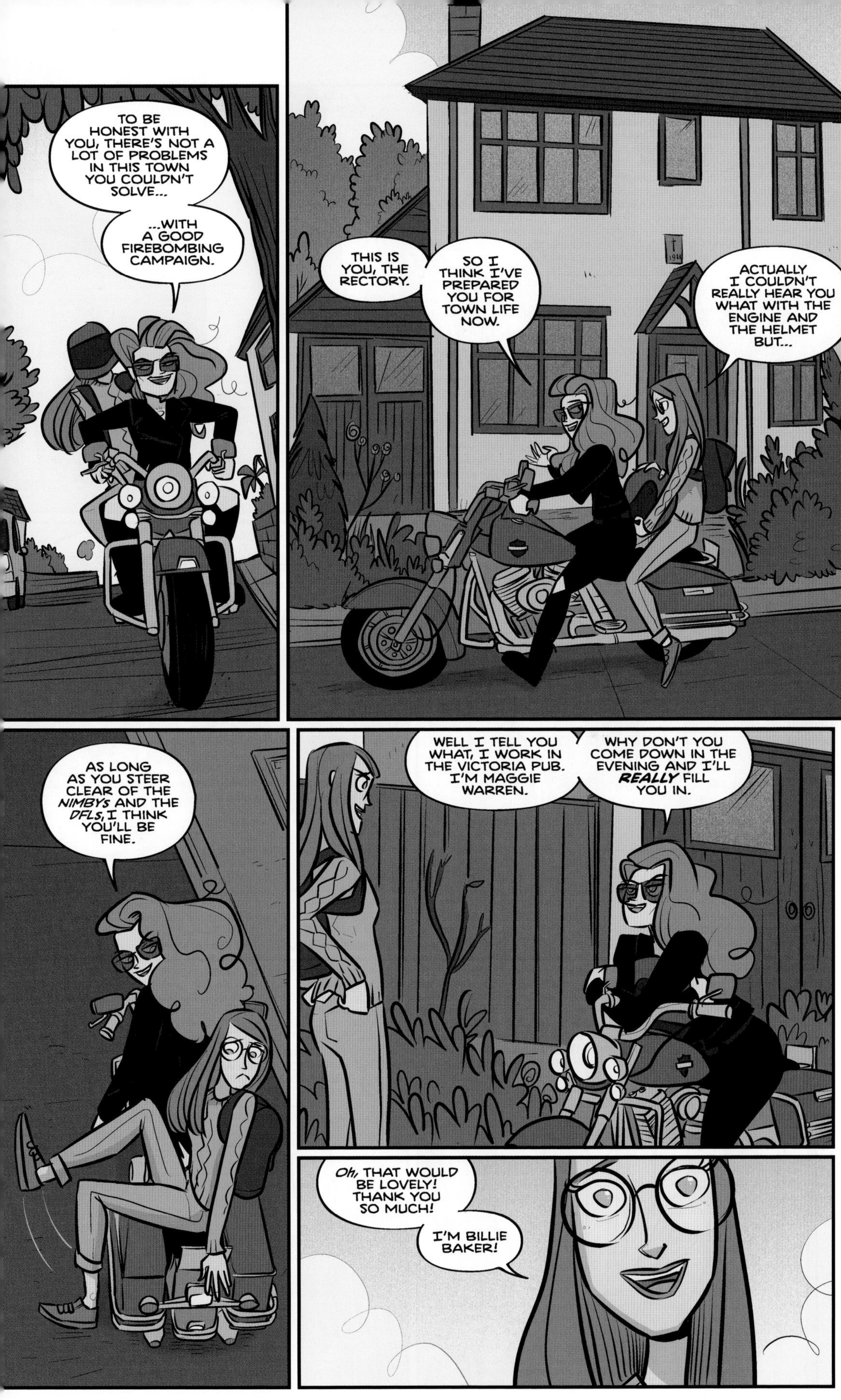

TO BE HONEST WITH YOU, THERE'S NOT A LOT OF PROBLEMS IN THIS TOWN YOU COULDN'T SOLVE...
...WITH A GOOD FIREBOMBING CAMPAIGN.
THIS IS YOU, THE RECTORY.
SO I THINK I'VE PREPARED YOU FOR TOWN LIFE NOW.
ACTUALLY I COULDN'T REALLY HEAR YOU WHAT WITH THE ENGINE AND THE HELMET BUT...
AS LONG AS YOU STEER CLEAR OF THE *NIMBYS* AND THE *DFLS*, I THINK YOU'LL BE FINE.
WELL I TELL YOU WHAT, I WORK IN THE VICTORIA PUB. I'M MAGGIE WARREN.
WHY DON'T YOU COME DOWN IN THE EVENING AND I'LL *REALLY* FILL YOU IN.
Oh, THAT WOULD BE LOVELY! THANK YOU SO MUCH!
I'M BILLIE BAKER!

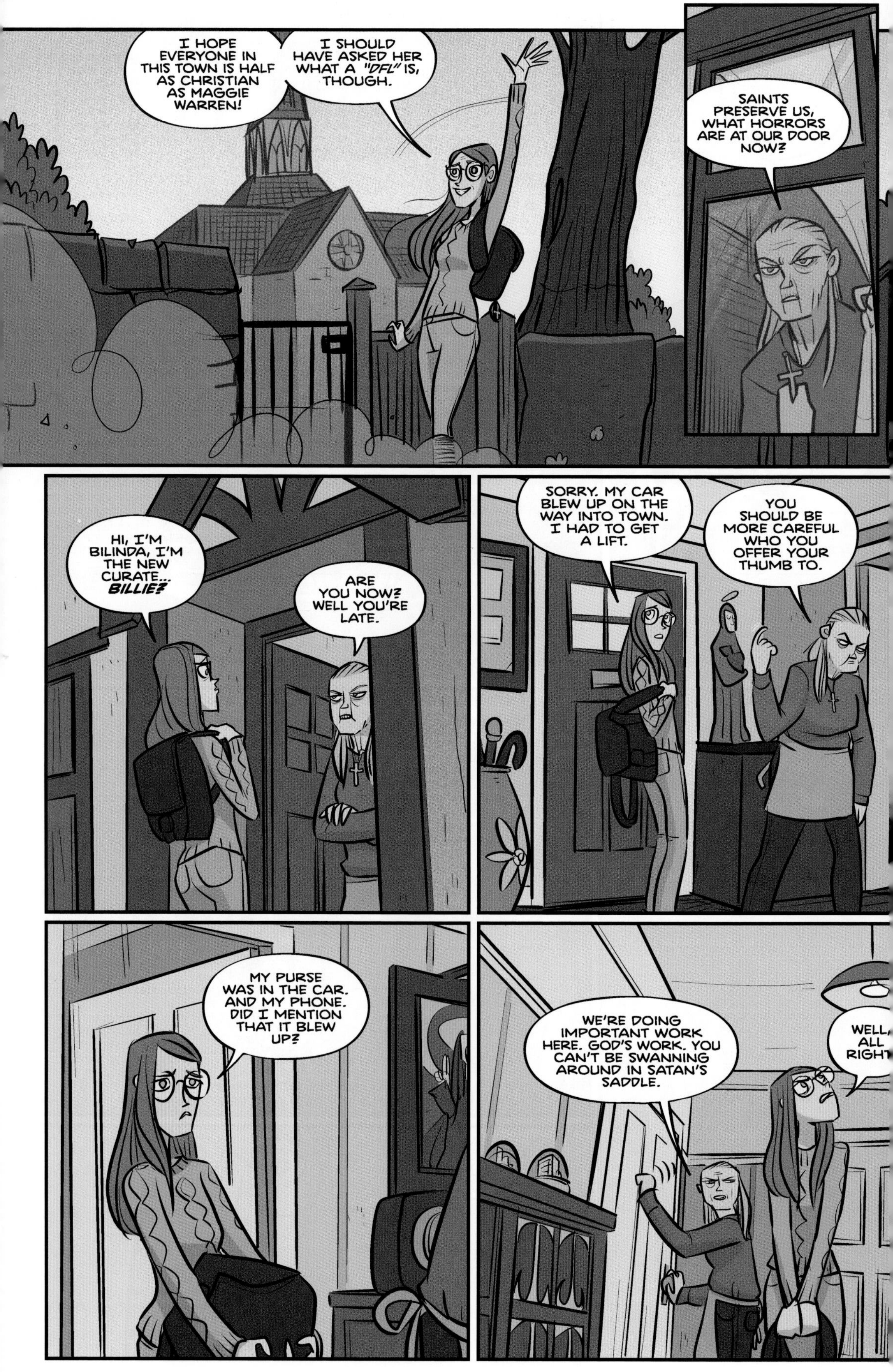
I HOPE EVERYONE IN THIS TOWN IS HALF AS CHRISTIAN AS MAGGIE WARREN!
I SHOULD HAVE ASKED HER WHAT A "DFL" IS, THOUGH.
SAINTS PRESERVE US, WHAT HORRORS ARE AT OUR DOOR NOW?
HI, I'M BILINDA, I'M THE NEW CURATE... ***BILLIE?***
ARE YOU NOW? WELL YOU'RE LATE.
SORRY. MY CAR BLEW UP ON THE WAY INTO TOWN. I HAD TO GET A LIFT.
YOU SHOULD BE MORE CAREFUL WHO YOU OFFER YOUR THUMB TO.
MY PURSE WAS IN THE CAR. AND MY PHONE. DID I MENTION THAT IT BLEW UP?
WE'RE DOING IMPORTANT WORK HERE. GOD'S WORK. YOU CAN'T BE SWANNING AROUND IN SATAN'S SADDLE.
WELL, ALL RIGHT

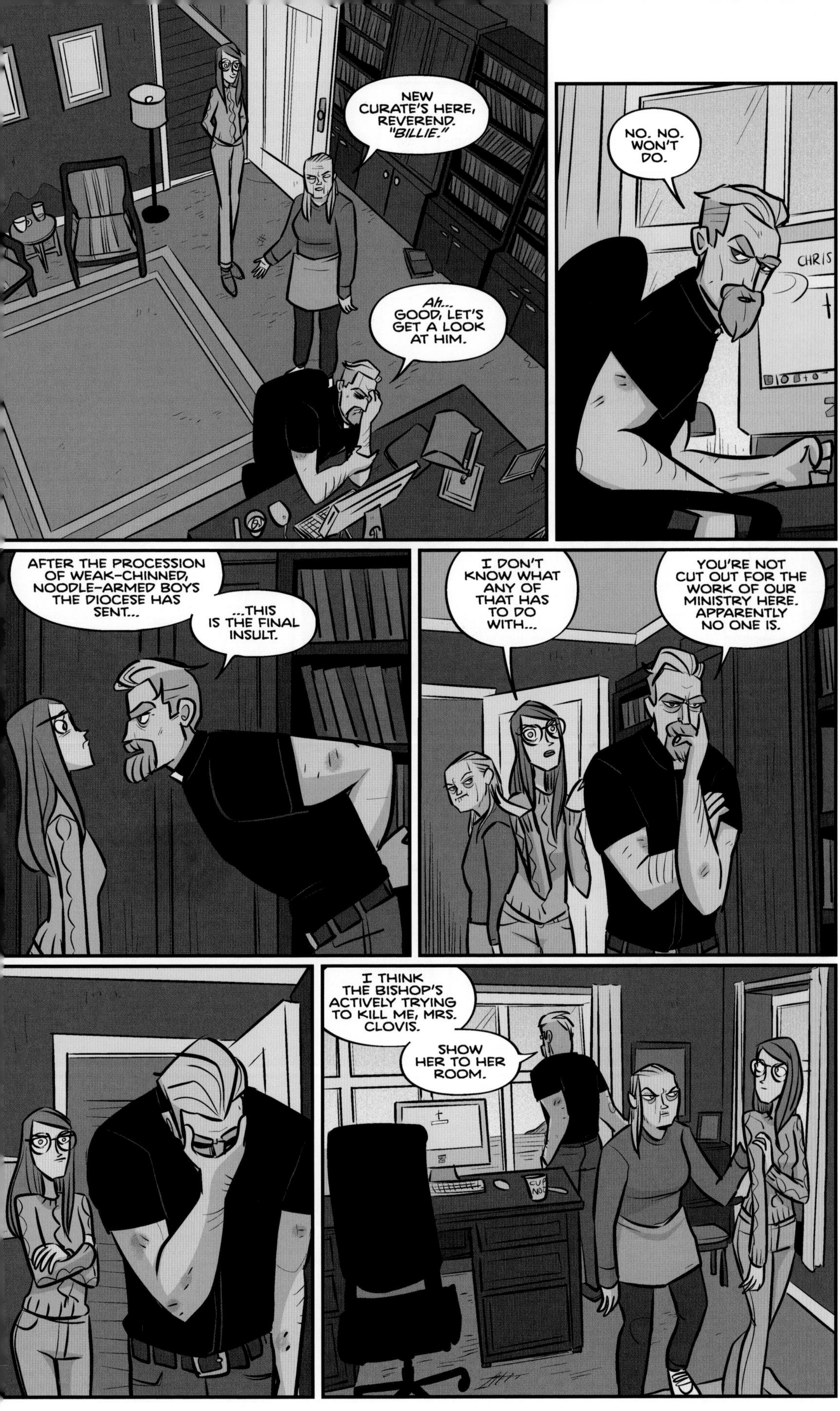
NEW CURATE'S HERE, REVEREND. "BILLIE."
Ah... GOOD, LET'S GET A LOOK AT HIM.
NO. NO. WON'T DO.
CHRIS
AFTER THE PROCESSION OF WEAK-CHINNED, NOODLE-ARMED BOYS THE DIOCESE HAS SENT...
...THIS IS THE FINAL INSULT.
I DON'T KNOW WHAT ANY OF THAT HAS TO DO WITH...
YOU'RE NOT CUT OUT FOR THE WORK OF OUR MINISTRY HERE. APPARENTLY NO ONE IS.
I THINK THE BISHOP'S ACTIVELY TRYING TO KILL ME, MRS. CLOVIS.
SHOW HER TO HER ROOM.

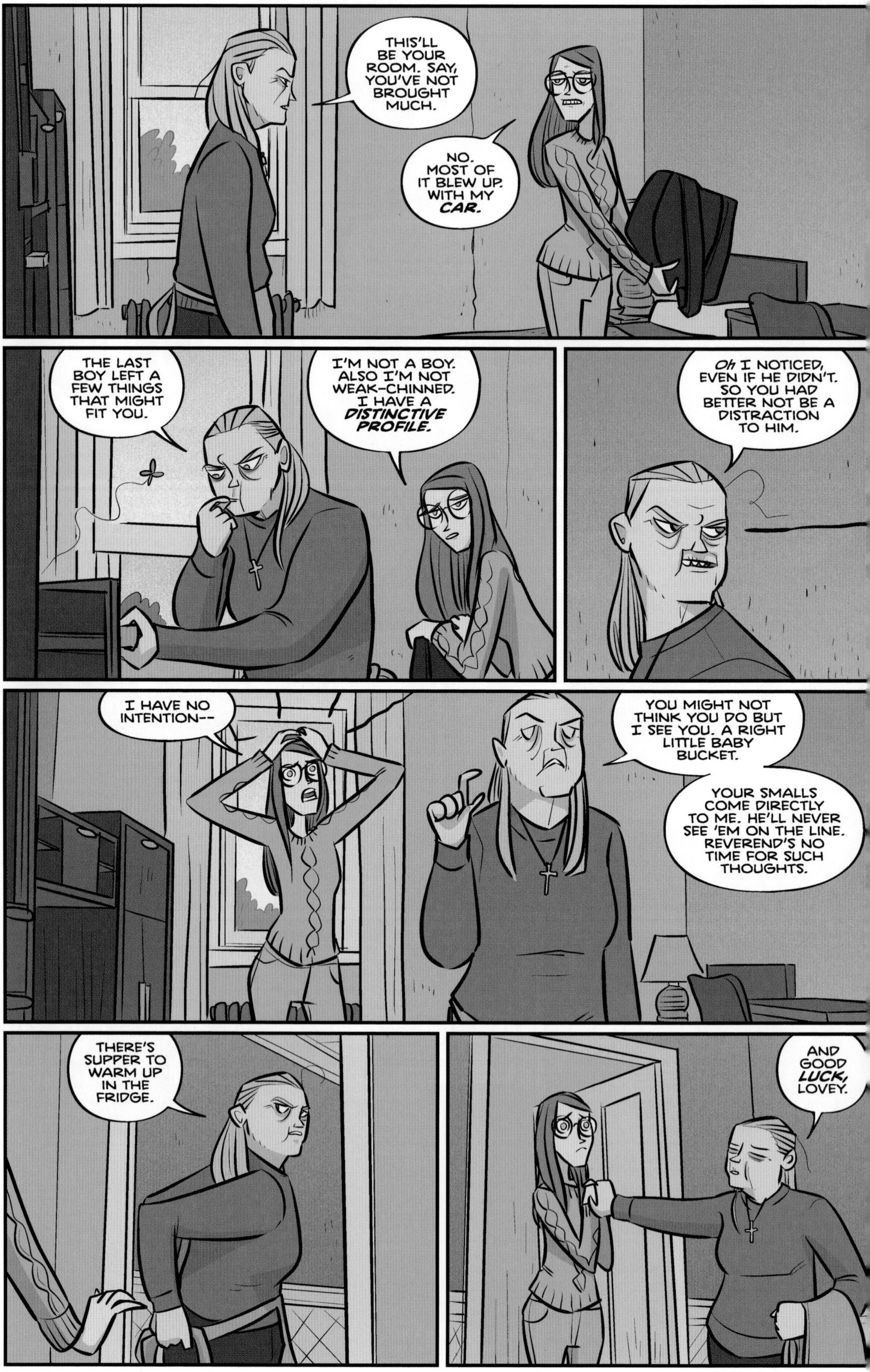
THIS'LL BE YOUR ROOM. SAY, YOU'VE NOT BROUGHT MUCH.
NO. MOST OF IT BLEW UP. WITH MY *CAR.*
THE LAST BOY LEFT A FEW THINGS THAT MIGHT FIT YOU.
I'M NOT A BOY. ALSO I'M NOT WEAK-CHINNED. I HAVE A ***DISTINCTIVE PROFILE.***
Oh I NOTICED, EVEN IF HE DIDN'T. SO YOU HAD BETTER NOT BE A DISTRACTION TO HIM.
I HAVE NO INTENTION--
YOU MIGHT NOT THINK YOU DO BUT I SEE YOU. A RIGHT LITTLE BABY BUCKET.
YOUR SMALLS COME DIRECTLY TO ME. HE'LL NEVER SEE 'EM ON THE LINE. REVEREND'S NO TIME FOR SUCH THOUGHTS.
THERE'S SUPPER TO WARM UP IN THE FRIDGE.
AND GOOD ***LUCK,*** LOVEY.

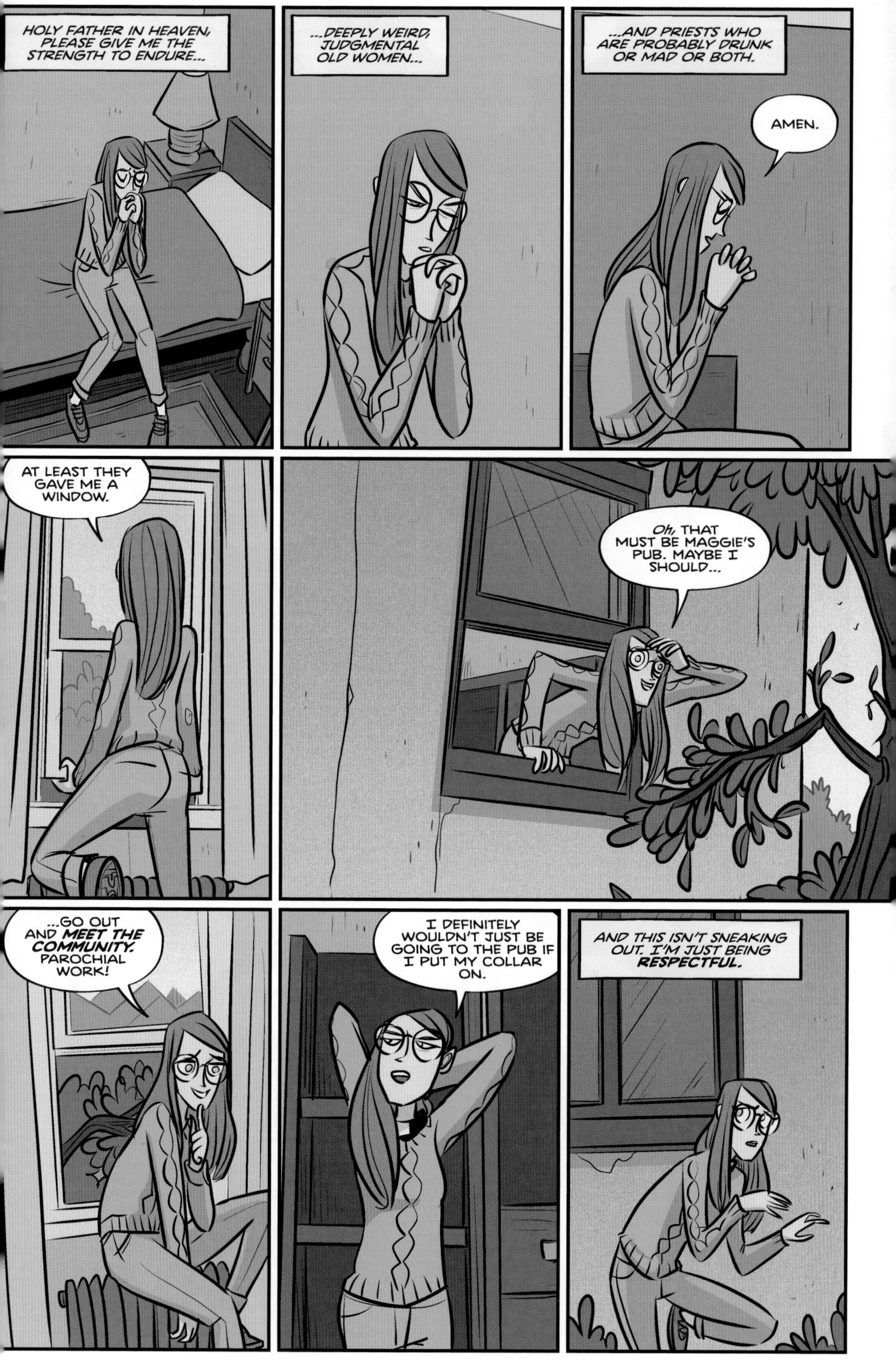
HOLY FATHER IN HEAVEN, PLEASE GIVE ME THE STRENGTH TO ENDURE...
...DEEPLY WEIRD, JUDGMENTAL OLD WOMEN...
...AND PRIESTS WHO ARE PROBABLY DRUNK OR MAD OR BOTH.
AMEN.
AT LEAST THEY GAVE ME A WINDOW.
Oh, THAT MUST BE MAGGIE'S PUB. MAYBE I SHOULD...
...GO OUT AND ***MEET THE COMMUNITY.*** PAROCHIAL WORK!
I DEFINITELY WOULDN'T JUST BE GOING TO THE PUB IF I PUT MY COLLAR ON.
AND THIS ISN'T SNEAKING OUT. I'M JUST BEING ***RESPECTFUL.***

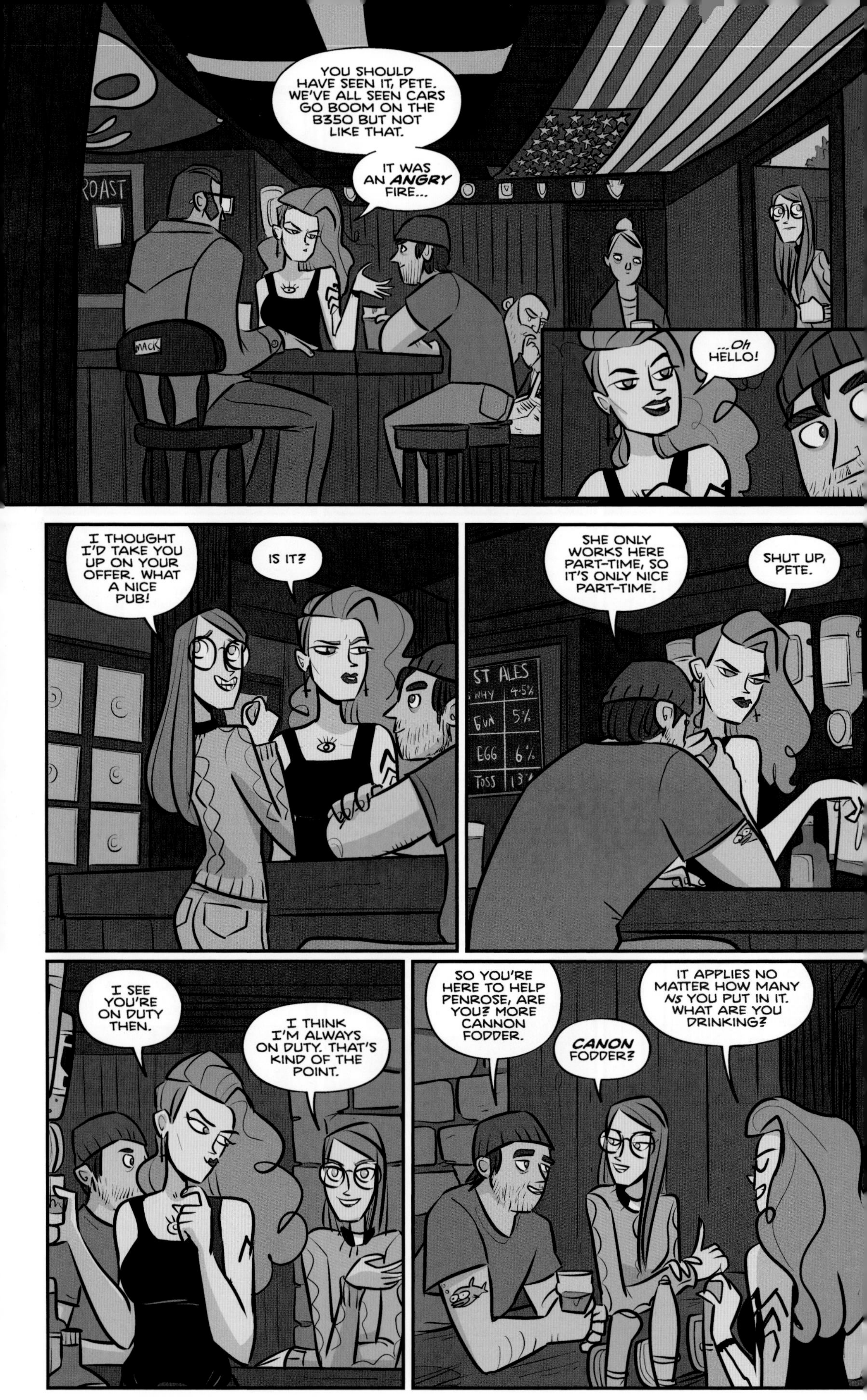
YOU SHOULD HAVE SEEN IT, PETE. WE'VE ALL SEEN CARS GO BOOM ON THE B350 BUT NOT LIKE THAT.
IT WAS AN ANGRY FIRE...
ROAST
MACK
...Oh HELLO!
I THOUGHT I'D TAKE YOU UP ON YOUR OFFER. WHAT A NICE PUB!
IS IT?
SHE ONLY WORKS HERE PART-TIME, SO IT'S ONLY NICE PART-TIME.
SHUT UP, PETE.
ST ALES
4.5%
5%
EGG 6%
I SEE YOU'RE ON DUTY THEN.
I THINK I'M ALWAYS ON DUTY. THAT'S KIND OF THE POINT.
SO YOU'RE HERE TO HELP PENROSE, ARE YOU? MORE CANNON FODDER.
CANON FODDER?
IT APPLIES NO MATTER HOW MANY Ns YOU PUT IN IT. WHAT ARE YOU DRINKING?

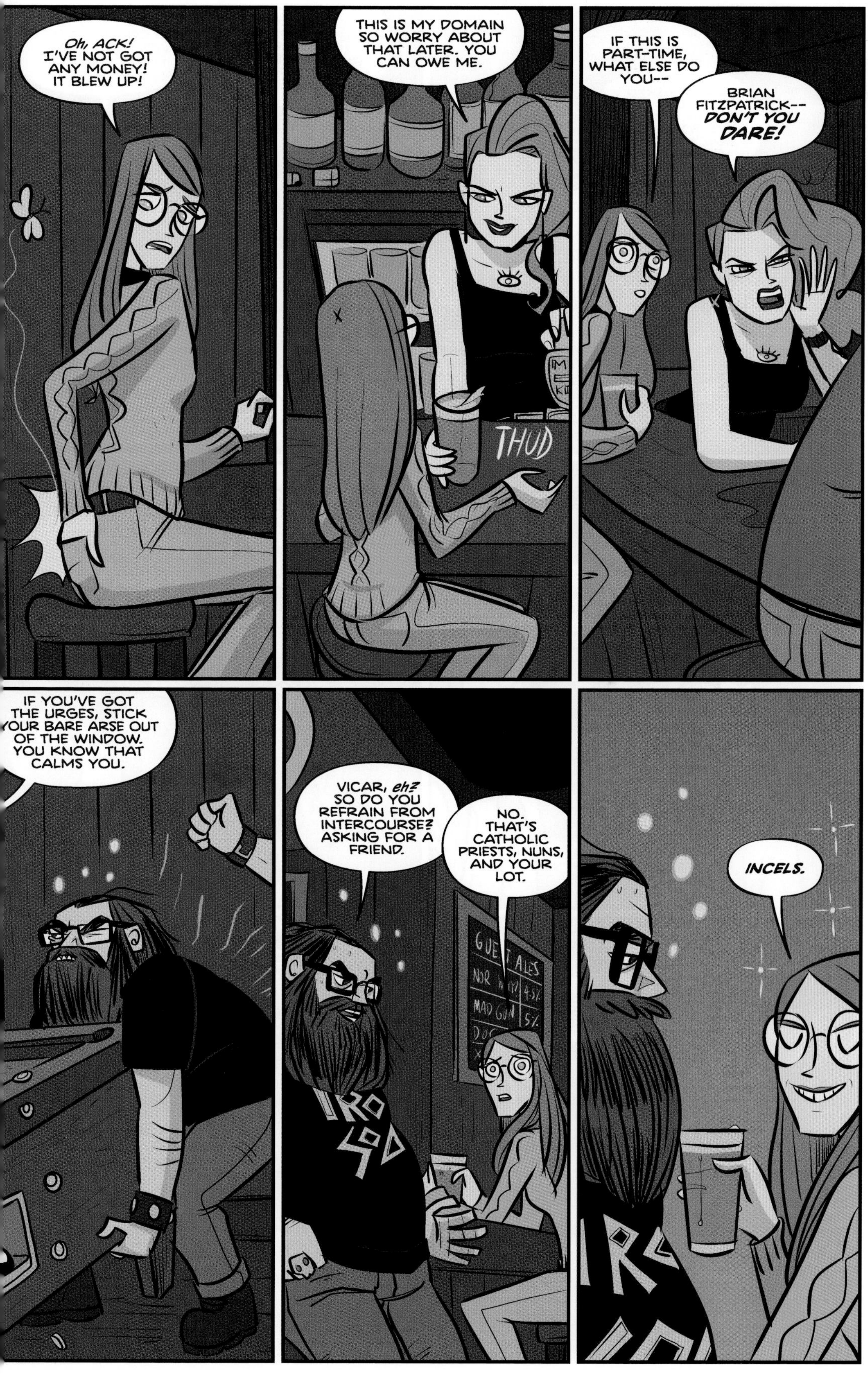
Oh, ACK! I'VE NOT GOT ANY MONEY! IT BLEW UP!
THIS IS MY DOMAIN SO WORRY ABOUT THAT LATER. YOU CAN OWE ME.
THUD
IF THIS IS PART-TIME, WHAT ELSE DO YOU--
BRIAN FITZPATRICK-- DON'T YOU DARE!
IF YOU'VE GOT THE URGES, STICK YOUR BARE ARSE OUT OF THE WINDOW. YOU KNOW THAT CALMS YOU.
VICAR, eh? SO DO YOU REFRAIN FROM INTERCOURSE? ASKING FOR A FRIEND.
NO. THAT'S CATHOLIC PRIESTS, NUNS, AND YOUR LOT.
INCELS.

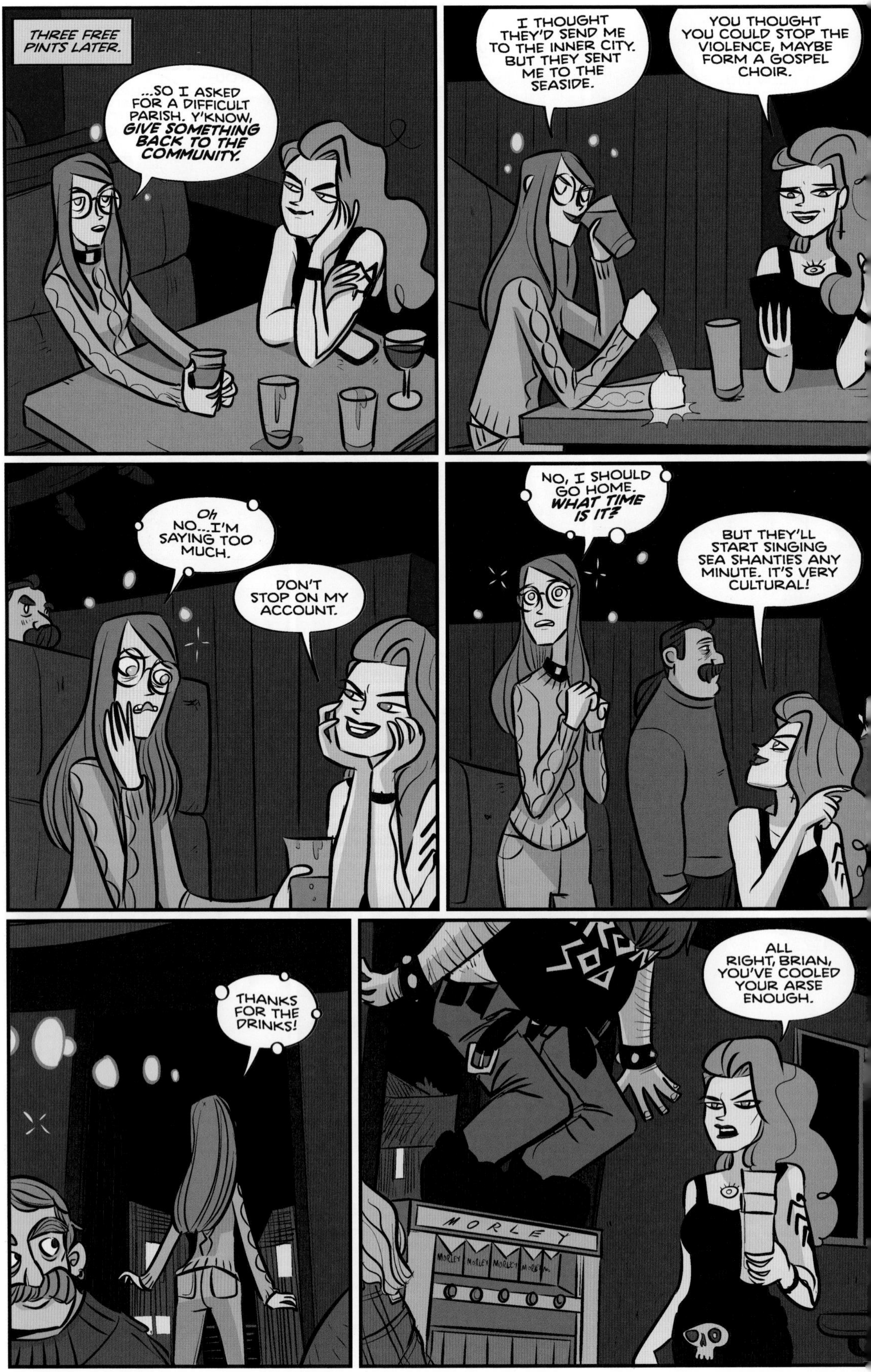
THREE FREE PINTS LATER.
...SO I ASKED FOR A DIFFICULT PARISH. Y'KNOW, GIVE SOMETHING BACK TO THE COMMUNITY.
I THOUGHT THEY'D SEND ME TO THE INNER CITY. BUT THEY SENT ME TO THE SEASIDE.
YOU THOUGHT YOU COULD STOP THE VIOLENCE, MAYBE FORM A GOSPEL CHOIR.
Oh NO...I'M SAYING TOO MUCH.
DON'T STOP ON MY ACCOUNT.
NO, I SHOULD GO HOME. WHAT TIME IS IT?
BUT THEY'LL START SINGING SEA SHANTIES ANY MINUTE. IT'S VERY CULTURAL!
THANKS FOR THE DRINKS!
ALL RIGHT, BRIAN, YOU'VE COOLED YOUR ARSE ENOUGH.
MORLEY

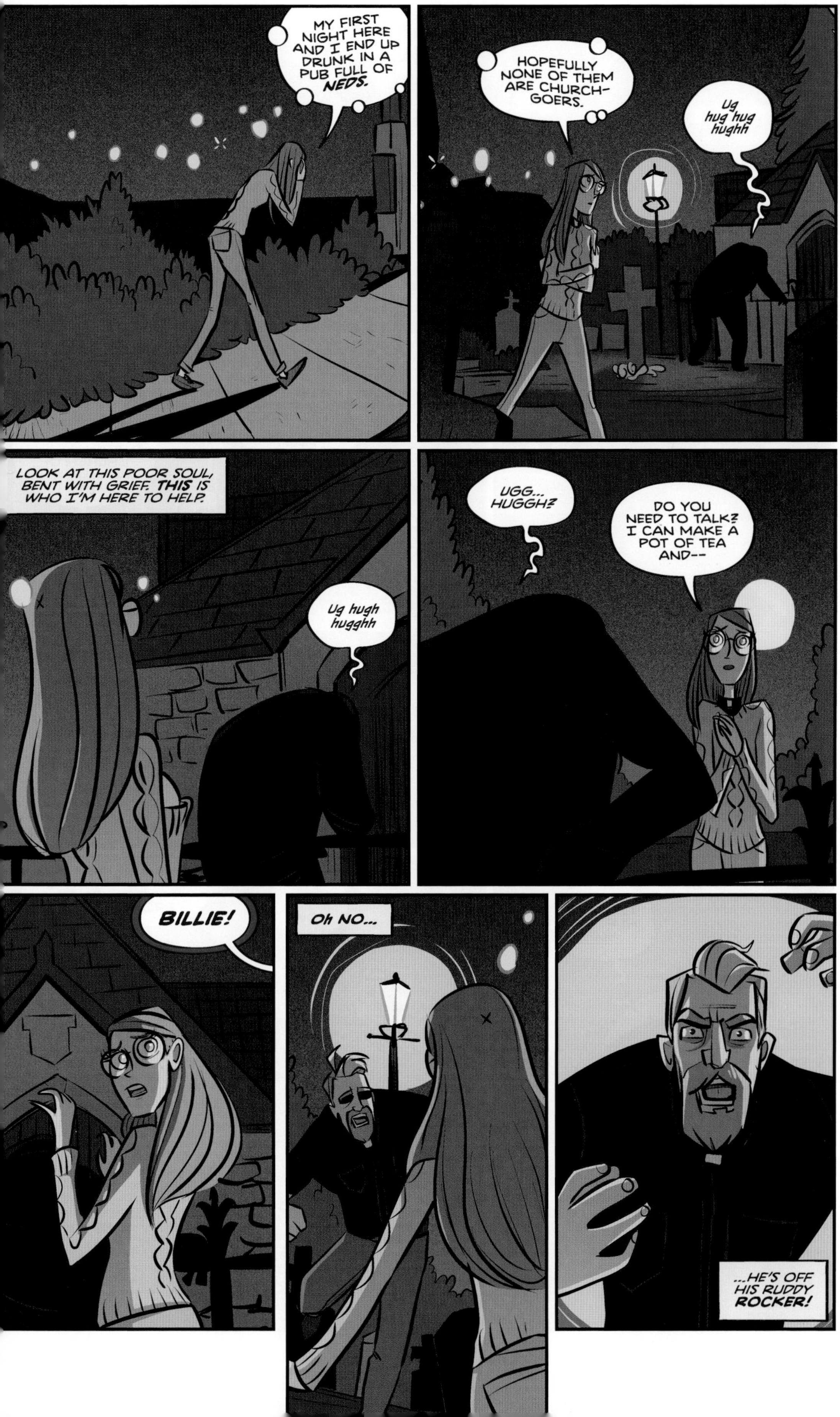

MY FIRST NIGHT HERE AND I END UP DRUNK IN A PUB FULL OF NEDS.
HOPEFULLY NONE OF THEM ARE CHURCH-GOERS.
Ug hug hug hughh
LOOK AT THIS POOR SOUL, BENT WITH GRIEF. THIS IS WHO I'M HERE TO HELP.
Ug hugh hugghh
UGG... HUGGH?
DO YOU NEED TO TALK? I CAN MAKE A POT OF TEA AND--
BILLIE!
Oh NO...
...HE'S OFF HIS RUDDY ROCKER!

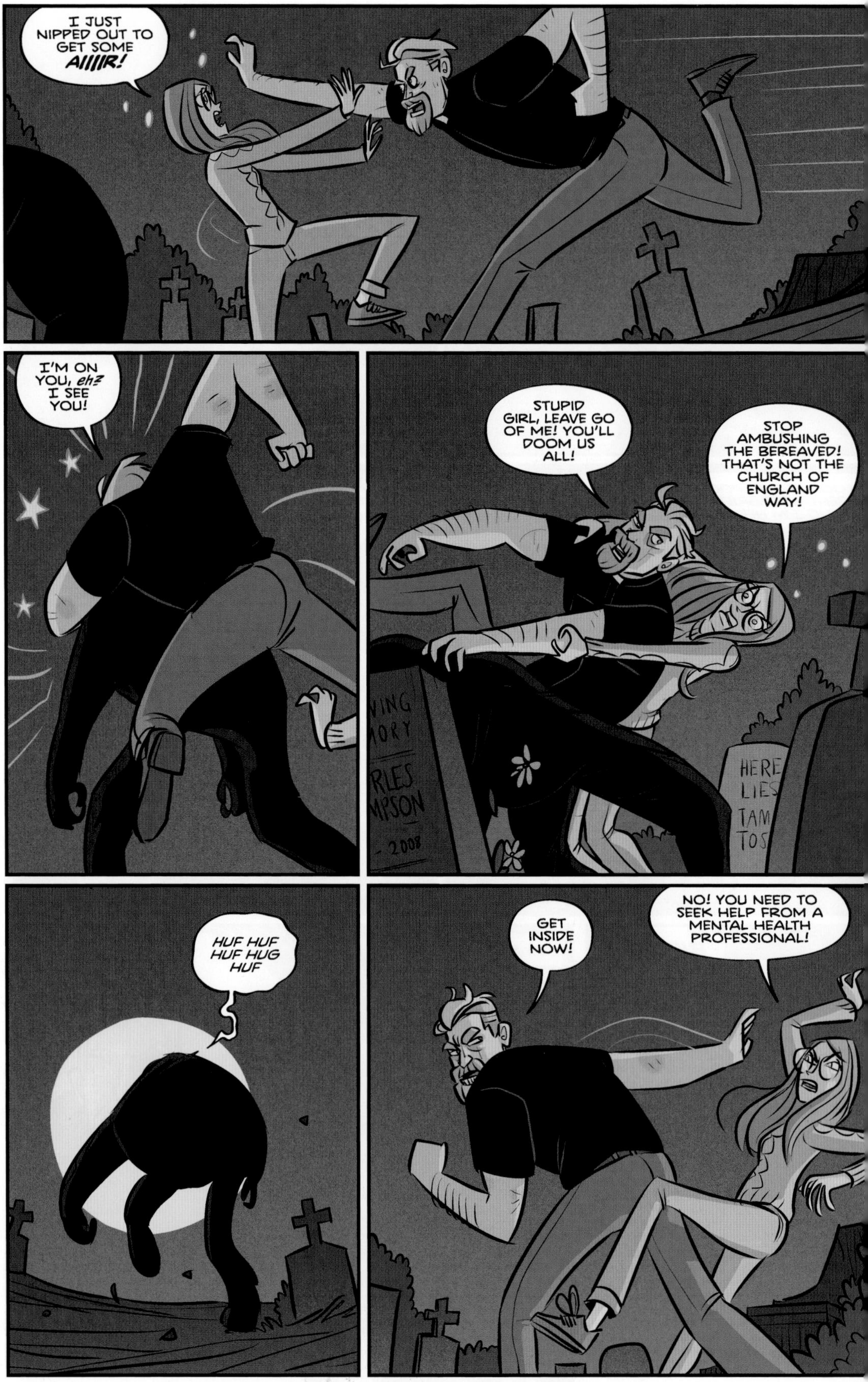
I JUST NIPPED OUT TO GET SOME *AIIIIR!*
I'M ON YOU, *eh?* I SEE YOU!
STUPID GIRL, LEAVE GO OF ME! YOU'LL DOOM US ALL!
STOP AMBUSHING THE BEREAVED! THAT'S NOT THE CHURCH OF ENGLAND WAY!
HERE LIES TAM TOS
HUF HUF HUF HUG HUF
GET INSIDE NOW!
NO! YOU NEED TO SEEK HELP FROM A MENTAL HEALTH PROFESSIONAL!

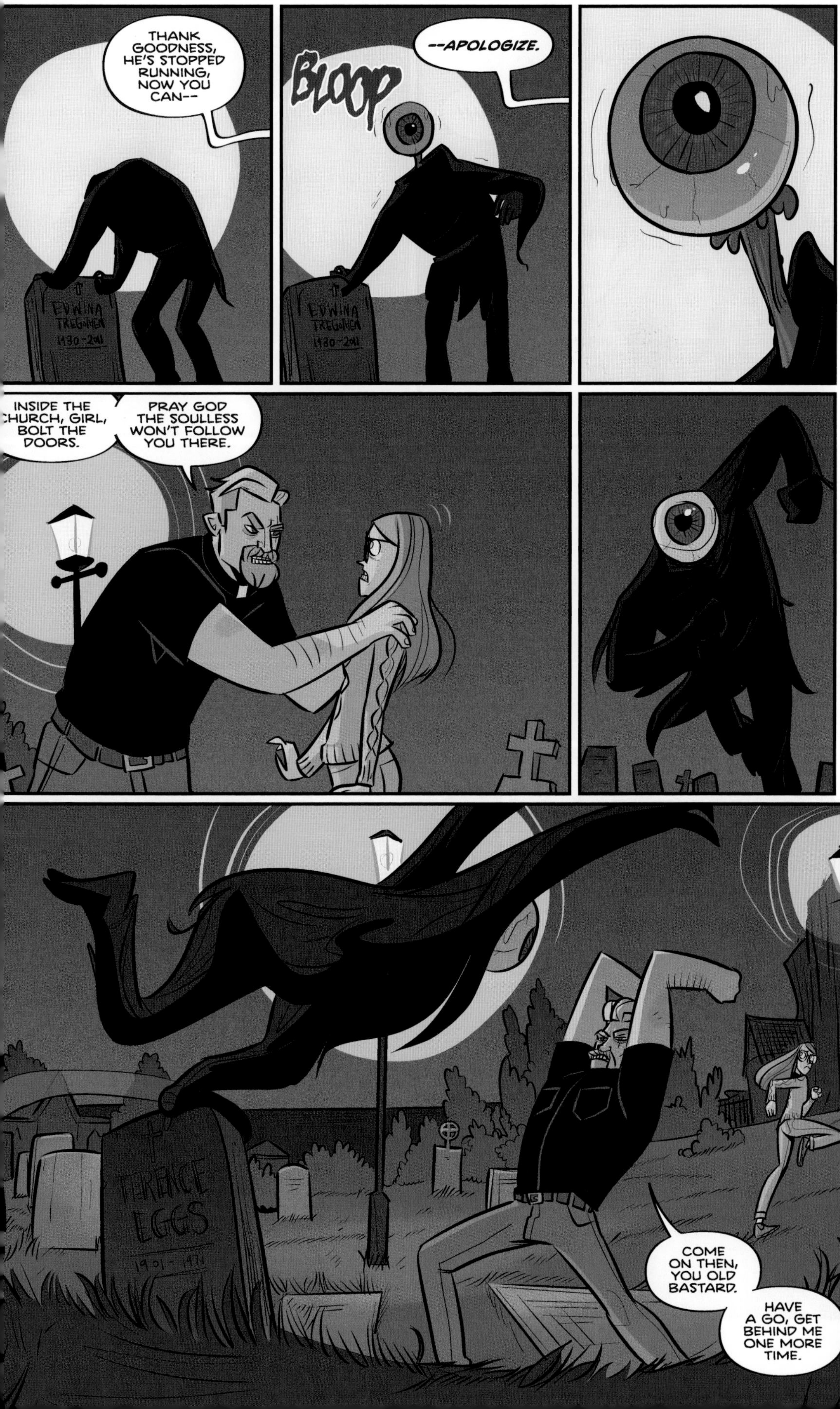
THANK GOODNESS, HE'S STOPPED RUNNING, NOW YOU CAN--
BLOOP
EDWINA TREGOWEN 1930-2011
--APOLOGIZE.
INSIDE THE CHURCH, GIRL, BOLT THE DOORS.
PRAY GOD THE SOULLESS WON'T FOLLOW YOU THERE.
TERENCE EGGS
COME ON THEN, YOU OLD BASTARD.
HAVE A GO, GET BEHIND ME ONE MORE TIME.

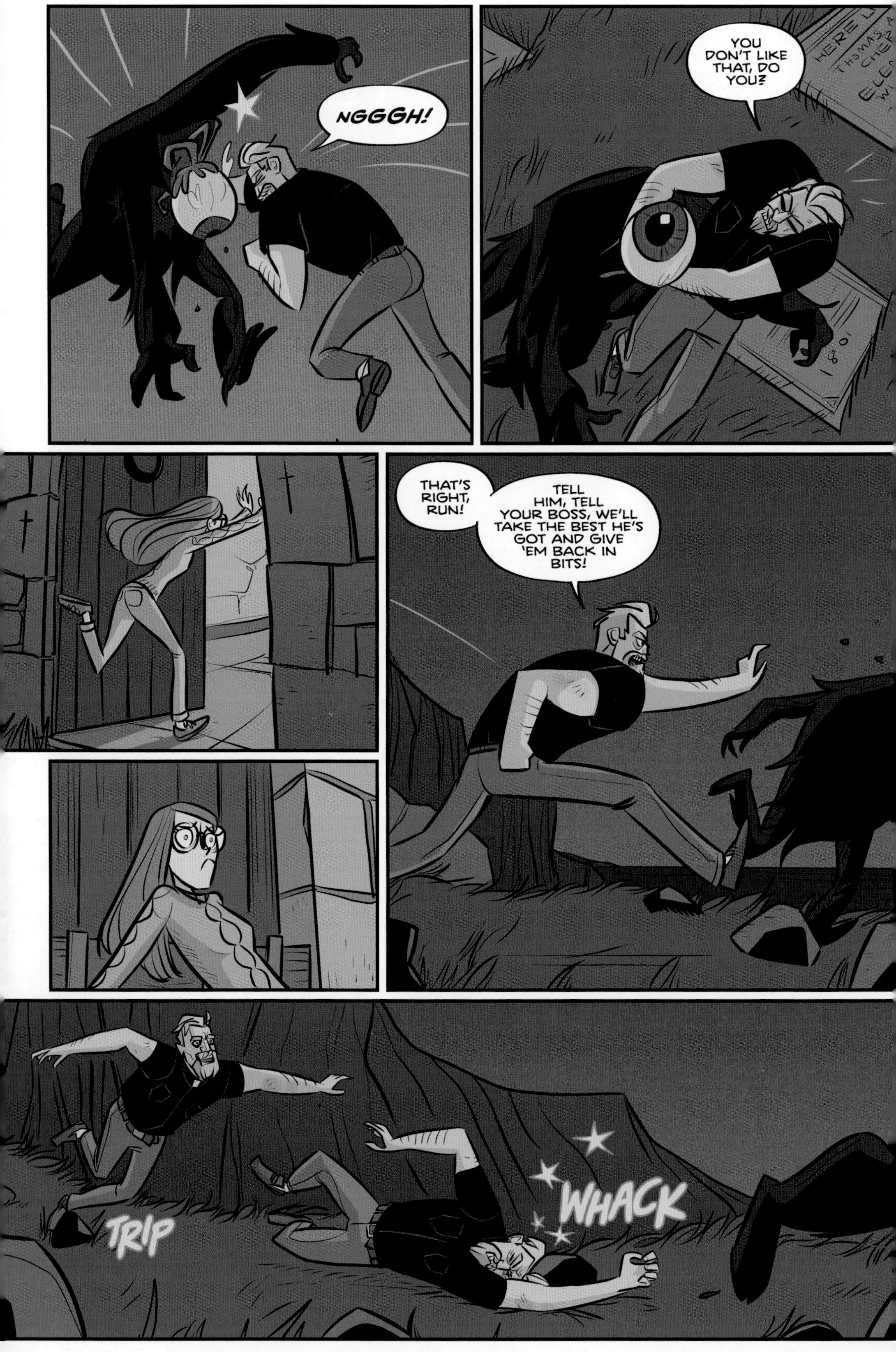
NGGGH!
YOU DON'T LIKE THAT, DO YOU?
THAT'S RIGHT, RUN!
TELL HIM, TELL YOUR BOSS, WE'LL TAKE THE BEST HE'S GOT AND GIVE 'EM BACK IN BITS!
TRIP
WHACK

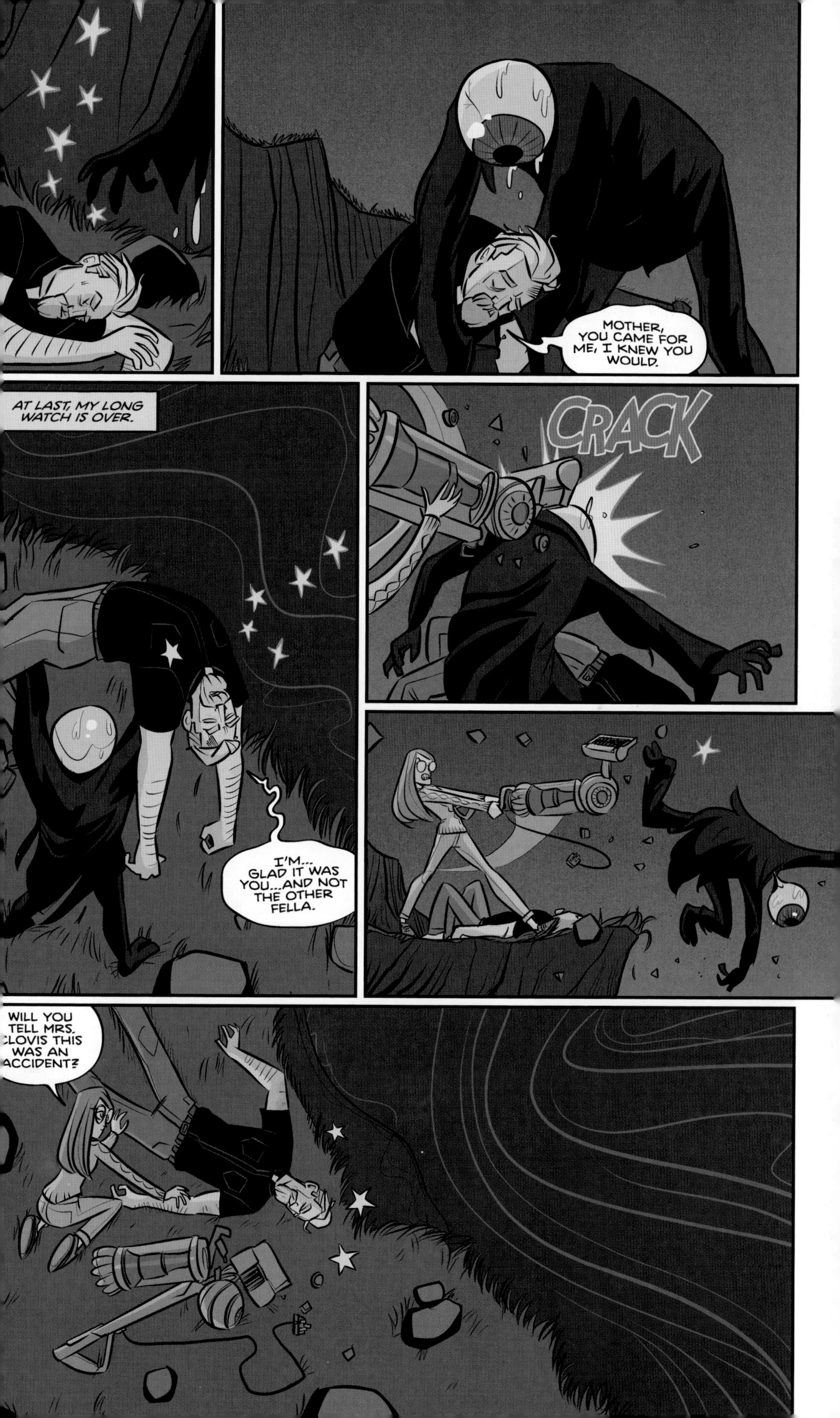
MOTHER, YOU CAME FOR ME, I KNEW YOU WOULD.
AT LAST, MY LONG WATCH IS OVER.
CRACK
I'M... GLAD IT WAS YOU...AND NOT THE OTHER FELLA.
WILL YOU TELL MRS. CLOVIS THIS WAS AN ACCIDENT?

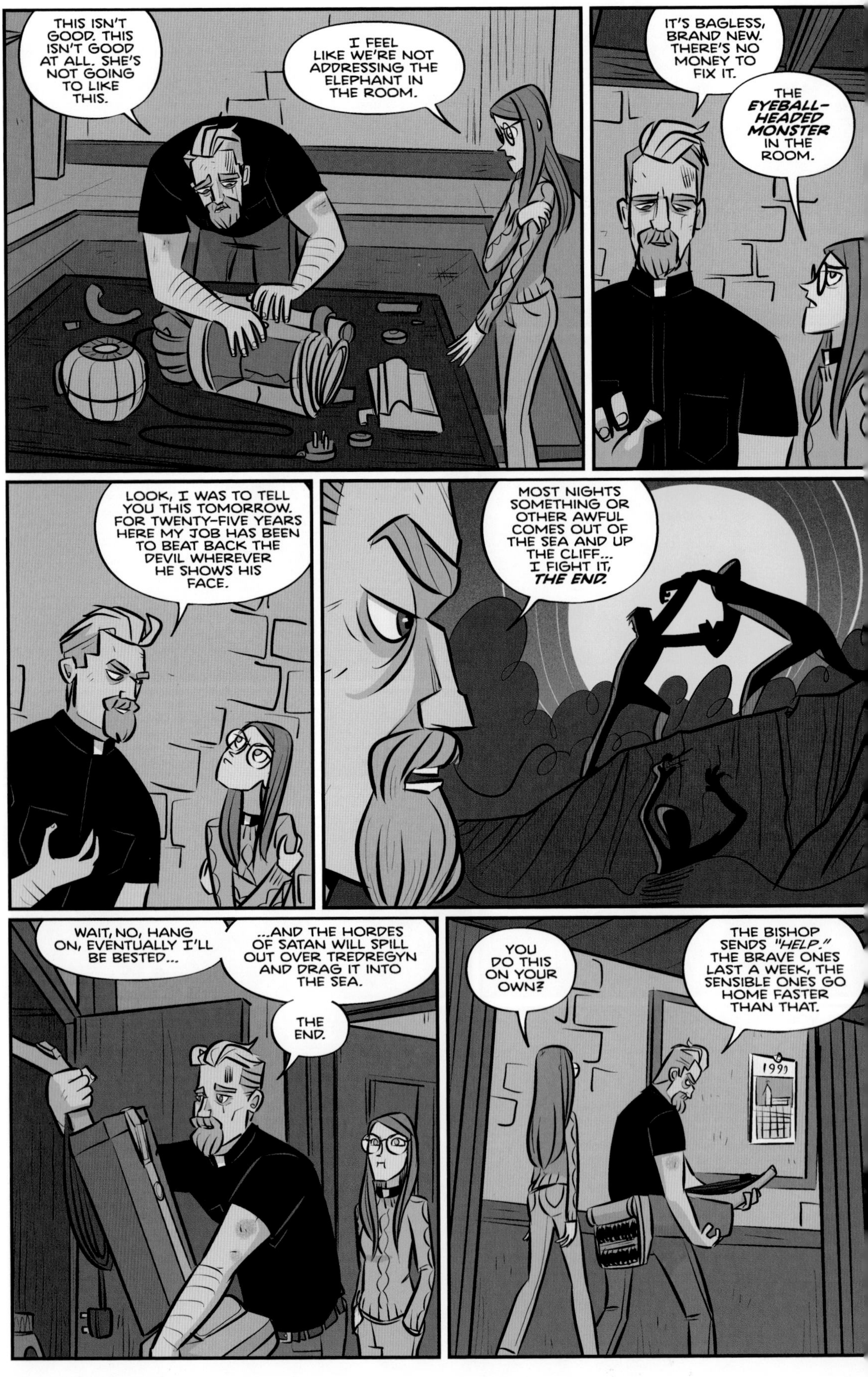
THIS ISN'T GOOD. THIS ISN'T GOOD AT ALL. SHE'S NOT GOING TO LIKE THIS.
I FEEL LIKE WE'RE NOT ADDRESSING THE ELEPHANT IN THE ROOM.
IT'S BAGLESS, BRAND NEW. THERE'S NO MONEY TO FIX IT.
THE ***EYEBALL-HEADED MONSTER*** IN THE ROOM.
LOOK, I WAS TO TELL YOU THIS TOMORROW. FOR TWENTY-FIVE YEARS HERE MY JOB HAS BEEN TO BEAT BACK THE DEVIL WHEREVER HE SHOWS HIS FACE.
MOST NIGHTS SOMETHING OR OTHER AWFUL COMES OUT OF THE SEA AND UP THE CLIFF... I FIGHT IT, ***THE END.***
WAIT, NO, HANG ON, EVENTUALLY I'LL BE BESTED...
...AND THE HORDES OF SATAN WILL SPILL OUT OVER TREDREGYN AND DRAG IT INTO THE SEA.
THE END.
YOU DO THIS ON YOUR OWN?
THE BISHOP SENDS *"HELP."* THE BRAVE ONES LAST A WEEK, THE SENSIBLE ONES GO HOME FASTER THAN THAT.
1999

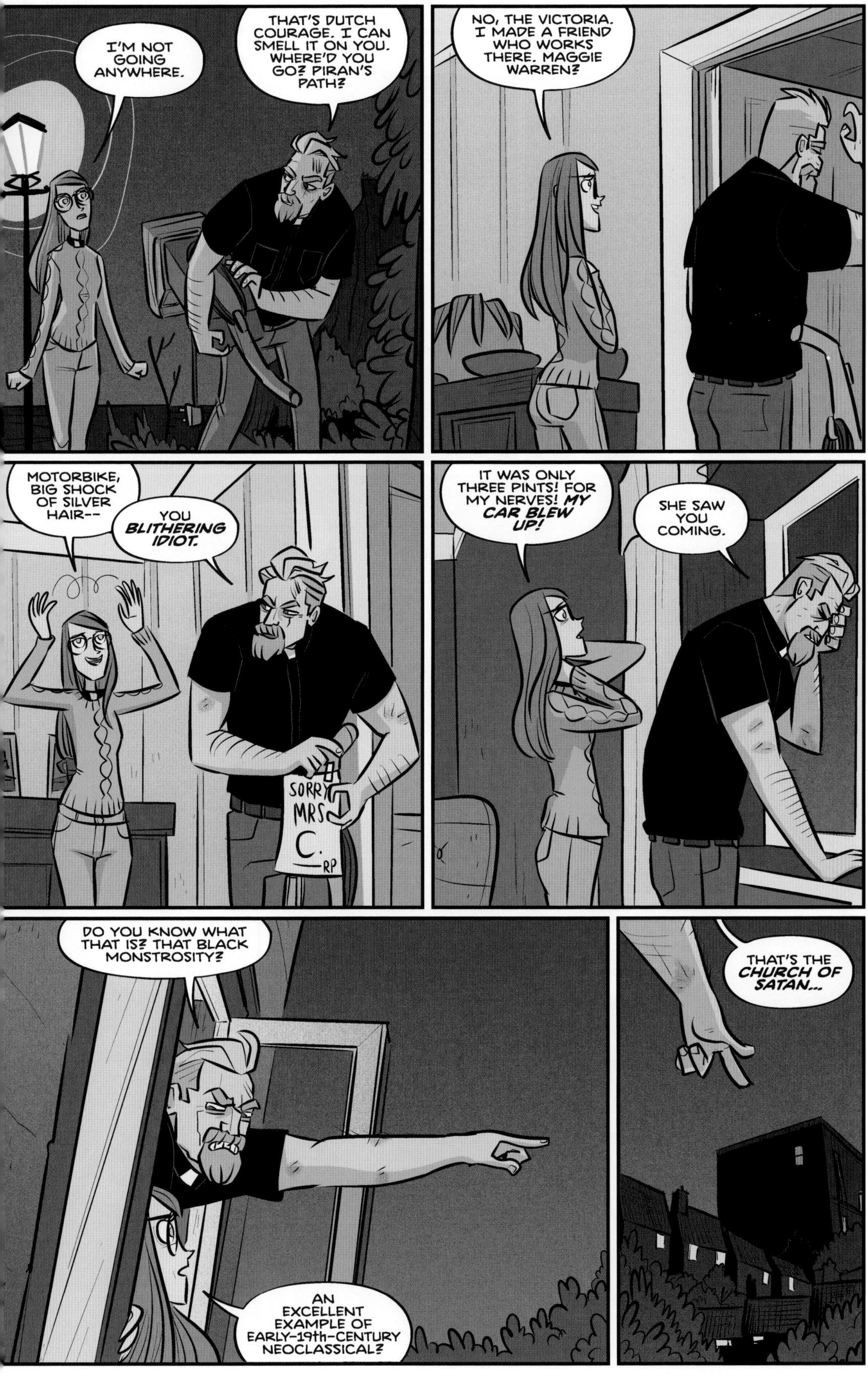
I'M NOT GOING ANYWHERE.
THAT'S DUTCH COURAGE. I CAN SMELL IT ON YOU. WHERE'D YOU GO? PIRAN'S PATH?
NO, THE VICTORIA. I MADE A FRIEND WHO WORKS THERE. MAGGIE WARREN?
MOTORBIKE, BIG SHOCK OF SILVER HAIR--
YOU *BLITHERING IDIOT.*
SORRY MRS C. RP
IT WAS ONLY THREE PINTS! FOR MY NERVES! *MY CAR BLEW UP!*
SHE SAW YOU COMING.
DO YOU KNOW WHAT THAT IS? THAT BLACK MONSTROSITY?
AN EXCELLENT EXAMPLE OF EARLY-19th-CENTURY NEOCLASSICAL?
THAT'S THE *CHURCH OF SATAN...*

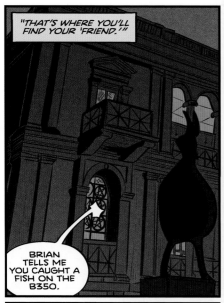

"THAT'S WHERE YOU'LL FIND YOUR 'FRIEND.'"

BRIAN TELLS ME YOU CAUGHT A FISH ON THE B350.

I DID NO SUCH THING. LEAVE ME ALONE, TOM.

A SWEET LITTLE THING. PENROSE'S NEW HELPER.

IT GOES WITHOUT SAYING THAT YOU DISGUST ME.

YOU'LL LIKE HER, TOM...

...PERFECT FOR TURNING. PLENTY OF LASAGNA IF ANYONE WANTS SOME.

EACH OF US MUST DO OUR PART FOR BELIAL, MARGARET.

UPSTAIRS TOILET'S BLOCKED AGAIN, BY THE BY.

DON'T YOU BOTH LOOK AT ME! I'VE BEEN BUNGED-UP FOR DAYS!

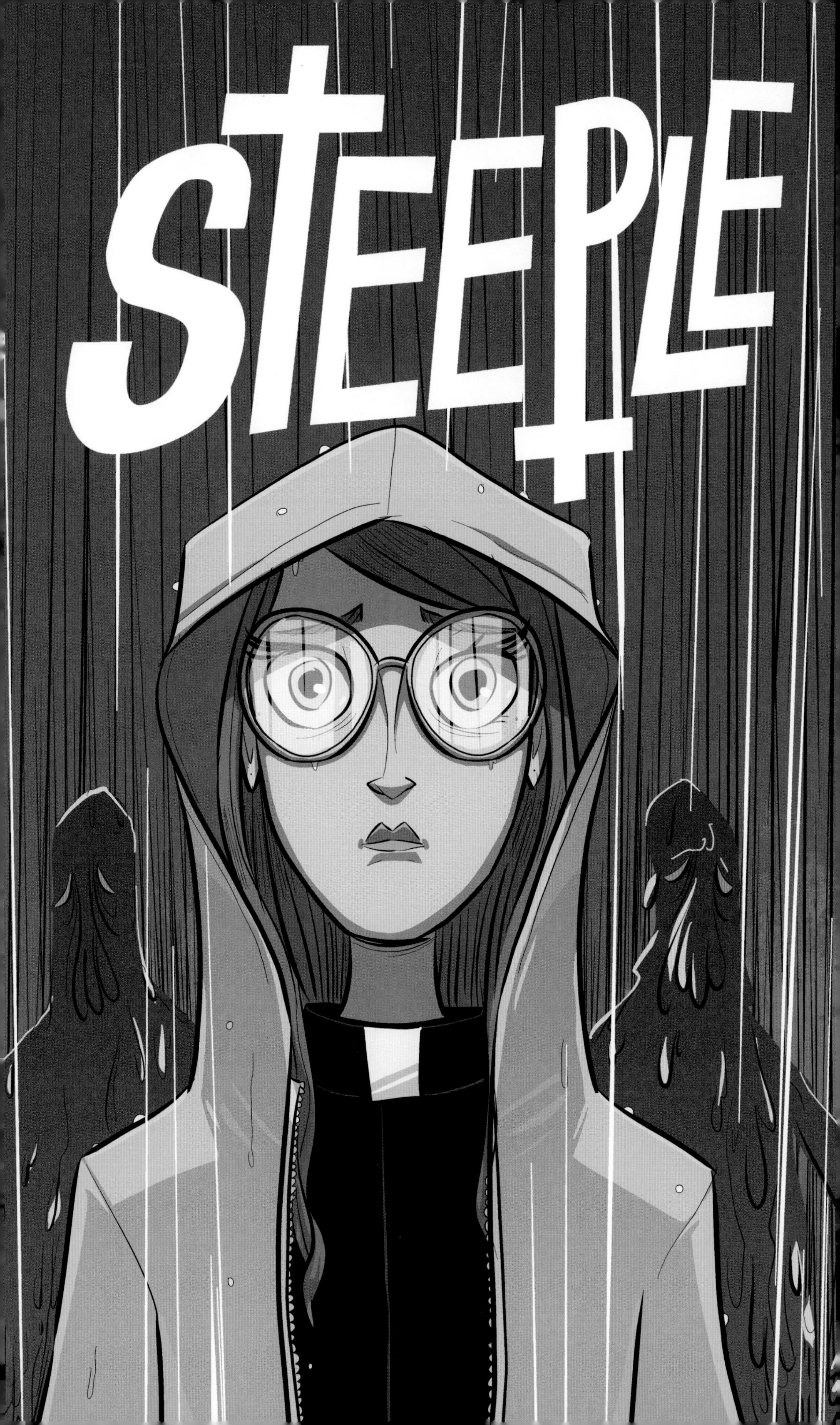
STEEPLE

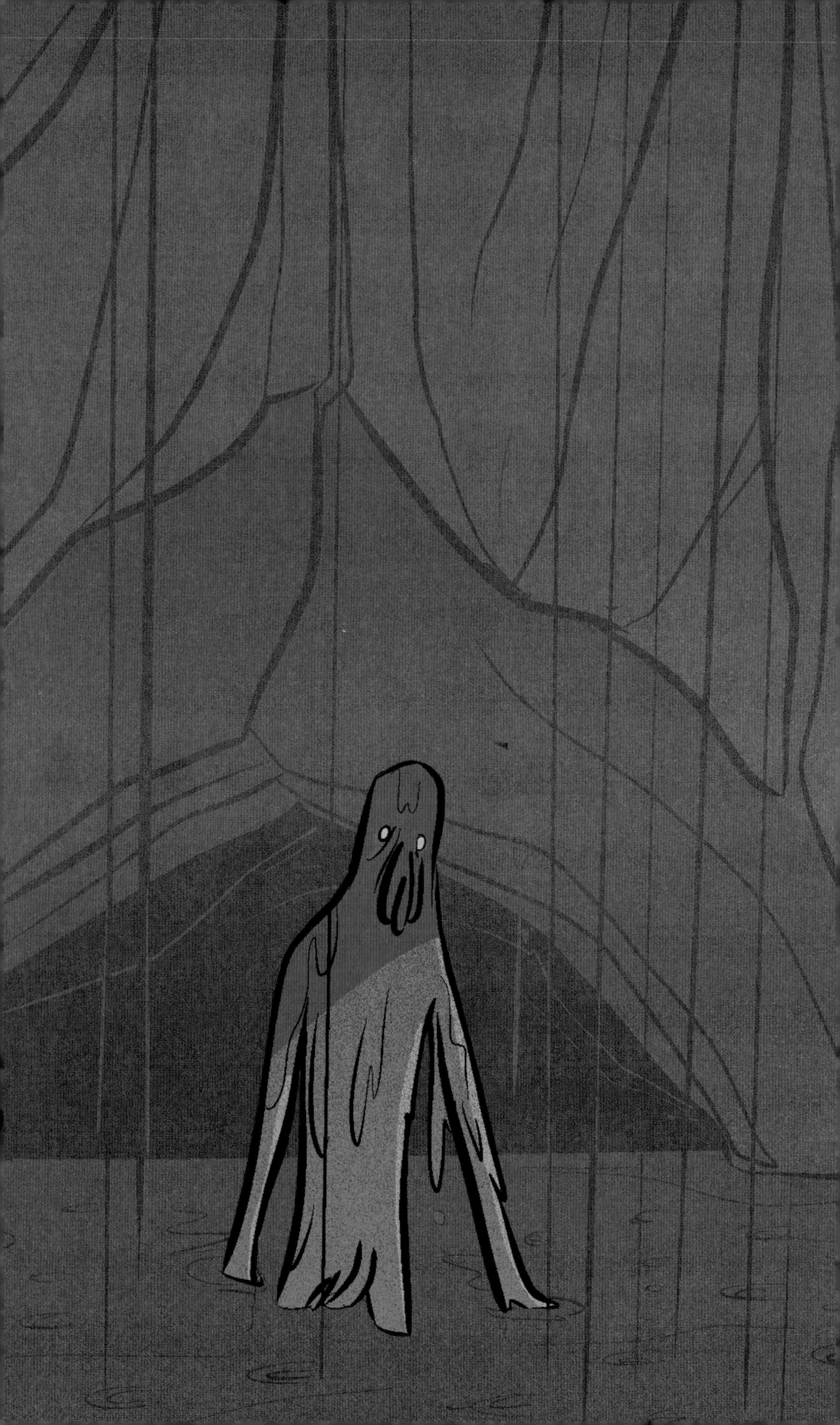

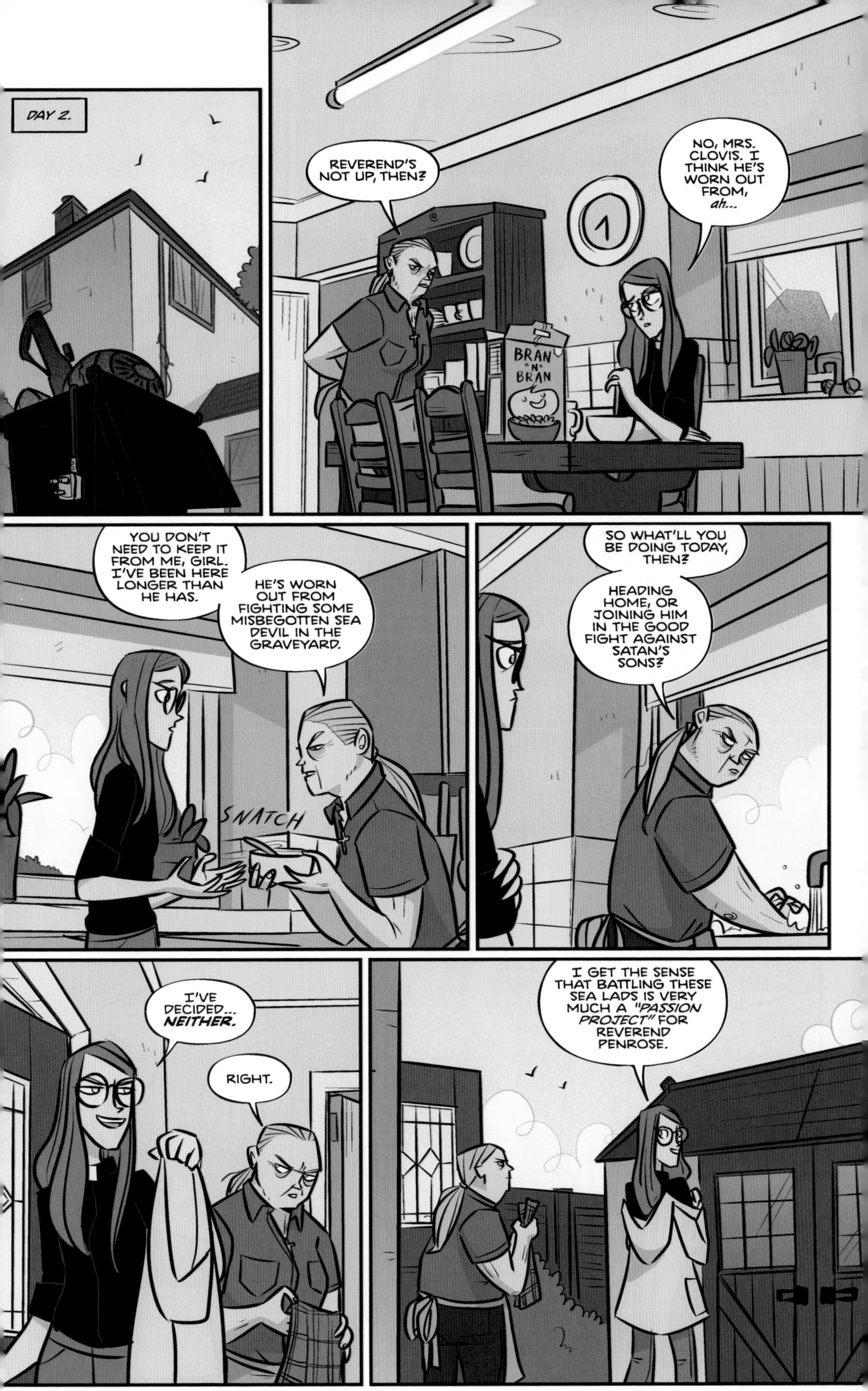
DAY 2.
REVEREND'S NOT UP, THEN?
NO, MRS. CLOVIS. I THINK HE'S WORN OUT FROM, *ah...*
BRAN "N" BRAN
YOU DON'T NEED TO KEEP IT FROM ME, GIRL. I'VE BEEN HERE LONGER THAN HE HAS.
HE'S WORN OUT FROM FIGHTING SOME MISBEGOTTEN SEA DEVIL IN THE GRAVEYARD.
SNATCH
SO WHAT'LL YOU BE DOING TODAY, THEN?
HEADING HOME, OR JOINING HIM IN THE GOOD FIGHT AGAINST SATAN'S SONS?
I'VE DECIDED... ***NEITHER.***
RIGHT.
I GET THE SENSE THAT BATTLING THESE SEA LADS IS VERY MUCH A *"PASSION PROJECT"* FOR REVEREND PENROSE.

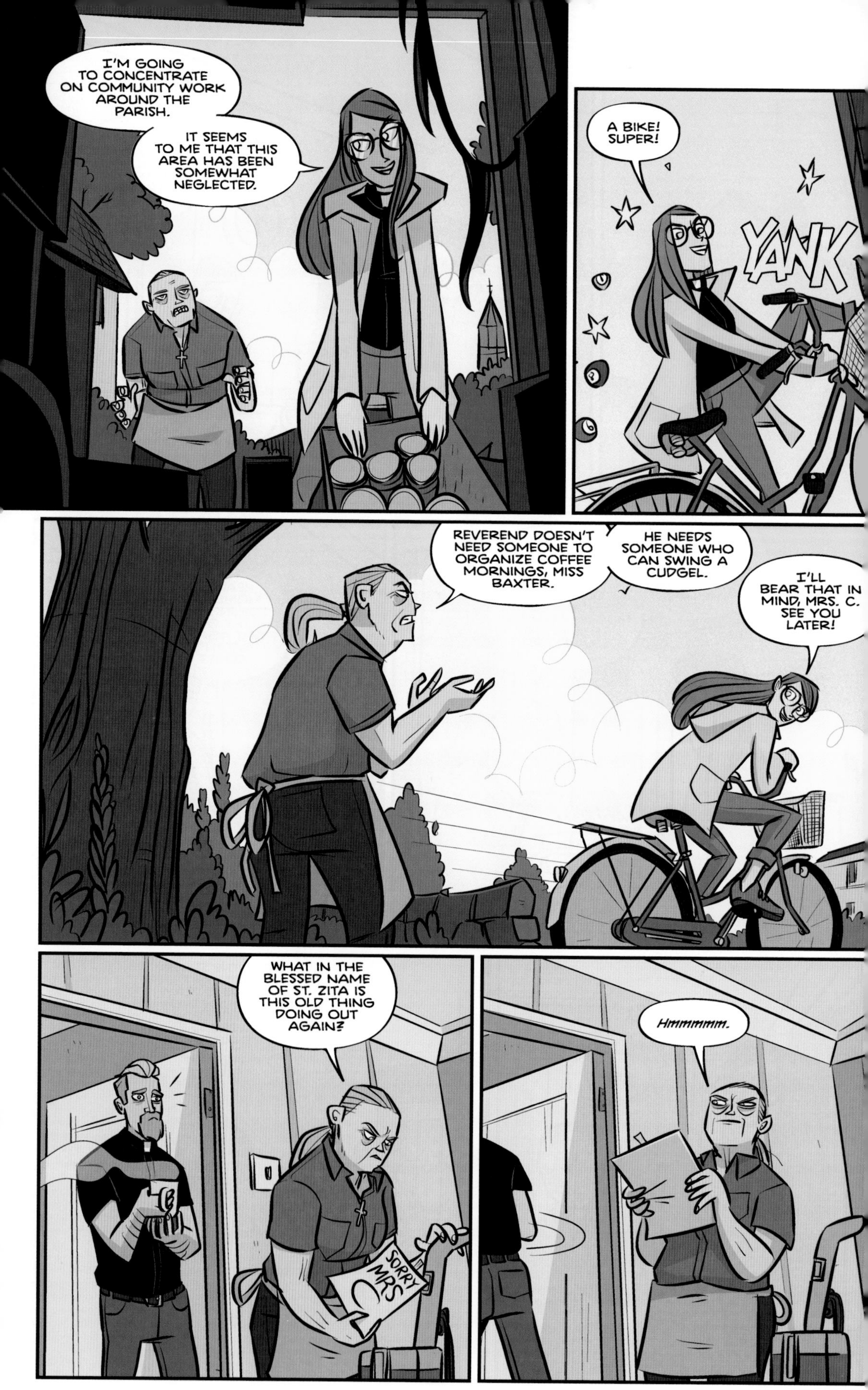
I'M GOING TO CONCENTRATE ON COMMUNITY WORK AROUND THE PARISH.
IT SEEMS TO ME THAT THIS AREA HAS BEEN SOMEWHAT NEGLECTED.
A BIKE! SUPER!
YANK
REVEREND DOESN'T NEED SOMEONE TO ORGANIZE COFFEE MORNINGS, MISS BAXTER.
HE NEEDS SOMEONE WHO CAN SWING A CUDGEL.
I'LL BEAR THAT IN MIND, MRS. C. SEE YOU LATER!
WHAT IN THE BLESSED NAME OF ST. ZITA IS THIS OLD THING DOING OUT AGAIN?
SORRY MRS C
Hmmmmmm.

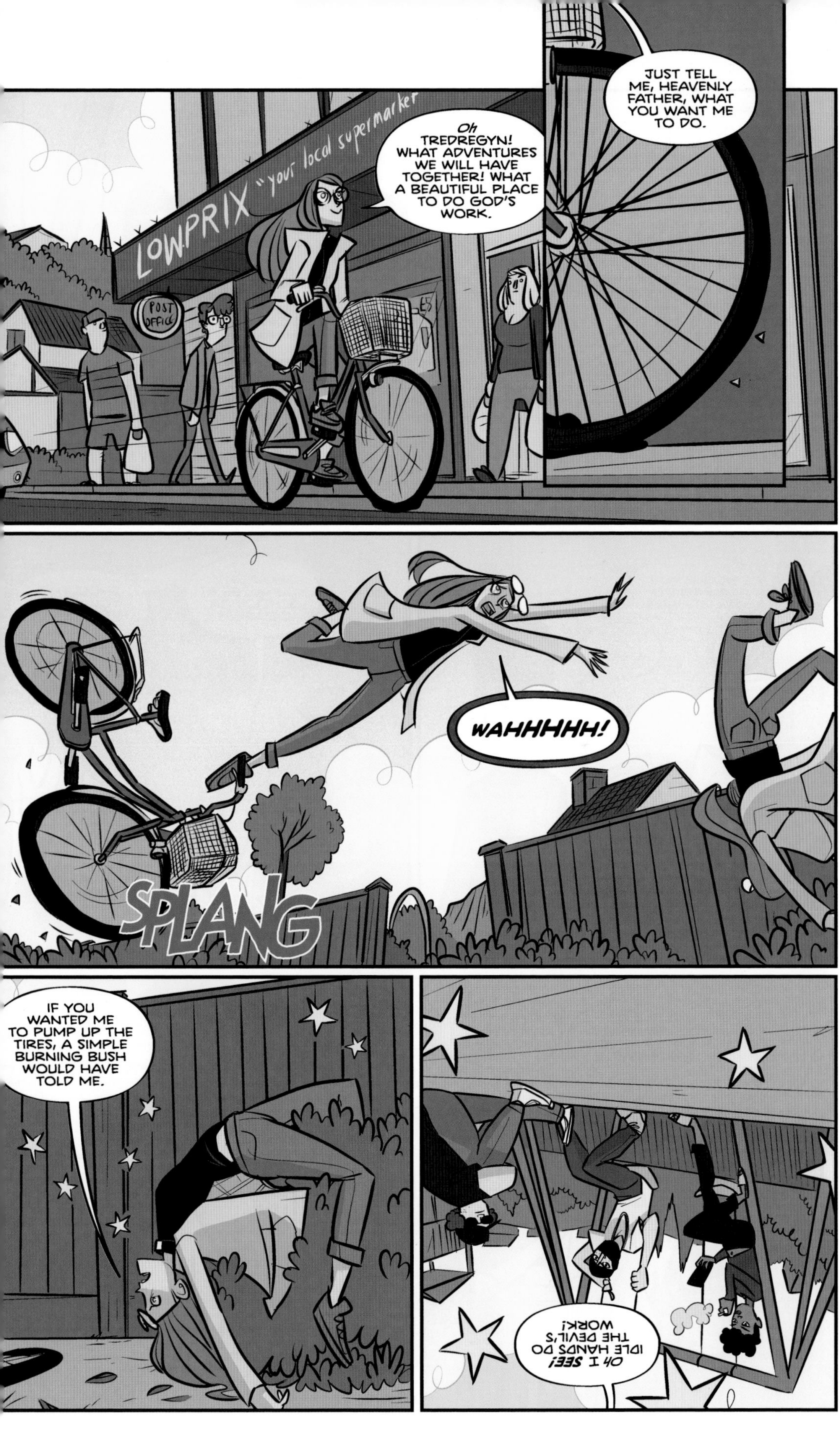
LOWPRIX "your local supermarket"
POST OFFICE
Oh TREDREGYN! WHAT ADVENTURES WE WILL HAVE TOGETHER! WHAT A BEAUTIFUL PLACE TO DO GOD'S WORK.
JUST TELL ME, HEAVENLY FATHER, WHAT YOU WANT ME TO DO.
WAHHHHH!
SPLANG
IF YOU WANTED ME TO PUMP UP THE TIRES, A SIMPLE BURNING BUSH WOULD HAVE TOLD ME.
OH I SEE! IDLE HANDS DO THE DEVIL'S WORK!

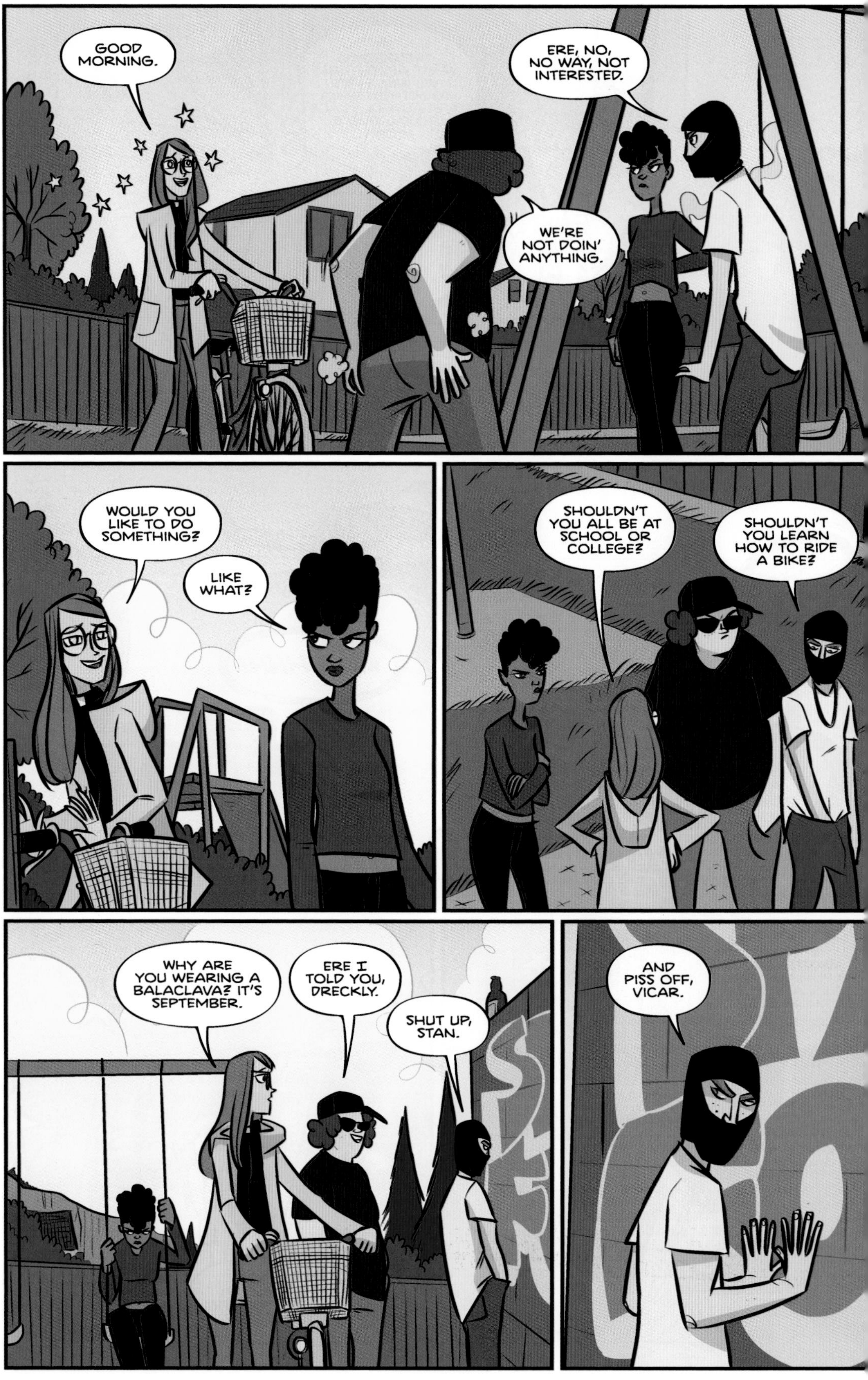
GOOD MORNING.
ERE, NO, NO WAY, NOT INTERESTED.
WE'RE NOT DOIN' ANYTHING.
WOULD YOU LIKE TO DO SOMETHING?
LIKE WHAT?
SHOULDN'T YOU ALL BE AT SCHOOL OR COLLEGE?
SHOULDN'T YOU LEARN HOW TO RIDE A BIKE?
WHY ARE YOU WEARING A BALACLAVA? IT'S SEPTEMBER.
ERE I TOLD YOU, DRECKLY.
SHUT UP, STAN.
AND PISS OFF, VICAR.

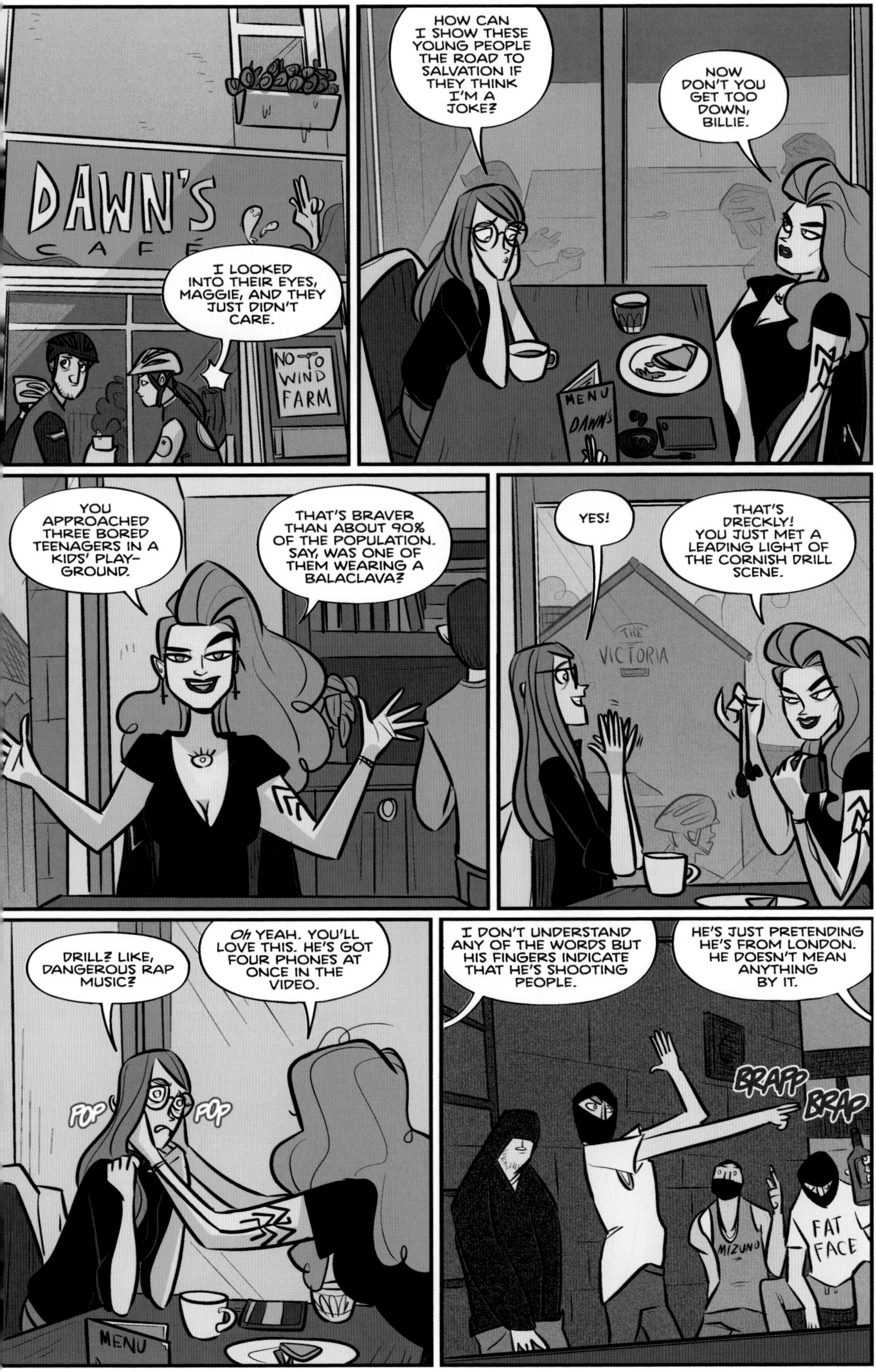
DAWN'S CAFE
I LOOKED INTO THEIR EYES, MAGGIE, AND THEY JUST DIDN'T CARE.
NO TO WIND FARM
HOW CAN I SHOW THESE YOUNG PEOPLE THE ROAD TO SALVATION IF THEY THINK I'M A JOKE?
NOW DON'T YOU GET TOO DOWN, BILLIE.
MENU
DAWN'S
YOU APPROACHED THREE BORED TEENAGERS IN A KIDS' PLAY-GROUND.
THAT'S BRAVER THAN ABOUT 90% OF THE POPULATION. SAY, WAS ONE OF THEM WEARING A BALACLAVA?
YES!
THAT'S DRECKLY! YOU JUST MET A LEADING LIGHT OF THE CORNISH DRILL SCENE.
THE VICTORIA
DRILL? LIKE, DANGEROUS RAP MUSIC?
Oh YEAH. YOU'LL LOVE THIS. HE'S GOT FOUR PHONES AT ONCE IN THE VIDEO.
POP
POP
MENU
I DON'T UNDERSTAND ANY OF THE WORDS BUT HIS FINGERS INDICATE THAT HE'S SHOOTING PEOPLE.
HE'S JUST PRETENDING HE'S FROM LONDON. HE DOESN'T MEAN ANYTHING BY IT.
BRAPP
BRAP
MIZUNO
FAT FACE

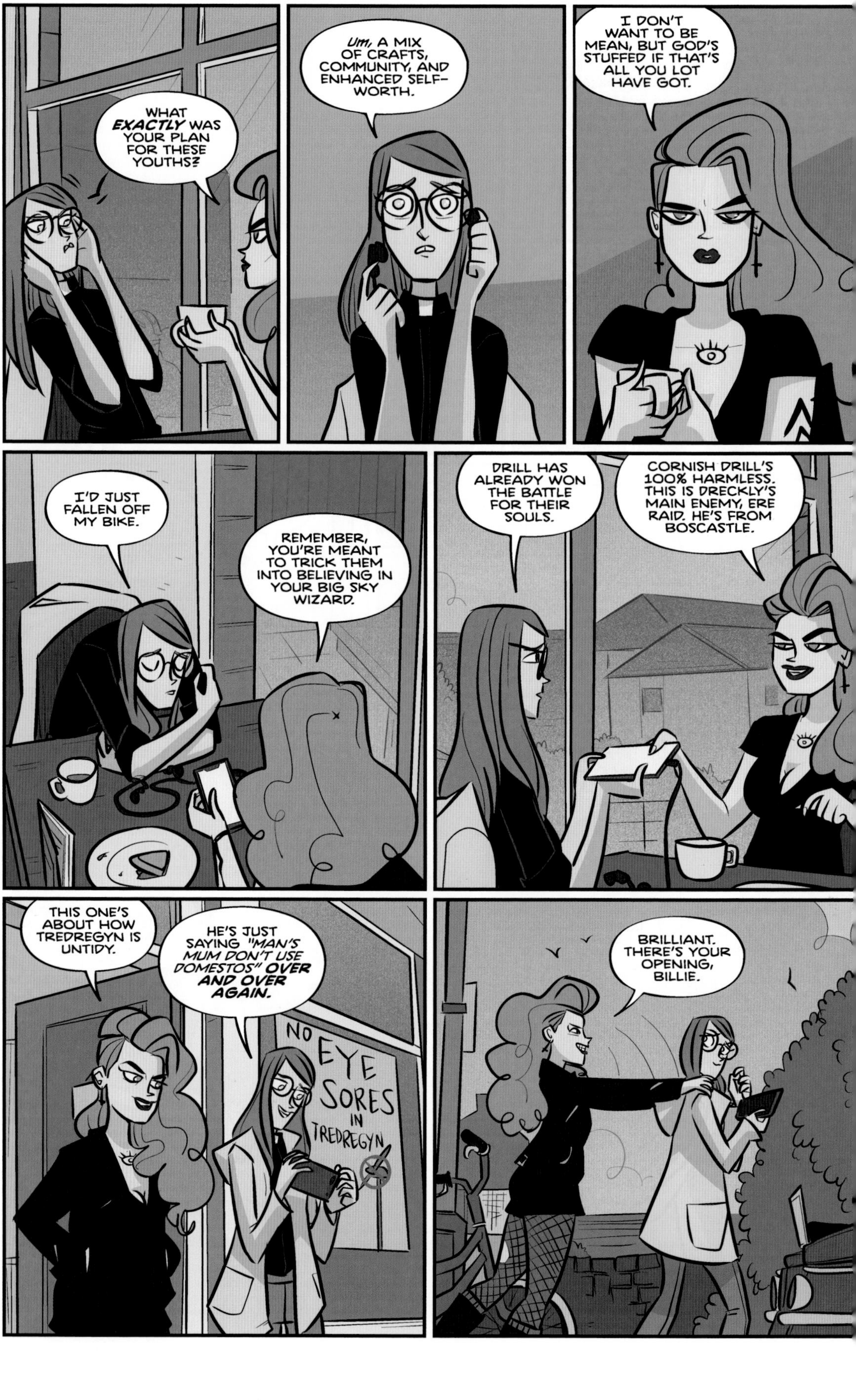
WHAT *EXACTLY* WAS YOUR PLAN FOR THESE YOUTHS?
Um, A MIX OF CRAFTS, COMMUNITY, AND ENHANCED SELF-WORTH.
I DON'T WANT TO BE MEAN, BUT GOD'S STUFFED IF THAT'S ALL YOU LOT HAVE GOT.
I'D JUST FALLEN OFF MY BIKE.
REMEMBER, YOU'RE MEANT TO TRICK THEM INTO BELIEVING IN YOUR BIG SKY WIZARD.
DRILL HAS ALREADY WON THE BATTLE FOR THEIR SOULS.
CORNISH DRILL'S 100% HARMLESS. THIS IS DRECKLY'S MAIN ENEMY, ERE RAID. HE'S FROM BOSCASTLE.
THIS ONE'S ABOUT HOW TREDREGYN IS UNTIDY.
HE'S JUST SAYING *"MAN'S MUM DON'T USE DOMESTOS"* **OVER AND OVER AGAIN.**
NO EYE SORES IN TREDREGYN
BRILLIANT. THERE'S YOUR OPENING, BILLIE.

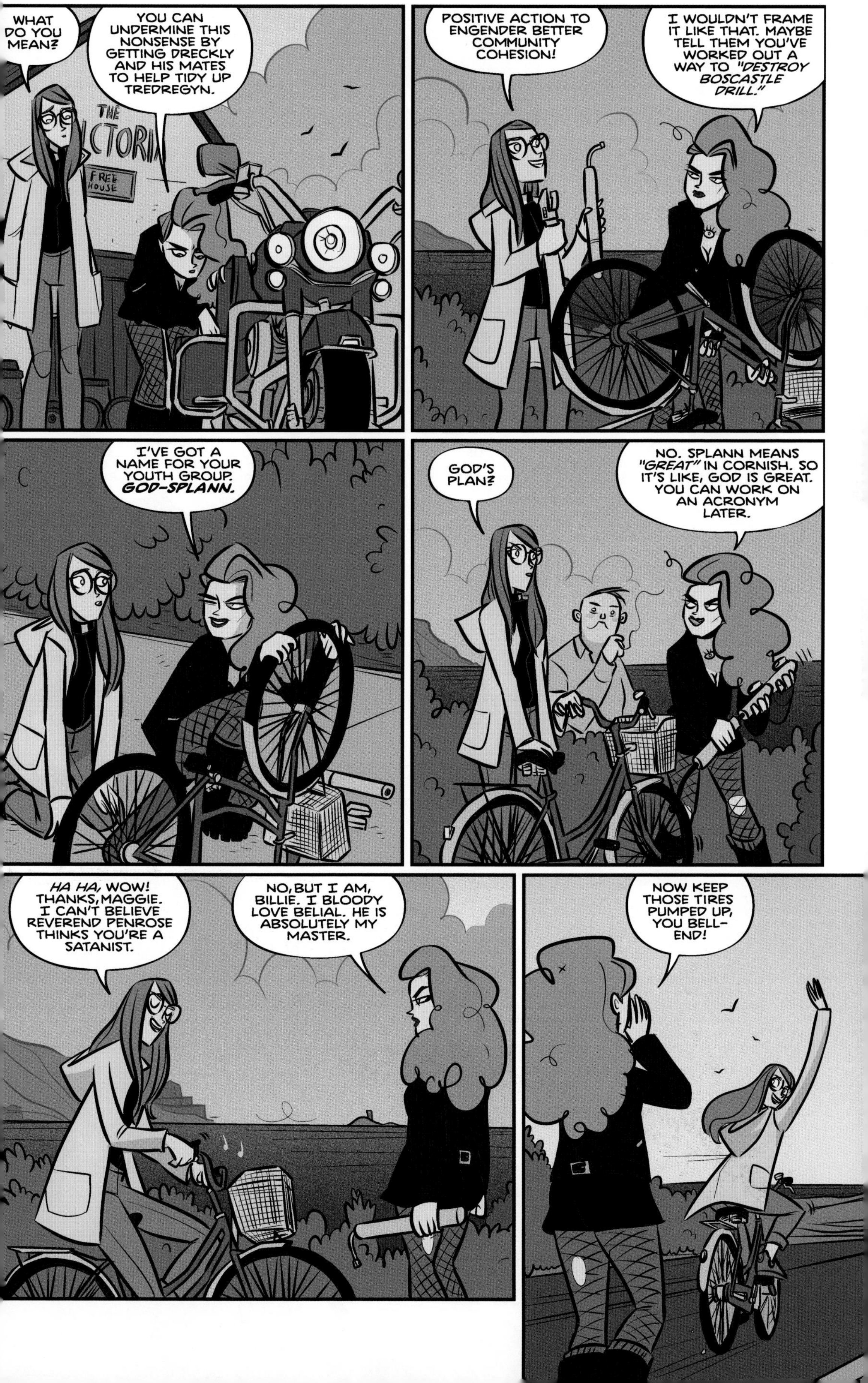
WHAT DO YOU MEAN?
YOU CAN UNDERMINE THIS NONSENSE BY GETTING DRECKLY AND HIS MATES TO HELP TIDY UP TREDREGYN.
THE VICTORI
FREE HOUSE
POSITIVE ACTION TO ENGENDER BETTER COMMUNITY COHESION!
I WOULDN'T FRAME IT LIKE THAT. MAYBE TELL THEM YOU'VE WORKED OUT A WAY TO *"DESTROY BOSCASTLE DRILL."*
I'VE GOT A NAME FOR YOUR YOUTH GROUP. ***GOD-SPLANN.***
GOD'S PLAN?
NO. SPLANN MEANS *"GREAT"* IN CORNISH. SO IT'S LIKE, GOD IS GREAT. YOU CAN WORK ON AN ACRONYM LATER.
HA HA, WOW! THANKS, MAGGIE. I CAN'T BELIEVE REVEREND PENROSE THINKS YOU'RE A SATANIST.
NO, BUT I AM, BILLIE. I BLOODY LOVE BELIAL. HE IS ABSOLUTELY MY MASTER.
NOW KEEP THOSE TIRES PUMPED UP, YOU BELL-END!

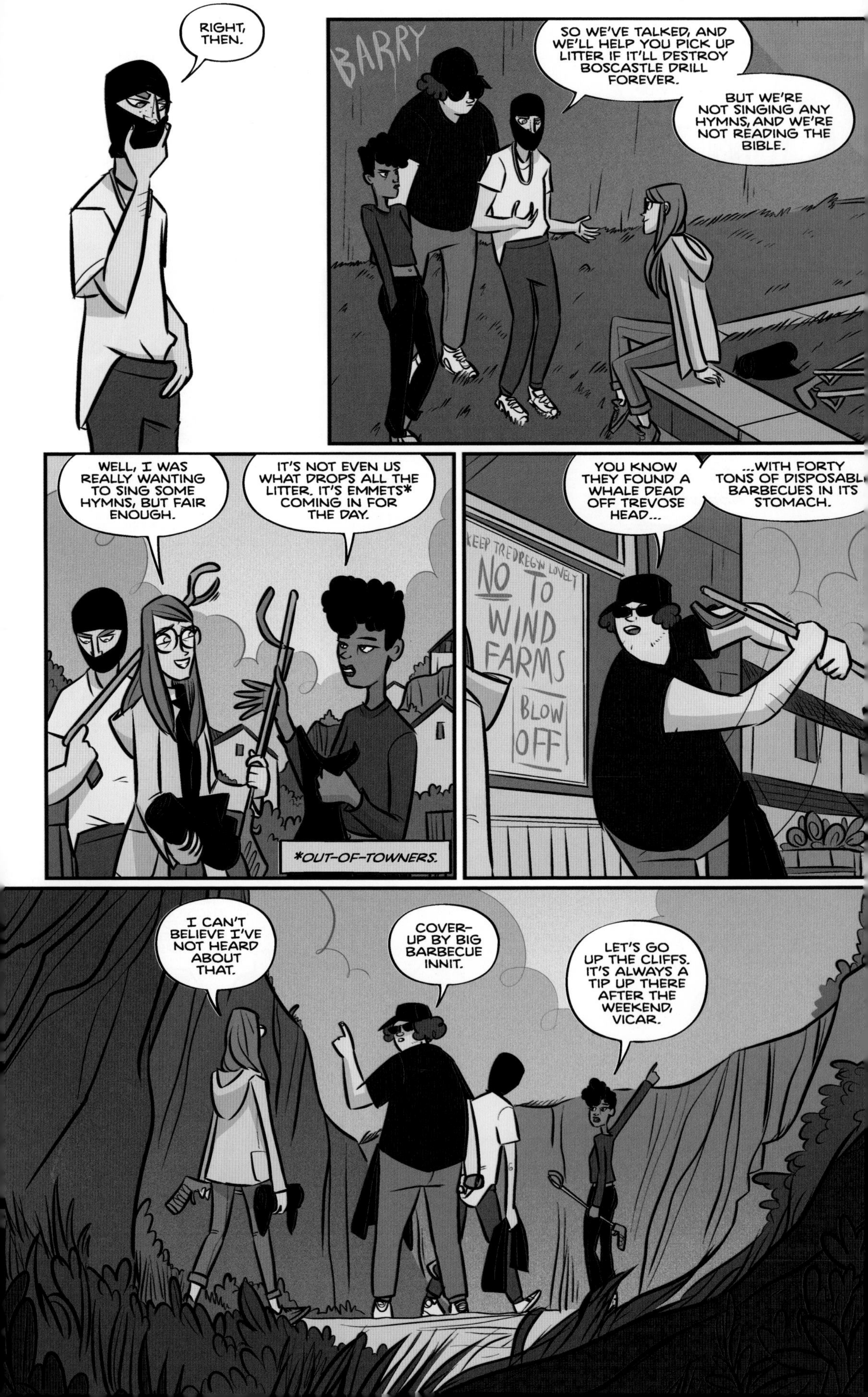
RIGHT, THEN.
BARRY
SO WE'VE TALKED, AND WE'LL HELP YOU PICK UP LITTER IF IT'LL DESTROY BOSCASTLE DRILL FOREVER.
BUT WE'RE NOT SINGING ANY HYMNS, AND WE'RE NOT READING THE BIBLE.
WELL, I WAS REALLY WANTING TO SING SOME HYMNS, BUT FAIR ENOUGH.
IT'S NOT EVEN US WHAT DROPS ALL THE LITTER. IT'S EMMETS* COMING IN FOR THE DAY.
*OUT-OF-TOWNERS.
YOU KNOW THEY FOUND A WHALE DEAD OFF TREVOSE HEAD...
...WITH FORTY TONS OF DISPOSABL BARBECUES IN ITS STOMACH.
KEEP TREDREGYN LOVELY
NO TO WIND FARMS
BLOW OFF
I CAN'T BELIEVE I'VE NOT HEARD ABOUT THAT.
COVER-UP BY BIG BARBECUE INNIT.
LET'S GO UP THE CLIFFS. IT'S ALWAYS A TIP UP THERE AFTER THE WEEKEND, VICAR.

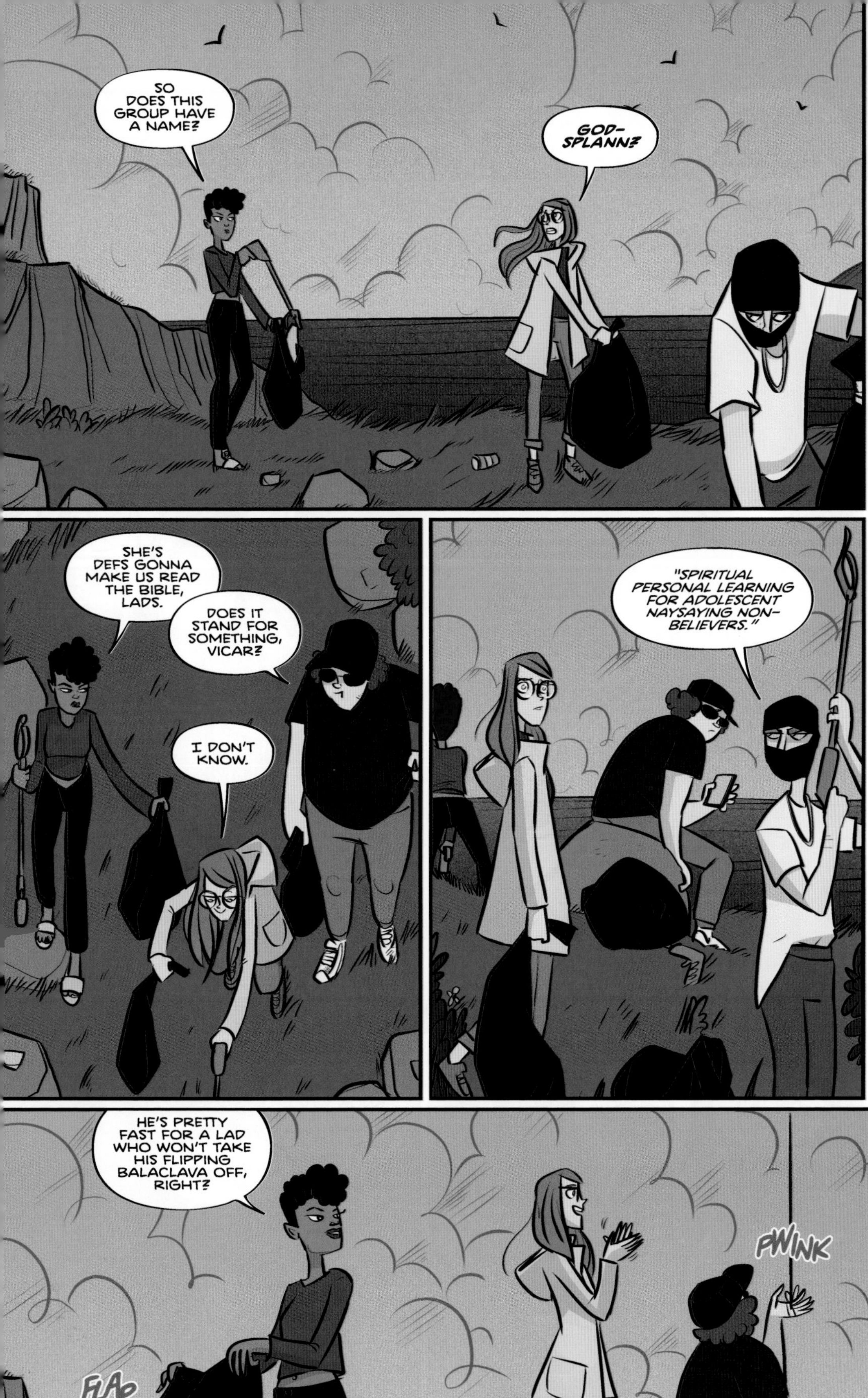
SO DOES THIS GROUP HAVE A NAME?
GOD-SPLANN?
SHE'S DEFS GONNA MAKE US READ THE BIBLE, LADS.
DOES IT STAND FOR SOMETHING, VICAR?
I DON'T KNOW.
"SPIRITUAL PERSONAL LEARNING FOR ADOLESCENT NAYSAYING NON-BELIEVERS."
HE'S PRETTY FAST FOR A LAD WHO WON'T TAKE HIS FLIPPING BALACLAVA OFF, RIGHT?
PWINK
FLAP

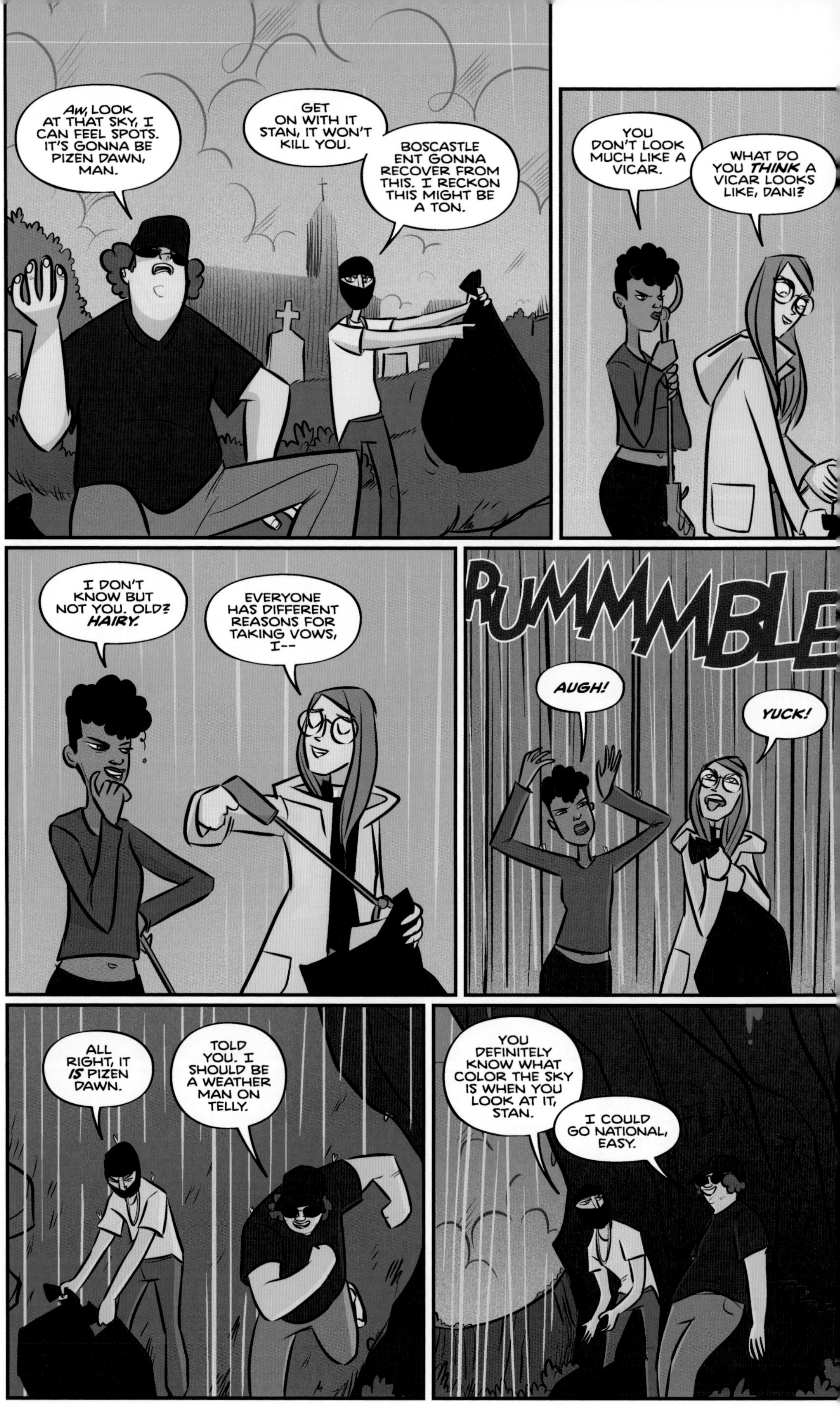
AW, LOOK AT THAT SKY, I CAN FEEL SPOTS. IT'S GONNA BE PIZEN DAWN, MAN.
GET ON WITH IT STAN, IT WON'T KILL YOU.
BOSCASTLE ENT GONNA RECOVER FROM THIS. I RECKON THIS MIGHT BE A TON.
YOU DON'T LOOK MUCH LIKE A VICAR.
WHAT DO YOU *THINK* A VICAR LOOKS LIKE, DANI?
I DON'T KNOW BUT NOT YOU. OLD? ***HAIRY.***
EVERYONE HAS DIFFERENT REASONS FOR TAKING VOWS, I--
RUMMMBLE
AUGH!
YUCK!
ALL RIGHT, IT *IS* PIZEN DAWN.
TOLD YOU. I SHOULD BE A WEATHER MAN ON TELLY.
YOU DEFINITELY KNOW WHAT COLOR THE SKY IS WHEN YOU LOOK AT IT, STAN.
I COULD GO NATIONAL, EASY.

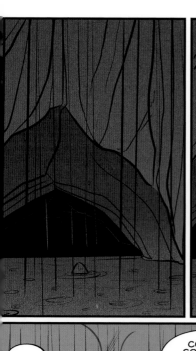

HA HA HA! RUN, EVERYONE!

NO.

COME ON, COME BACK TO THE CHURCH FOR TEA AND A BISCUIT.

WE CAN CARRY ON WHEN THE RAIN STOPS.

OKAY, VICAR.

WHAT KIND OF BISCUITS? IT BETTER NOT BE THEM *WAFERS.*

THE BODY OF CHRIST ISN'T A SNACK, STAN.

IT'S MORE OF A *TREAT.*

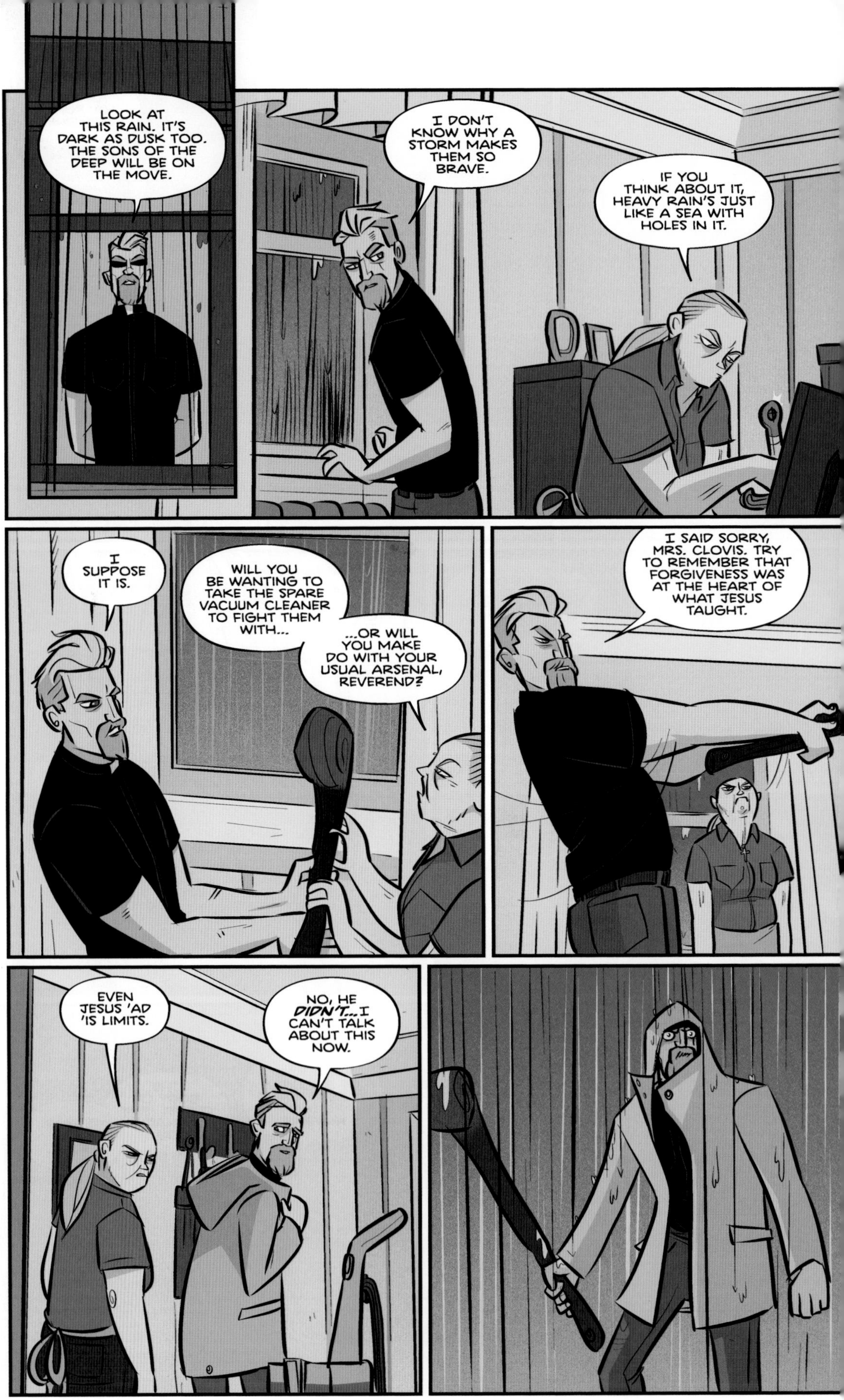
LOOK AT THIS RAIN. IT'S DARK AS DUSK TOO. THE SONS OF THE DEEP WILL BE ON THE MOVE.
I DON'T KNOW WHY A STORM MAKES THEM SO BRAVE.
IF YOU THINK ABOUT IT, HEAVY RAIN'S JUST LIKE A SEA WITH HOLES IN IT.
I SUPPOSE IT IS.
WILL YOU BE WANTING TO TAKE THE SPARE VACUUM CLEANER TO FIGHT THEM WITH...
...OR WILL YOU MAKE DO WITH YOUR USUAL ARSENAL, REVEREND?
I SAID SORRY, MRS. CLOVIS. TRY TO REMEMBER THAT FORGIVENESS WAS AT THE HEART OF WHAT JESUS TAUGHT.
EVEN JESUS 'AD 'IS LIMITS.
NO, HE *DIDN'T*... I CAN'T TALK ABOUT THIS NOW.

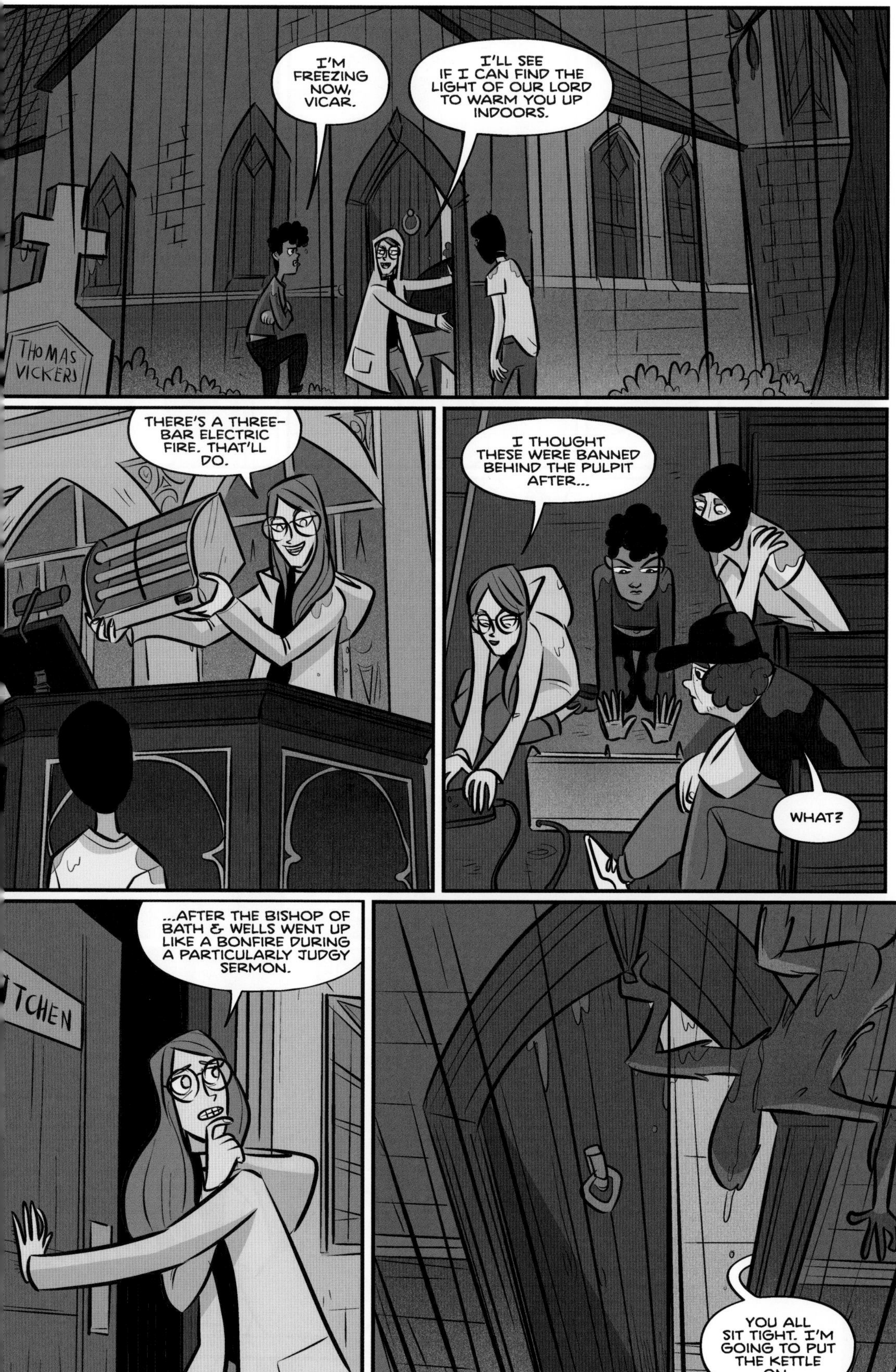
THOMAS VICKERS
I'M FREEZING NOW, VICAR.
I'LL SEE IF I CAN FIND THE LIGHT OF OUR LORD TO WARM YOU UP INDOORS.
THERE'S A THREE-BAR ELECTRIC FIRE. THAT'LL DO.
I THOUGHT THESE WERE BANNED BEHIND THE PULPIT AFTER...
WHAT?
...AFTER THE BISHOP OF BATH & WELLS WENT UP LIKE A BONFIRE DURING A PARTICULARLY JUDGY SERMON.
TCHEN
YOU ALL SIT TIGHT. I'M GOING TO PUT THE KETTLE ON.

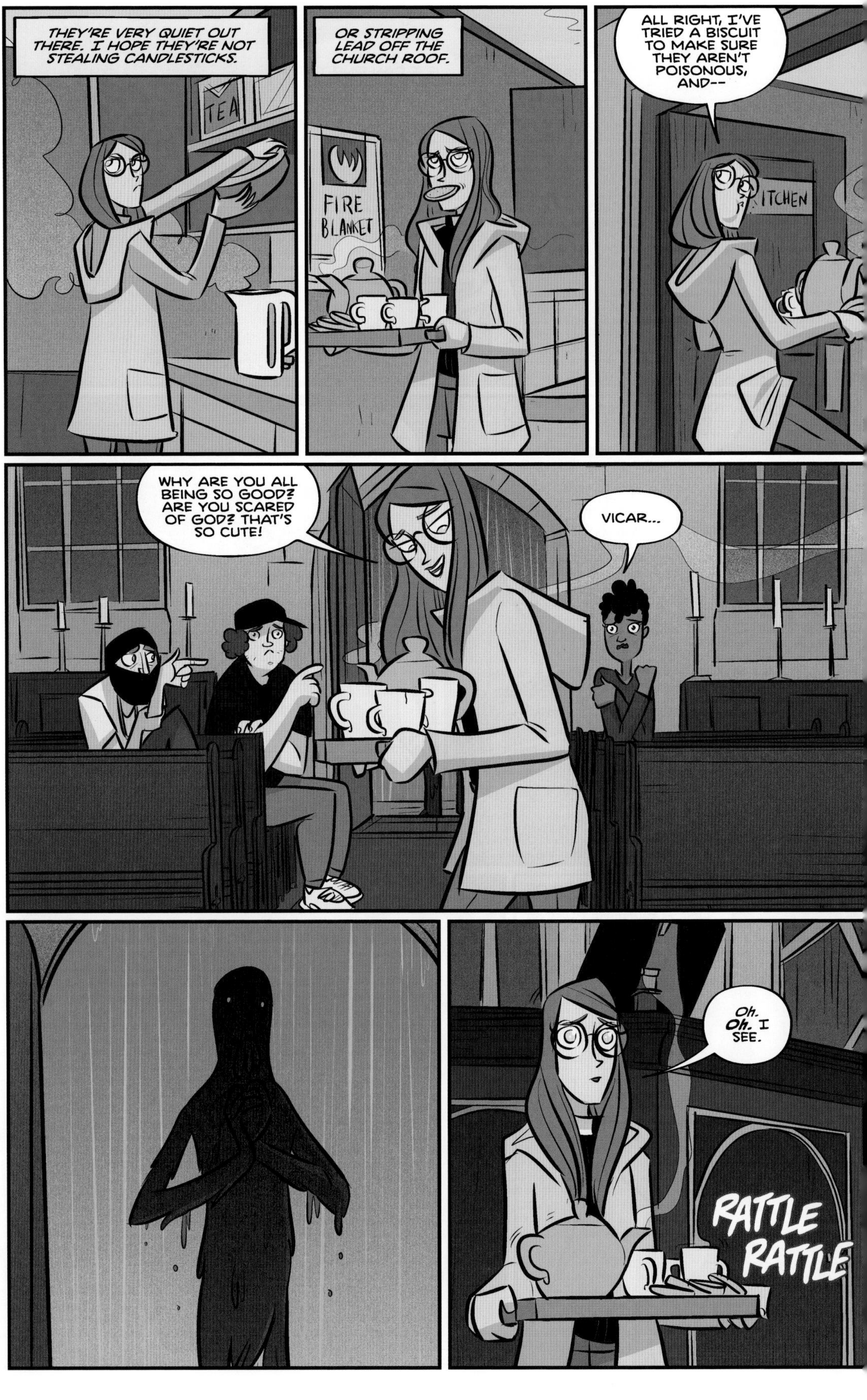

THEY'RE VERY QUIET OUT THERE. I HOPE THEY'RE NOT STEALING CANDLESTICKS.
TEA
OR STRIPPING LEAD OFF THE CHURCH ROOF.
FIRE BLANKET
ALL RIGHT, I'VE TRIED A BISCUIT TO MAKE SURE THEY AREN'T POISONOUS, AND--
ITCHEN
WHY ARE YOU ALL BEING SO GOOD? ARE YOU SCARED OF GOD? THAT'S SO CUTE!
VICAR...
Oh. Oh. I SEE.
RATTLE RATTLE

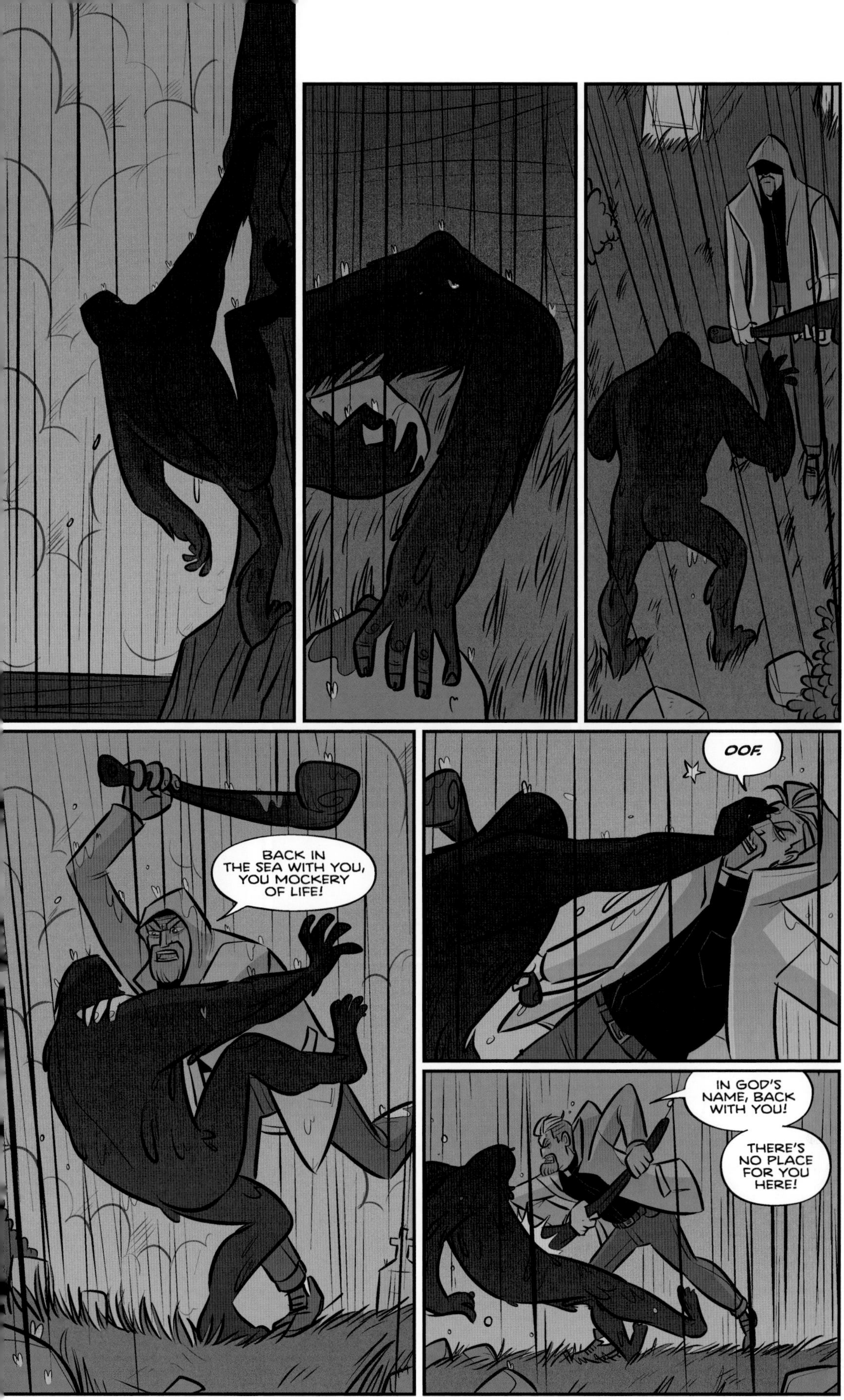
BACK IN THE SEA WITH YOU, YOU MOCKERY OF LIFE!
OOF.
IN GOD'S NAME, BACK WITH YOU!
THERE'S NO PLACE FOR YOU HERE!

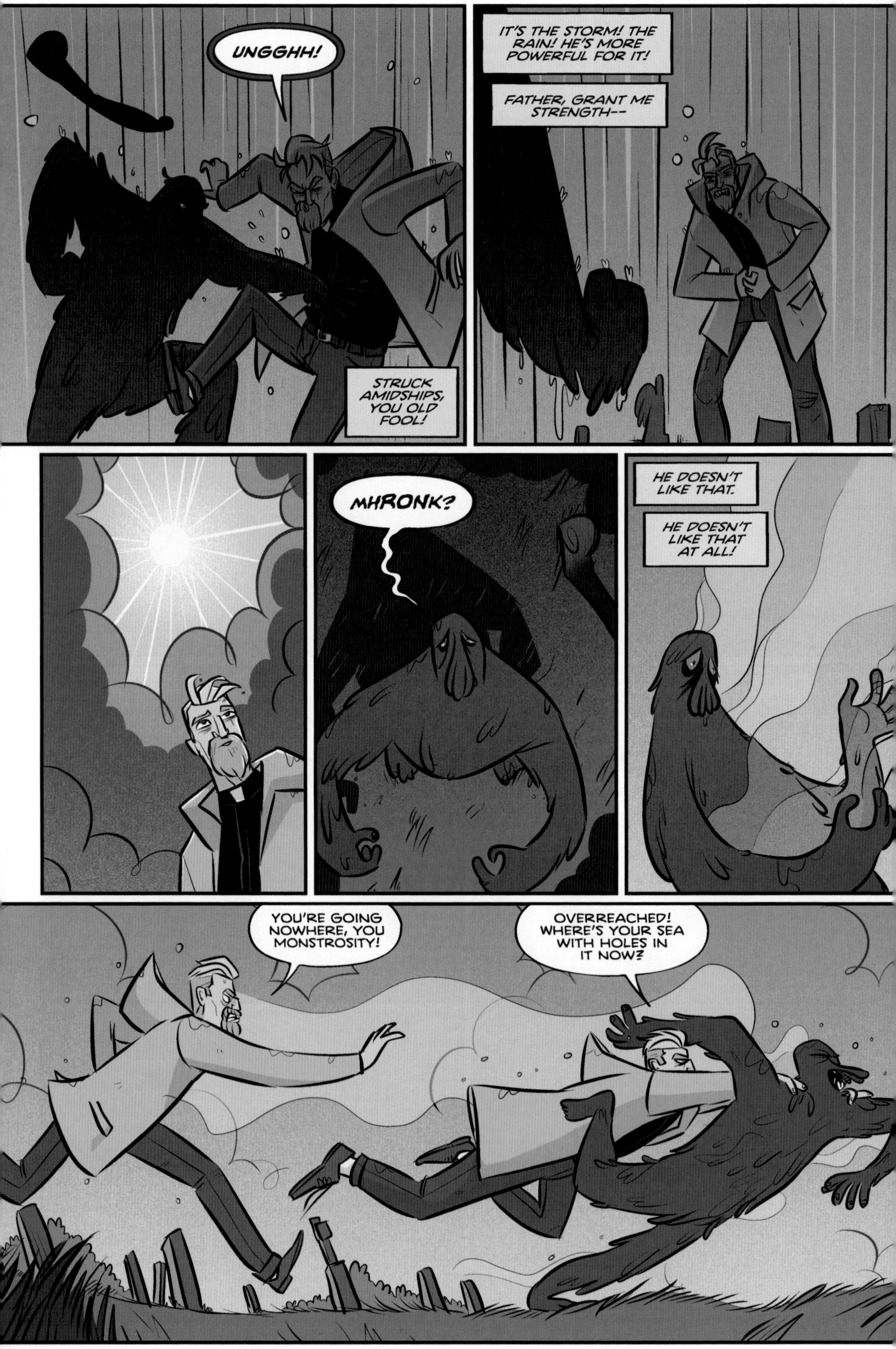
UNGGHH!
STRUCK AMIDSHIPS, YOU OLD FOOL!
IT'S THE STORM! THE RAIN! HE'S MORE POWERFUL FOR IT!
FATHER, GRANT ME STRENGTH--
MHRONK?
HE DOESN'T LIKE THAT.
HE DOESN'T LIKE THAT AT ALL!
YOU'RE GOING NOWHERE, YOU MONSTROSITY!
OVERREACHED! WHERE'S YOUR SEA WITH HOLES IN IT NOW?

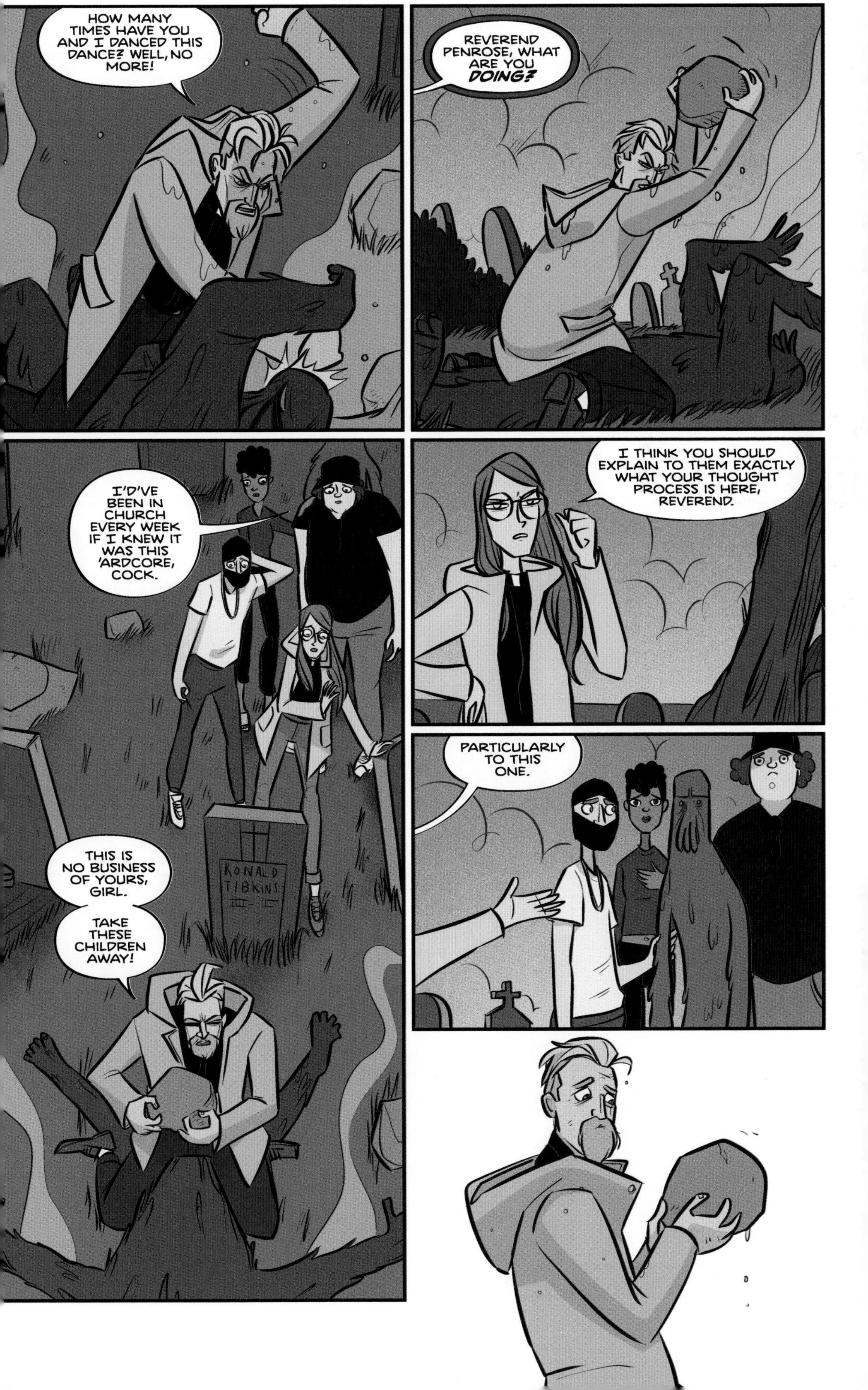
HOW MANY TIMES HAVE YOU AND I DANCED THIS DANCE? WELL, NO MORE!
REVEREND PENROSE, WHAT ARE YOU DOING?
I'D'VE BEEN IN CHURCH EVERY WEEK IF I KNEW IT WAS THIS 'ARDCORE, COCK.
RONALD TIBKINS
THIS IS NO BUSINESS OF YOURS, GIRL.
TAKE THESE CHILDREN AWAY!
I THINK YOU SHOULD EXPLAIN TO THEM EXACTLY WHAT YOUR THOUGHT PROCESS IS HERE, REVEREND.
PARTICULARLY TO THIS ONE.

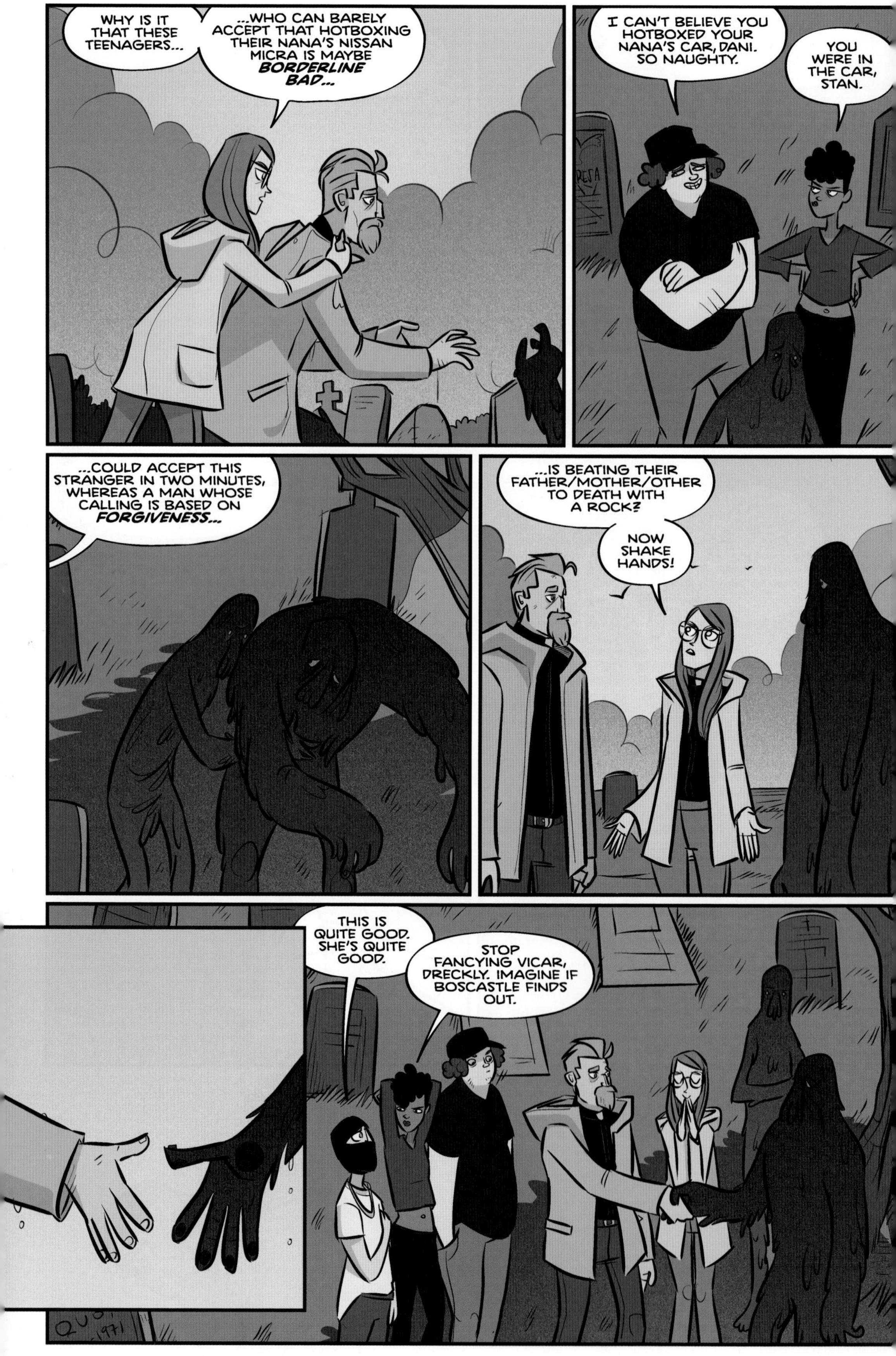
WHY IS IT THAT THESE TEENAGERS...
...WHO CAN BARELY ACCEPT THAT HOTBOXING THEIR NANA'S NISSAN MICRA IS MAYBE ***BORDERLINE BAD...***
I CAN'T BELIEVE YOU HOTBOXED YOUR NANA'S CAR, DANI. SO NAUGHTY.
YOU WERE IN THE CAR, STAN.
...COULD ACCEPT THIS STRANGER IN TWO MINUTES, WHEREAS A MAN WHOSE CALLING IS BASED ON ***FORGIVENESS...***
...IS BEATING THEIR FATHER/MOTHER/OTHER TO DEATH WITH A ROCK?
NOW SHAKE HANDS!
THIS IS QUITE GOOD. SHE'S QUITE GOOD.
STOP FANCYING VICAR, DRECKLY. IMAGINE IF BOSCASTLE FINDS OUT.

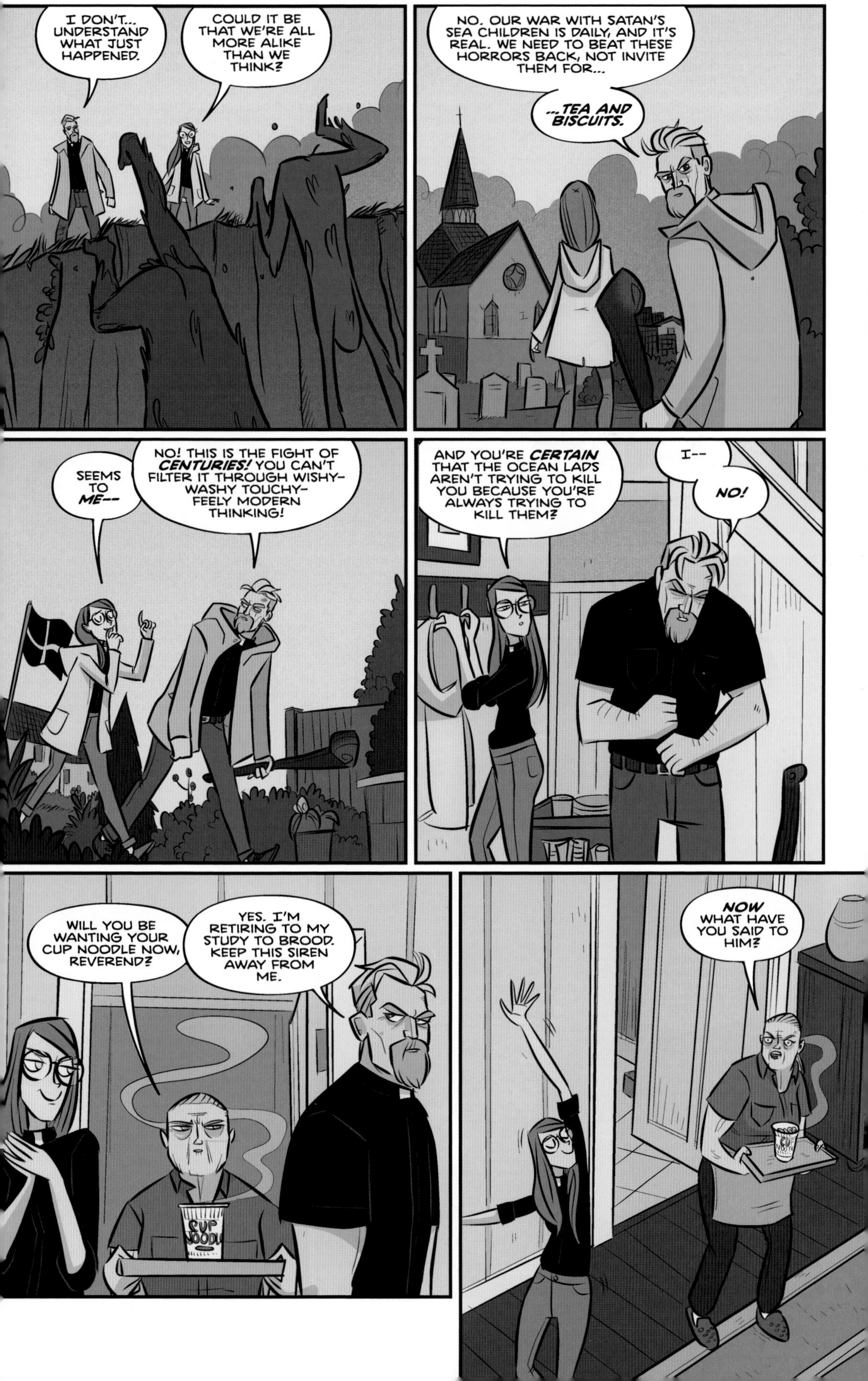
I DON'T... UNDERSTAND WHAT JUST HAPPENED.
COULD IT BE THAT WE'RE ALL MORE ALIKE THAN WE THINK?
NO. OUR WAR WITH SATAN'S SEA CHILDREN IS DAILY, AND IT'S REAL. WE NEED TO BEAT THESE HORRORS BACK, NOT INVITE THEM FOR...
...TEA AND BISCUITS.
SEEMS TO ME--
NO! THIS IS THE FIGHT OF CENTURIES! YOU CAN'T FILTER IT THROUGH WISHY-WASHY TOUCHY-FEELY MODERN THINKING!
AND YOU'RE CERTAIN THAT THE OCEAN LADS AREN'T TRYING TO KILL YOU BECAUSE YOU'RE ALWAYS TRYING TO KILL THEM?
I--
NO!
WILL YOU BE WANTING YOUR CUP NOODLE NOW, REVEREND?
YES. I'M RETIRING TO MY STUDY TO BROOD. KEEP THIS SIREN AWAY FROM ME.
NOW WHAT HAVE YOU SAID TO HIM?

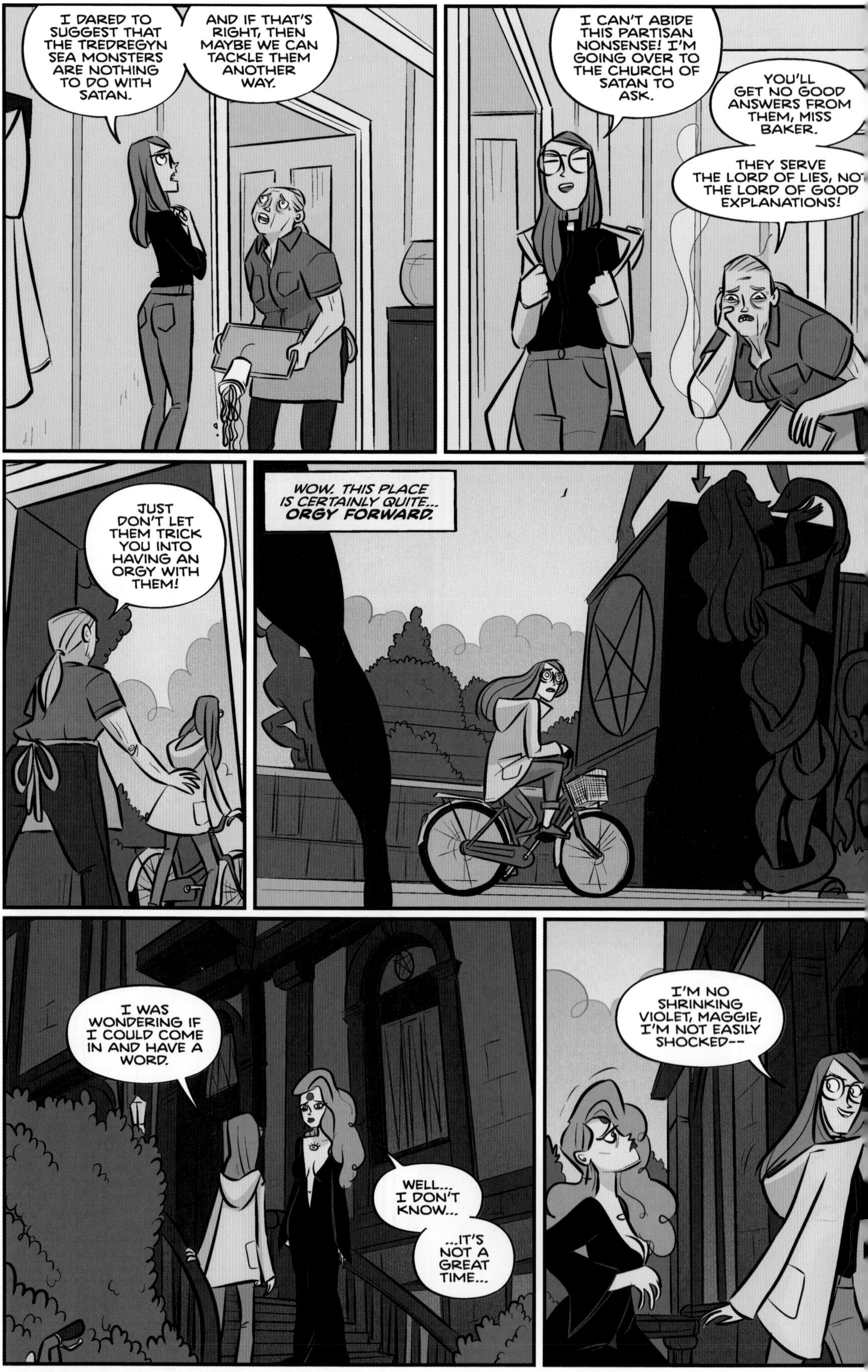
I DARED TO SUGGEST THAT THE TREDREGYN SEA MONSTERS ARE NOTHING TO DO WITH SATAN.
AND IF THAT'S RIGHT, THEN MAYBE WE CAN TACKLE THEM ANOTHER WAY.
I CAN'T ABIDE THIS PARTISAN NONSENSE! I'M GOING OVER TO THE CHURCH OF SATAN TO ASK.
YOU'LL GET NO GOOD ANSWERS FROM THEM, MISS BAKER.
THEY SERVE THE LORD OF LIES, NOT THE LORD OF GOOD EXPLANATIONS!
JUST DON'T LET THEM TRICK YOU INTO HAVING AN ORGY WITH THEM!
WOW. THIS PLACE IS CERTAINLY QUITE... ORGY FORWARD.
I WAS WONDERING IF I COULD COME IN AND HAVE A WORD.
WELL... I DON'T KNOW...
...IT'S NOT A GREAT TIME...
I'M NO SHRINKING VIOLET, MAGGIE, I'M NOT EASILY SHOCKED--

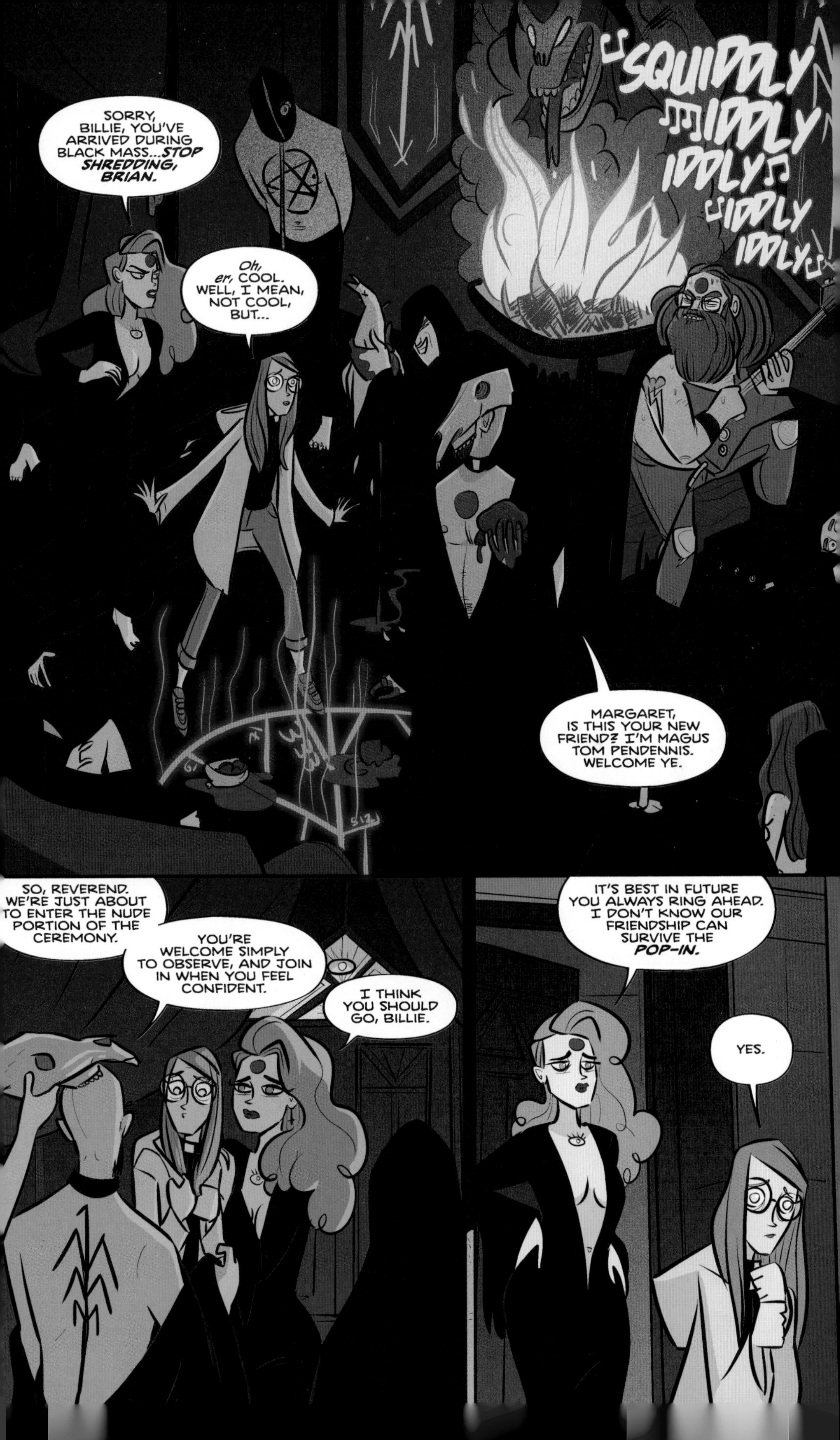
SORRY, BILLIE, YOU'VE ARRIVED DURING BLACK MASS...STOP SHREDDING, BRIAN.
SQUIDDLY IDDLY IDDLY IDDLY IDDLY
Oh, er, COOL. WELL, I MEAN, NOT COOL, BUT...
MARGARET, IS THIS YOUR NEW FRIEND? I'M MAGUS TOM PENDENNIS. WELCOME YE.
SO, REVEREND. WE'RE JUST ABOUT TO ENTER THE NUDE PORTION OF THE CEREMONY.
YOU'RE WELCOME SIMPLY TO OBSERVE, AND JOIN IN WHEN YOU FEEL CONFIDENT.
I THINK YOU SHOULD GO, BILLIE.
IT'S BEST IN FUTURE YOU ALWAYS RING AHEAD. I DON'T KNOW OUR FRIENDSHIP CAN SURVIVE THE POP-IN.
YES.

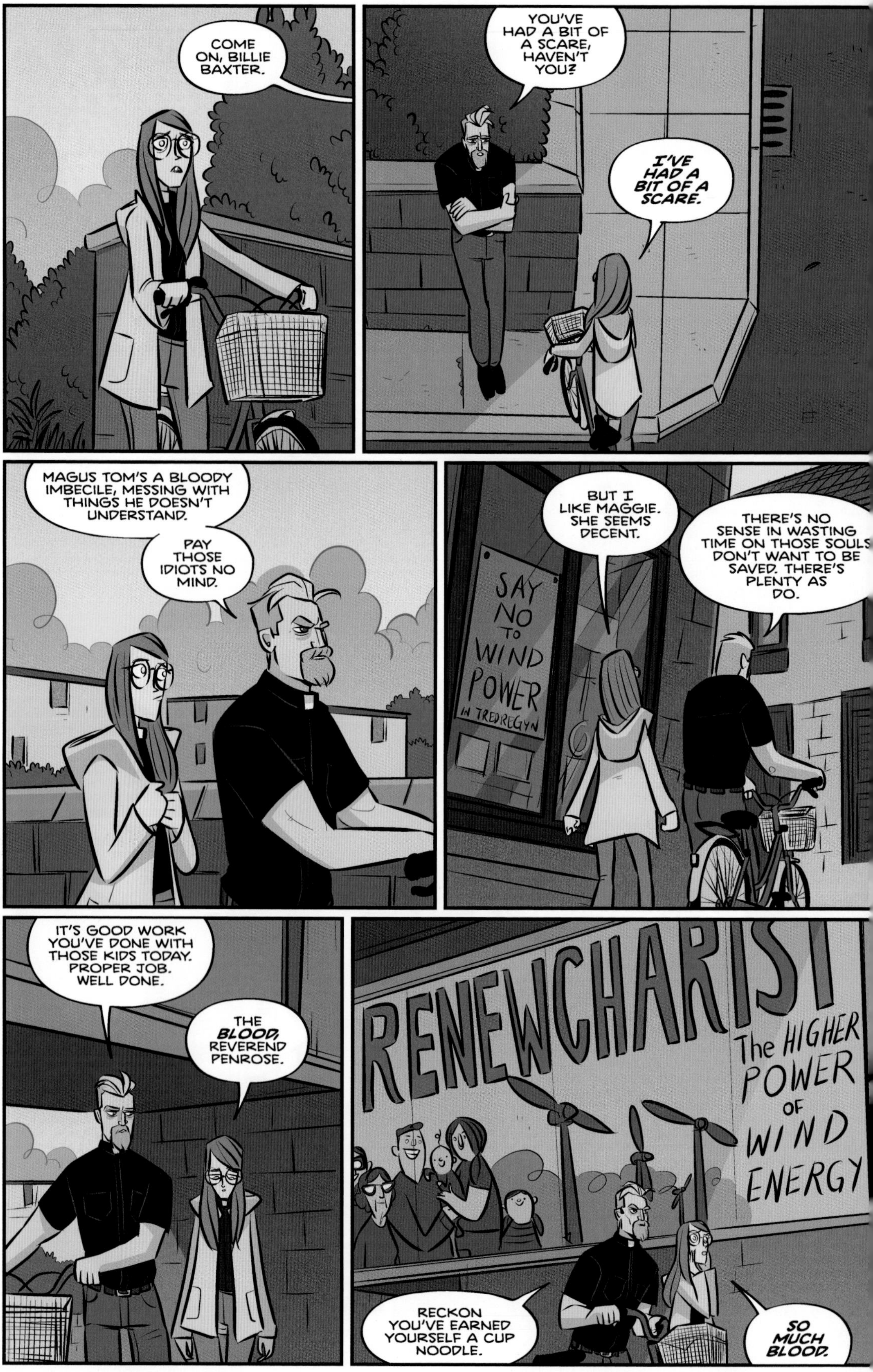
COME ON, BILLIE BAXTER.
YOU'VE HAD A BIT OF A SCARE, HAVEN'T YOU?
I'VE HAD A BIT OF A SCARE.
MAGUS TOM'S A BLOODY IMBECILE, MESSING WITH THINGS HE DOESN'T UNDERSTAND.
PAY THOSE IDIOTS NO MIND.
SAY NO TO WIND POWER IN TREDREGYN
BUT I LIKE MAGGIE. SHE SEEMS DECENT.
THERE'S NO SENSE IN WASTING TIME ON THOSE SOULS DON'T WANT TO BE SAVED. THERE'S PLENTY AS DO.
IT'S GOOD WORK YOU'VE DONE WITH THOSE KIDS TODAY. PROPER JOB. WELL DONE.
THE BLOOD, REVEREND PENROSE.
RENEWCHARIST
The HIGHER POWER OF WIND ENERGY
RECKON YOU'VE EARNED YOURSELF A CUP NOODLE.
SO MUCH BLOOD.

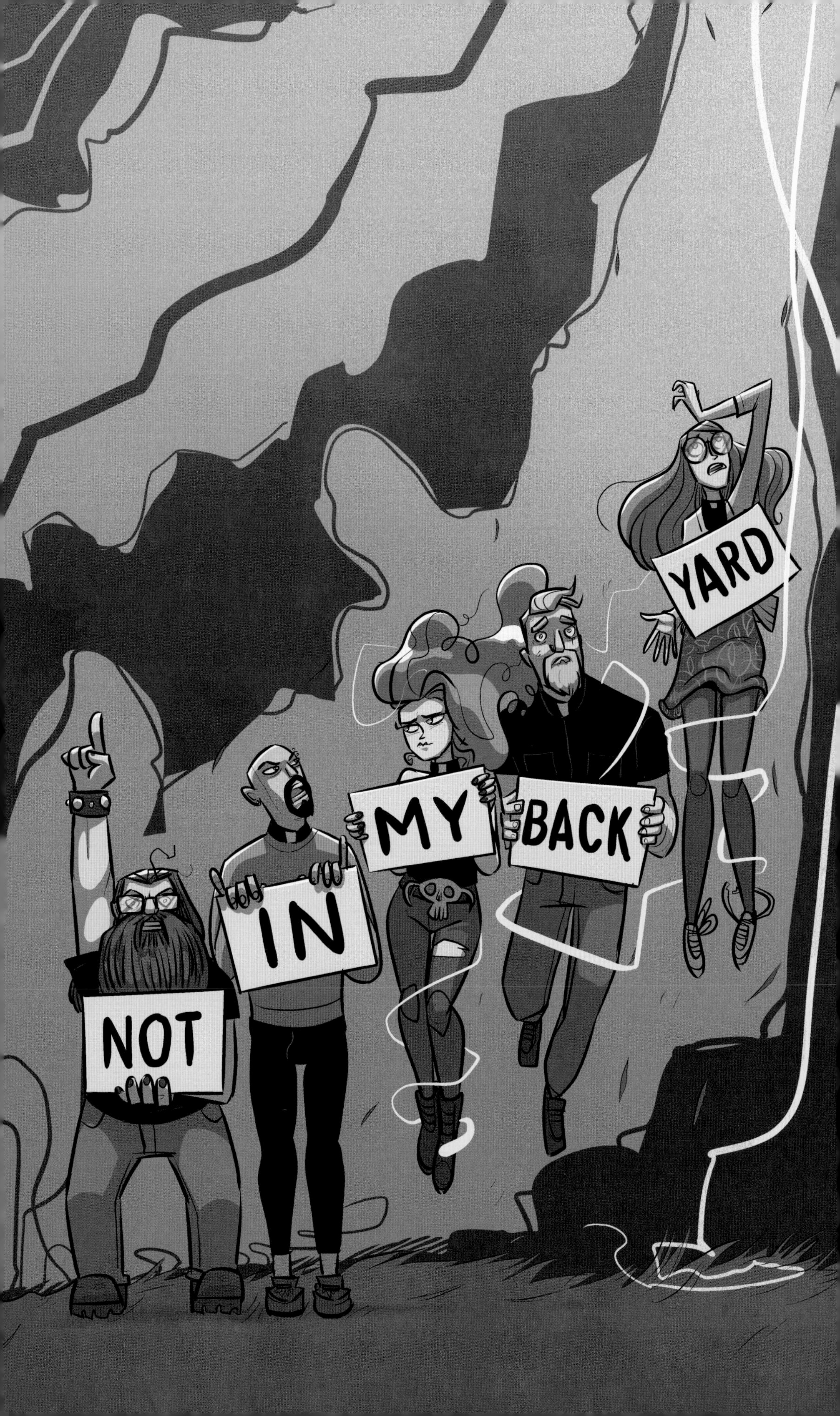
NOT
IN
MY
BACK
YARD

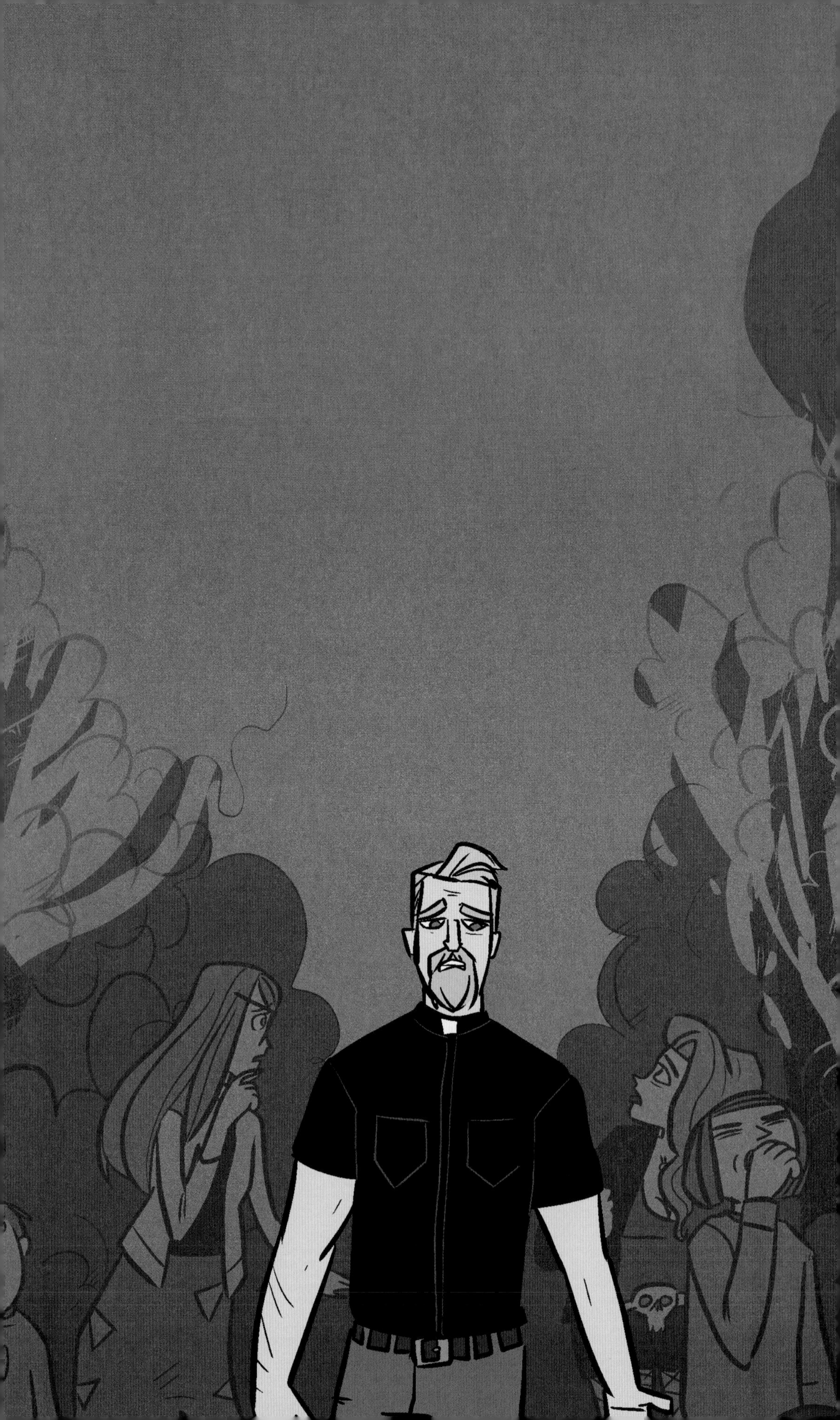

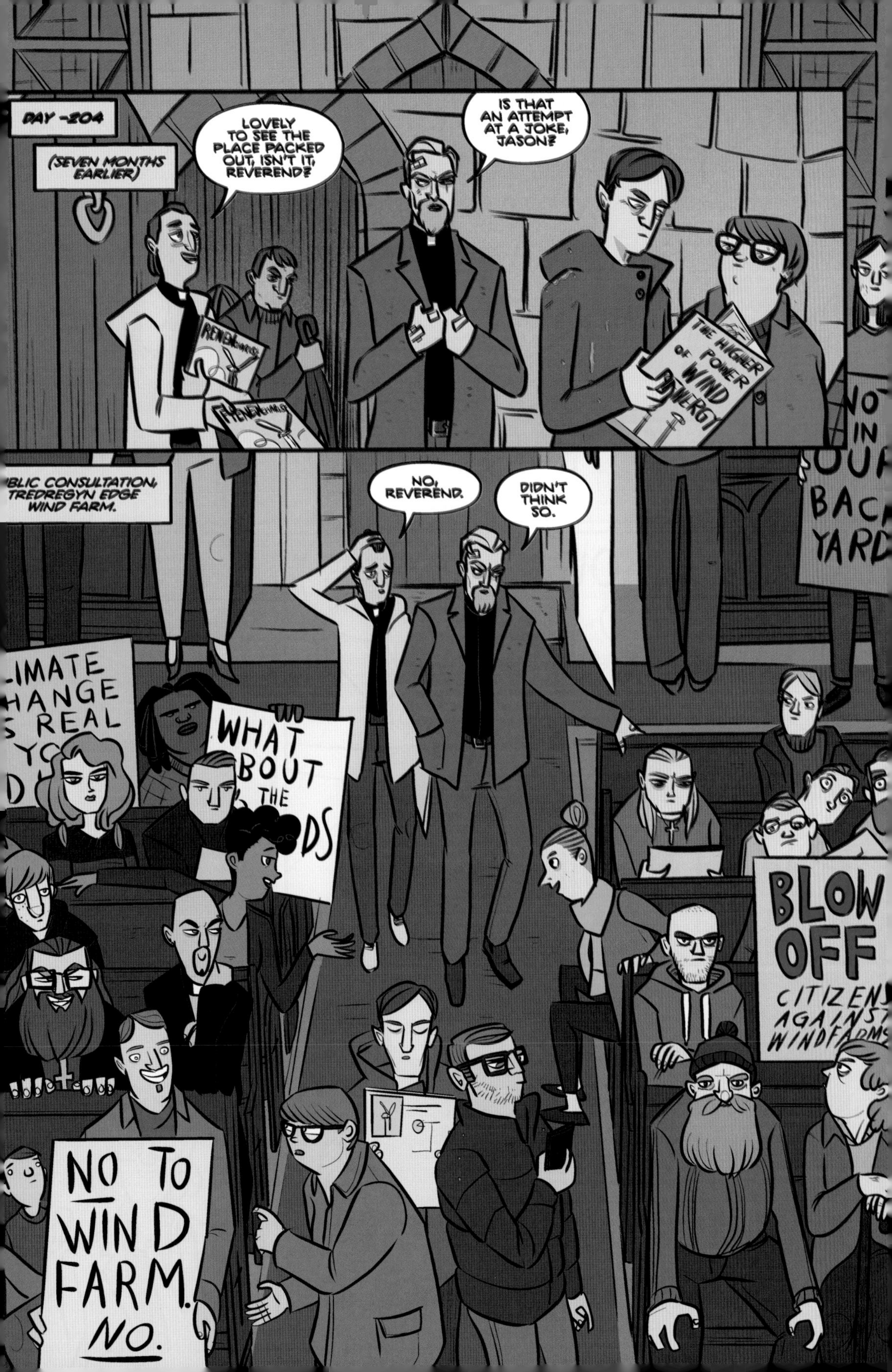
DAY -204
(SEVEN MONTHS EARLIER)
LOVELY TO SEE THE PLACE PACKED OUT, ISN'T IT, REVEREND?
IS THAT AN ATTEMPT AT A JOKE, JASON?
THE HIGHER POWER OF WIND
BLIC CONSULTATION, TREDREGYN EDGE WIND FARM.
NO, REVEREND.
DIDN'T THINK SO.
BLOW OFF
CITIZENS AGAINST WINDFARMS
NO TO WIND FARM. NO.

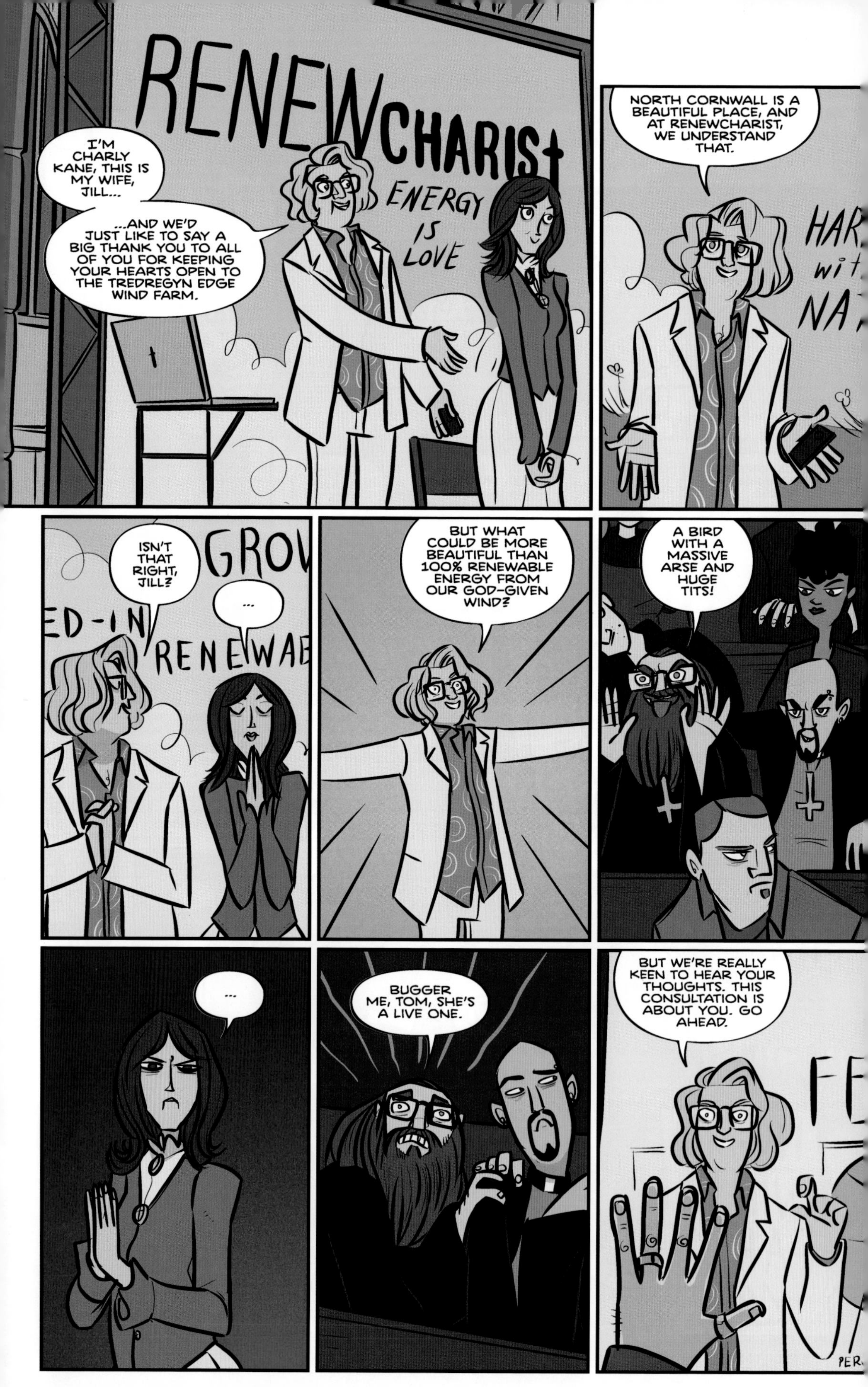
RENEWCHARIST
ENERGY IS LOVE
I'M CHARLY KANE, THIS IS MY WIFE, JILL...
...AND WE'D JUST LIKE TO SAY A BIG THANK YOU TO ALL OF YOU FOR KEEPING YOUR HEARTS OPEN TO THE TREDREGYN EDGE WIND FARM.
NORTH CORNWALL IS A BEAUTIFUL PLACE, AND AT RENEWCHARIST, WE UNDERSTAND THAT.
ISN'T THAT RIGHT, JILL?
...
BUT WHAT COULD BE MORE BEAUTIFUL THAN 100% RENEWABLE ENERGY FROM OUR GOD-GIVEN WIND?
A BIRD WITH A MASSIVE ARSE AND HUGE TITS!
...
BUGGER ME, TOM, SHE'S A LIVE ONE.
BUT WE'RE REALLY KEEN TO HEAR YOUR THOUGHTS. THIS CONSULTATION IS ABOUT YOU. GO AHEAD.

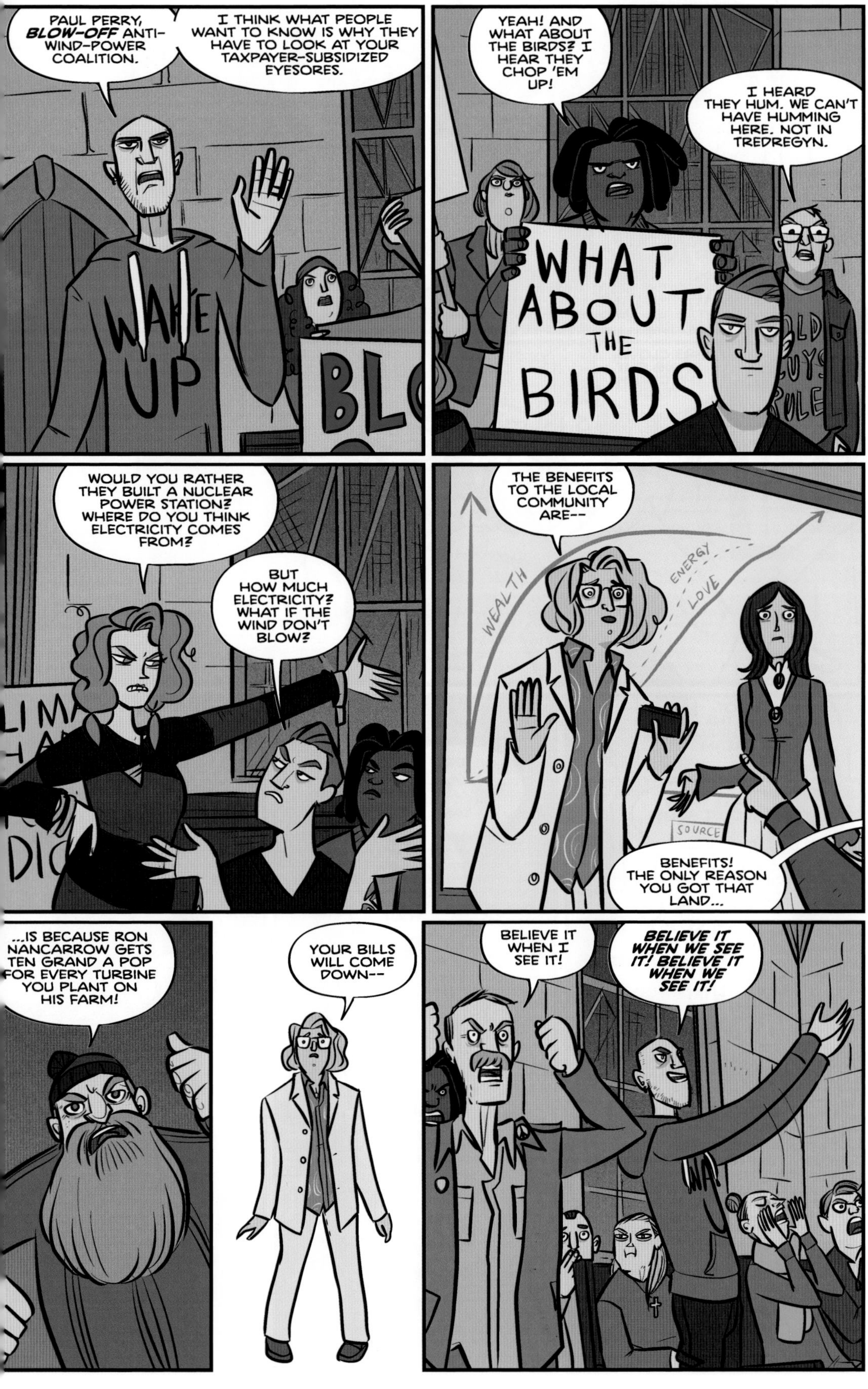

PAUL PERRY, BLOW-OFF ANTI-WIND-POWER COALITION.
I THINK WHAT PEOPLE WANT TO KNOW IS WHY THEY HAVE TO LOOK AT YOUR TAXPAYER-SUBSIDIZED EYESORES.
WAKE UP
YEAH! AND WHAT ABOUT THE BIRDS? I HEAR THEY CHOP 'EM UP!
I HEARD THEY HUM. WE CAN'T HAVE HUMMING HERE. NOT IN TREDREGYN.
WHAT ABOUT THE BIRDS
OLD GUYS RULE
WOULD YOU RATHER THEY BUILT A NUCLEAR POWER STATION? WHERE DO YOU THINK ELECTRICITY COMES FROM?
BUT HOW MUCH ELECTRICITY? WHAT IF THE WIND DON'T BLOW?
THE BENEFITS TO THE LOCAL COMMUNITY ARE--
WEALTH
ENERGY
LOVE
SOURCE
BENEFITS! THE ONLY REASON YOU GOT THAT LAND...
...IS BECAUSE RON NANCARROW GETS TEN GRAND A POP FOR EVERY TURBINE YOU PLANT ON HIS FARM!
YOUR BILLS WILL COME DOWN--
BELIEVE IT WHEN I SEE IT!
BELIEVE IT WHEN WE SEE IT! BELIEVE IT WHEN WE SEE IT!

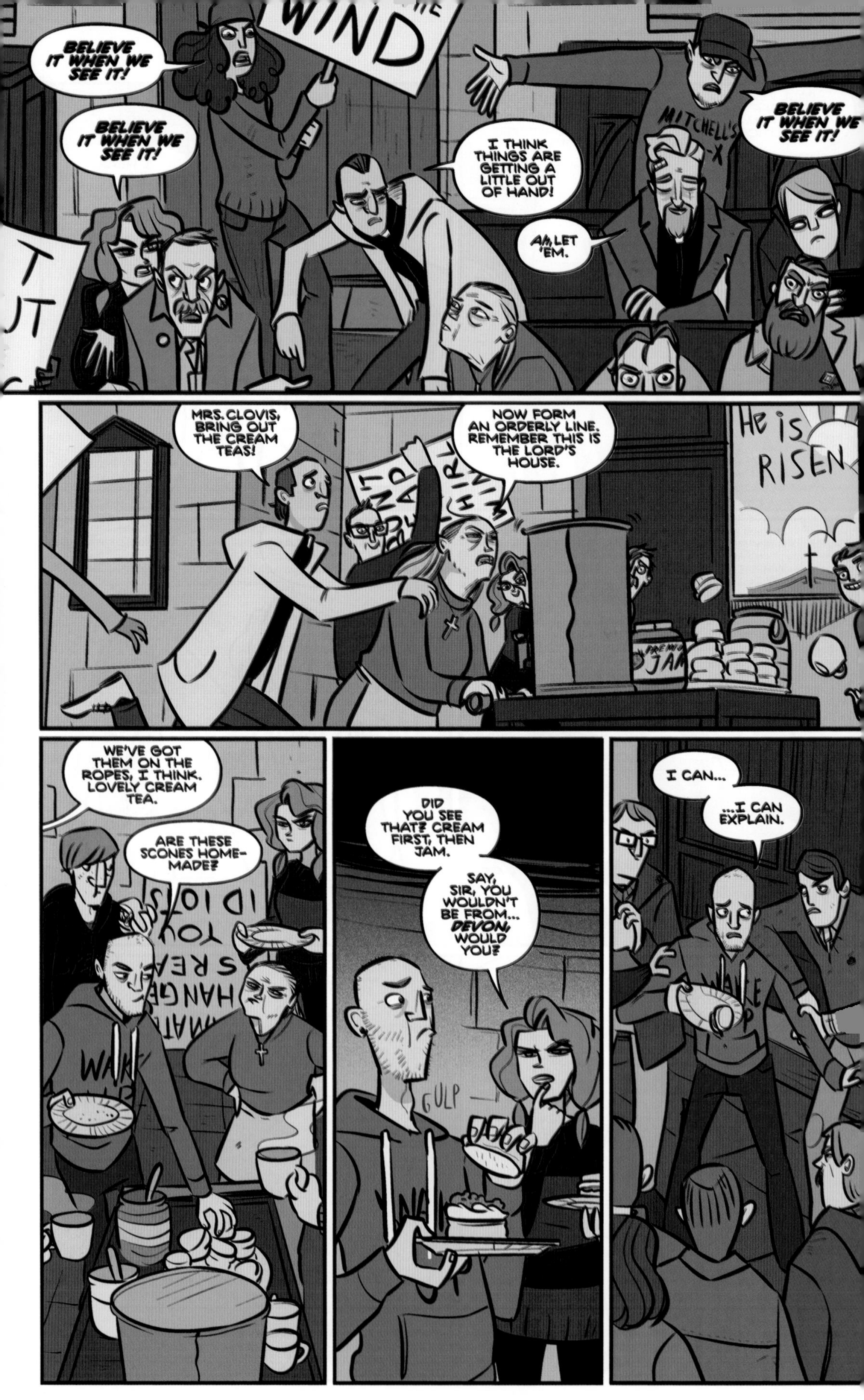
BELIEVE IT WHEN WE SEE IT!
BELIEVE IT WHEN WE SEE IT!
WIND
I THINK THINGS ARE GETTING A LITTLE OUT OF HAND!
AH, LET 'EM.
BELIEVE IT WHEN WE SEE IT!
MITCHELL'S
MRS. CLOVIS, BRING OUT THE CREAM TEAS!
NOW FORM AN ORDERLY LINE. REMEMBER THIS IS THE LORD'S HOUSE.
He is RISEN
JAM
WE'VE GOT THEM ON THE ROPES, I THINK. LOVELY CREAM TEA.
ARE THESE SCONES HOME-MADE?
DID YOU SEE THAT? CREAM FIRST, THEN JAM.
SAY, SIR, YOU WOULDN'T BE FROM... DEVON, WOULD YOU?
GULP
I CAN...
...I CAN EXPLAIN.

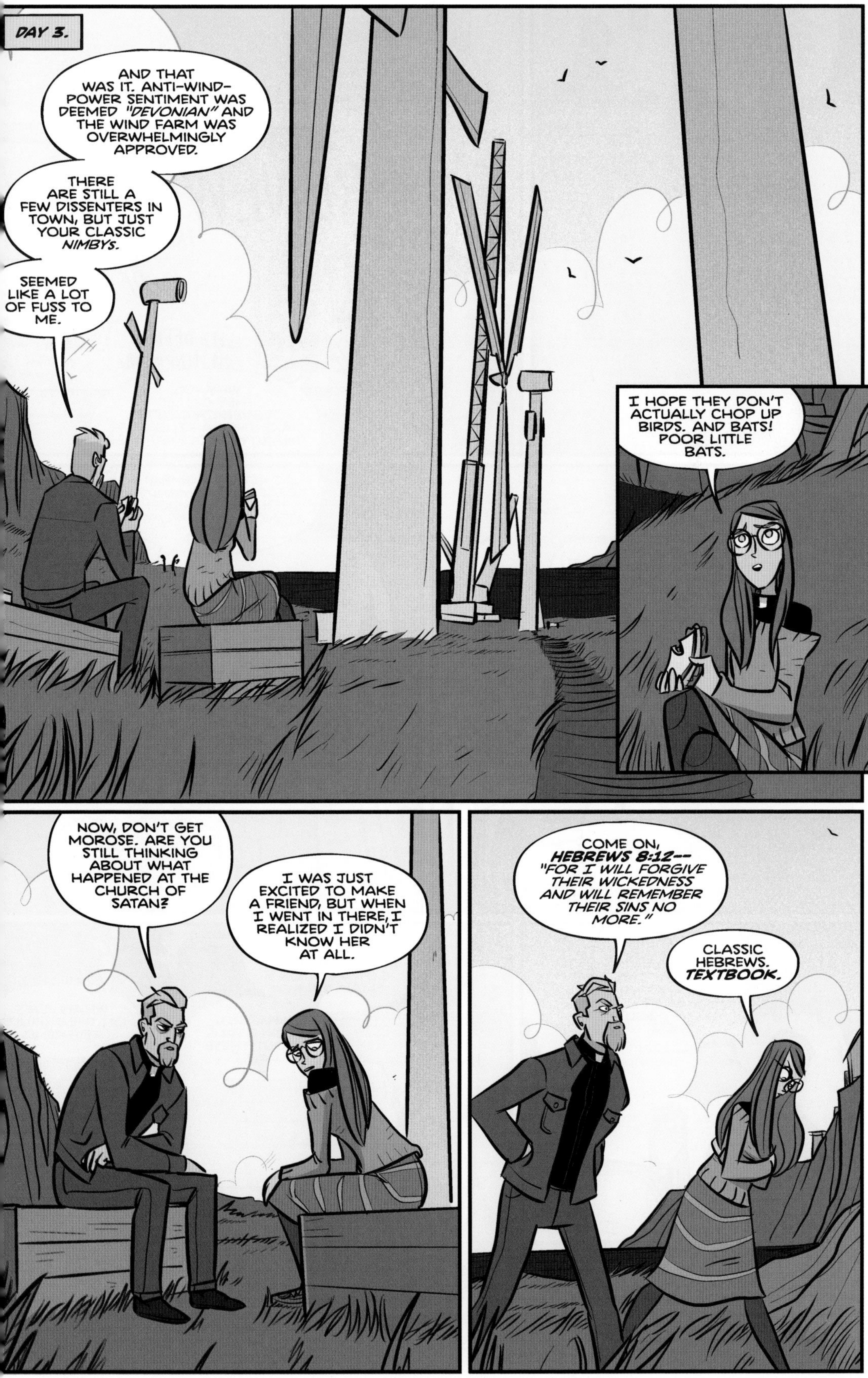
DAY 3.
AND THAT WAS IT. ANTI-WIND-POWER SENTIMENT WAS DEEMED "DEVONIAN" AND THE WIND FARM WAS OVERWHELMINGLY APPROVED.
THERE ARE STILL A FEW DISSENTERS IN TOWN, BUT JUST YOUR CLASSIC NIMBYS.
SEEMED LIKE A LOT OF FUSS TO ME.
I HOPE THEY DON'T ACTUALLY CHOP UP BIRDS. AND BATS! POOR LITTLE BATS.
NOW, DON'T GET MOROSE. ARE YOU STILL THINKING ABOUT WHAT HAPPENED AT THE CHURCH OF SATAN?
I WAS JUST EXCITED TO MAKE A FRIEND, BUT WHEN I WENT IN THERE, I REALIZED I DIDN'T KNOW HER AT ALL.
COME ON, HEBREWS 8:12-- "FOR I WILL FORGIVE THEIR WICKEDNESS AND WILL REMEMBER THEIR SINS NO MORE."
CLASSIC HEBREWS. TEXTBOOK.

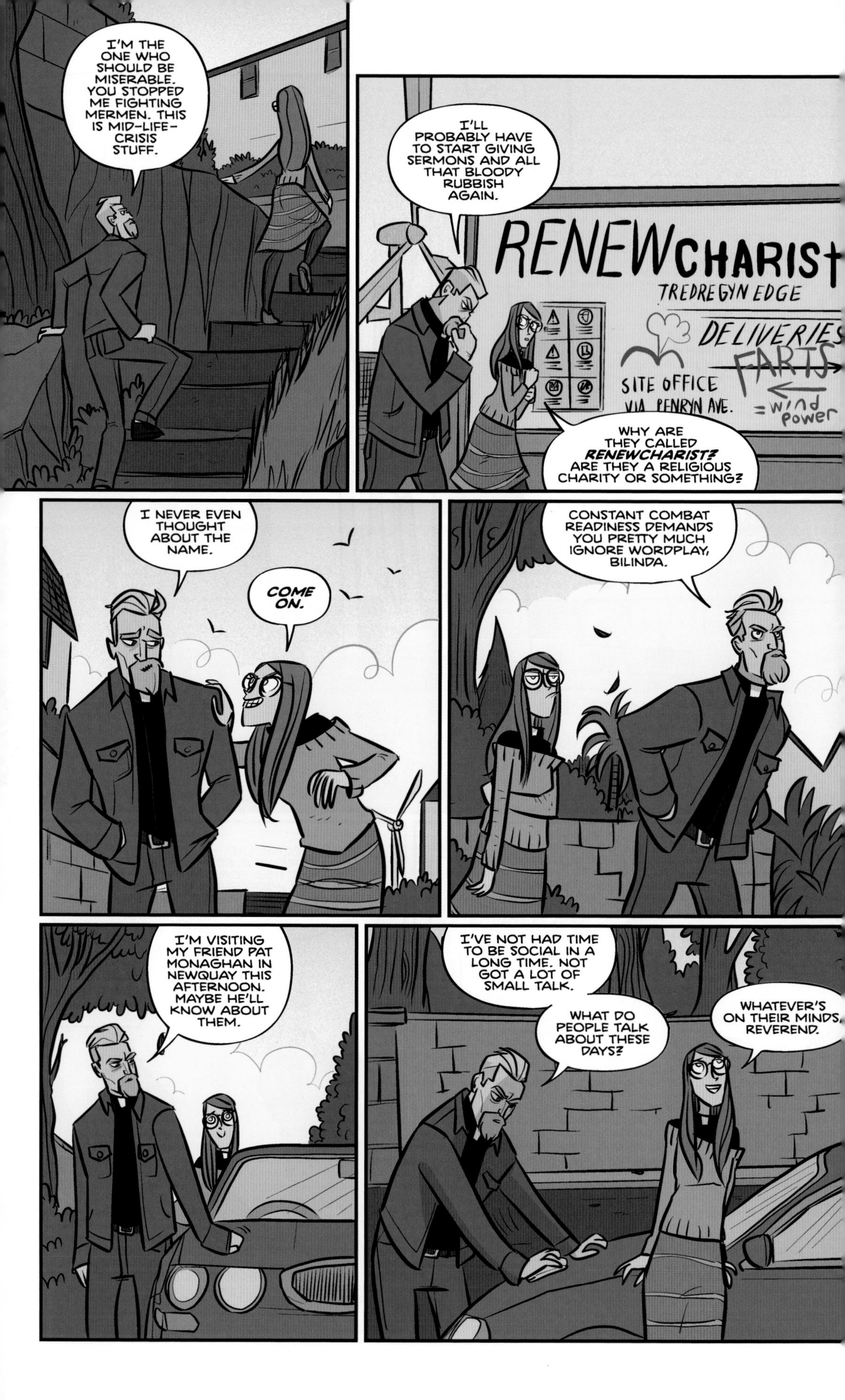
I'M THE ONE WHO SHOULD BE MISERABLE. YOU STOPPED ME FIGHTING MERMEN. THIS IS MID-LIFE-CRISIS STUFF.
I'LL PROBABLY HAVE TO START GIVING SERMONS AND ALL THAT BLOODY RUBBISH AGAIN.
RENEWCHARIST
TREDREGYN EDGE
DELIVERIES
FARTS
SITE OFFICE
VIA PENRYN AVE.
=wind power
WHY ARE THEY CALLED *RENEWCHARIST?* ARE THEY A RELIGIOUS CHARITY OR SOMETHING?
I NEVER EVEN THOUGHT ABOUT THE NAME.
COME ON.
CONSTANT COMBAT READINESS DEMANDS YOU PRETTY MUCH IGNORE WORDPLAY, BILINDA.
I'M VISITING MY FRIEND PAT MONAGHAN IN NEWQUAY THIS AFTERNOON. MAYBE HE'LL KNOW ABOUT THEM.
I'VE NOT HAD TIME TO BE SOCIAL IN A LONG TIME. NOT GOT A LOT OF SMALL TALK.
WHAT DO PEOPLE TALK ABOUT THESE DAYS?
WHATEVER'S ON THEIR MINDS, REVEREND.

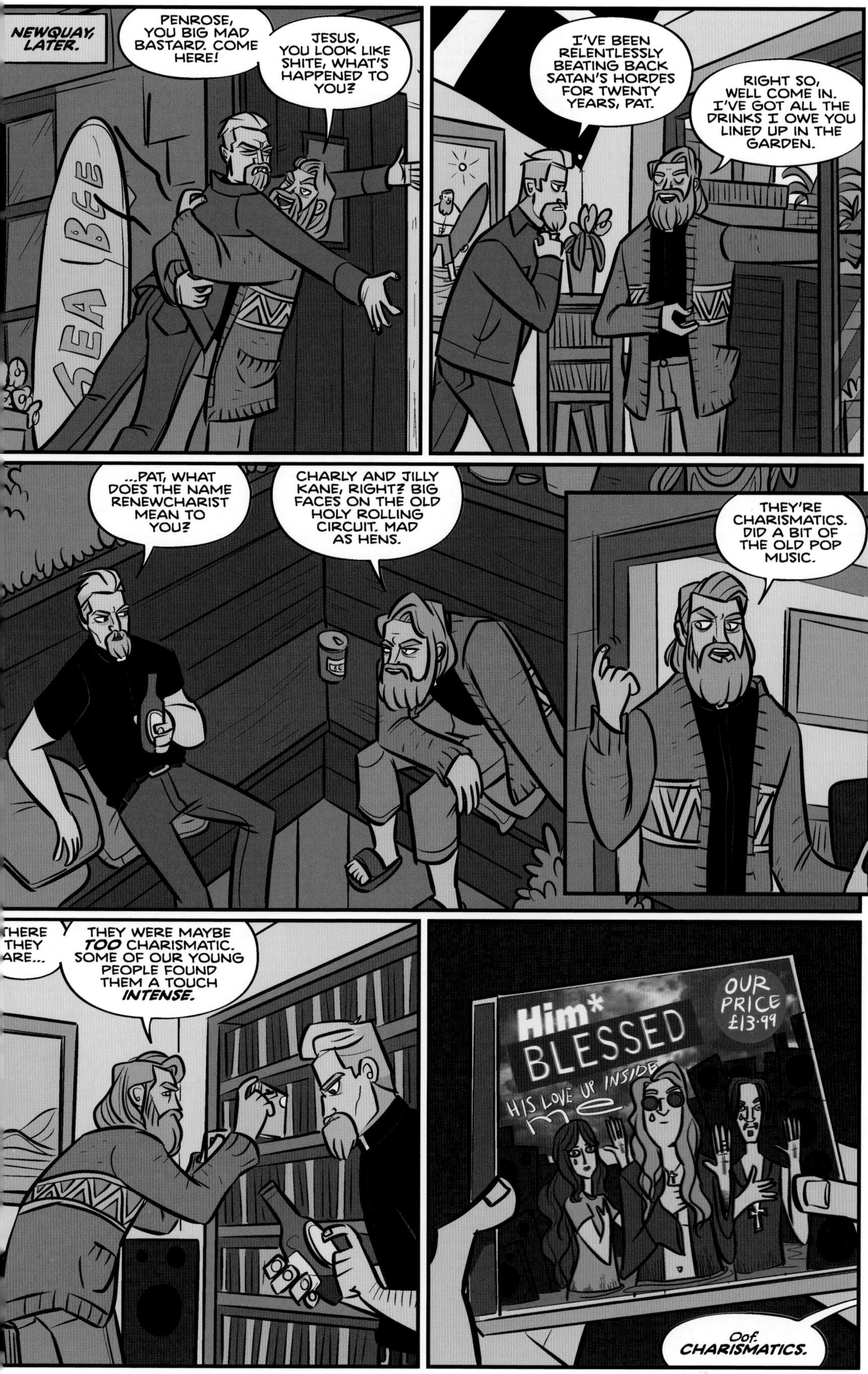

NEWQUAY, LATER.
PENROSE, YOU BIG MAD BASTARD. COME HERE!
JESUS, YOU LOOK LIKE SHITE, WHAT'S HAPPENED TO YOU?
SEA BEE
I'VE BEEN RELENTLESSLY BEATING BACK SATAN'S HORDES FOR TWENTY YEARS, PAT.
RIGHT SO, WELL COME IN. I'VE GOT ALL THE DRINKS I OWE YOU LINED UP IN THE GARDEN.
...PAT, WHAT DOES THE NAME RENEWCHARIST MEAN TO YOU?
CHARLY AND JILLY KANE, RIGHT? BIG FACES ON THE OLD HOLY ROLLING CIRCUIT. MAD AS HENS.
THEY'RE CHARISMATICS. DID A BIT OF THE OLD POP MUSIC.
THERE THEY ARE...
THEY WERE MAYBE *TOO* CHARISMATIC. SOME OF OUR YOUNG PEOPLE FOUND THEM A TOUCH ***INTENSE.***
OUR PRICE £13.99
Him*
BLESSED
HIS LOVE UP INSIDE me
Oof. ***CHARISMATICS.***

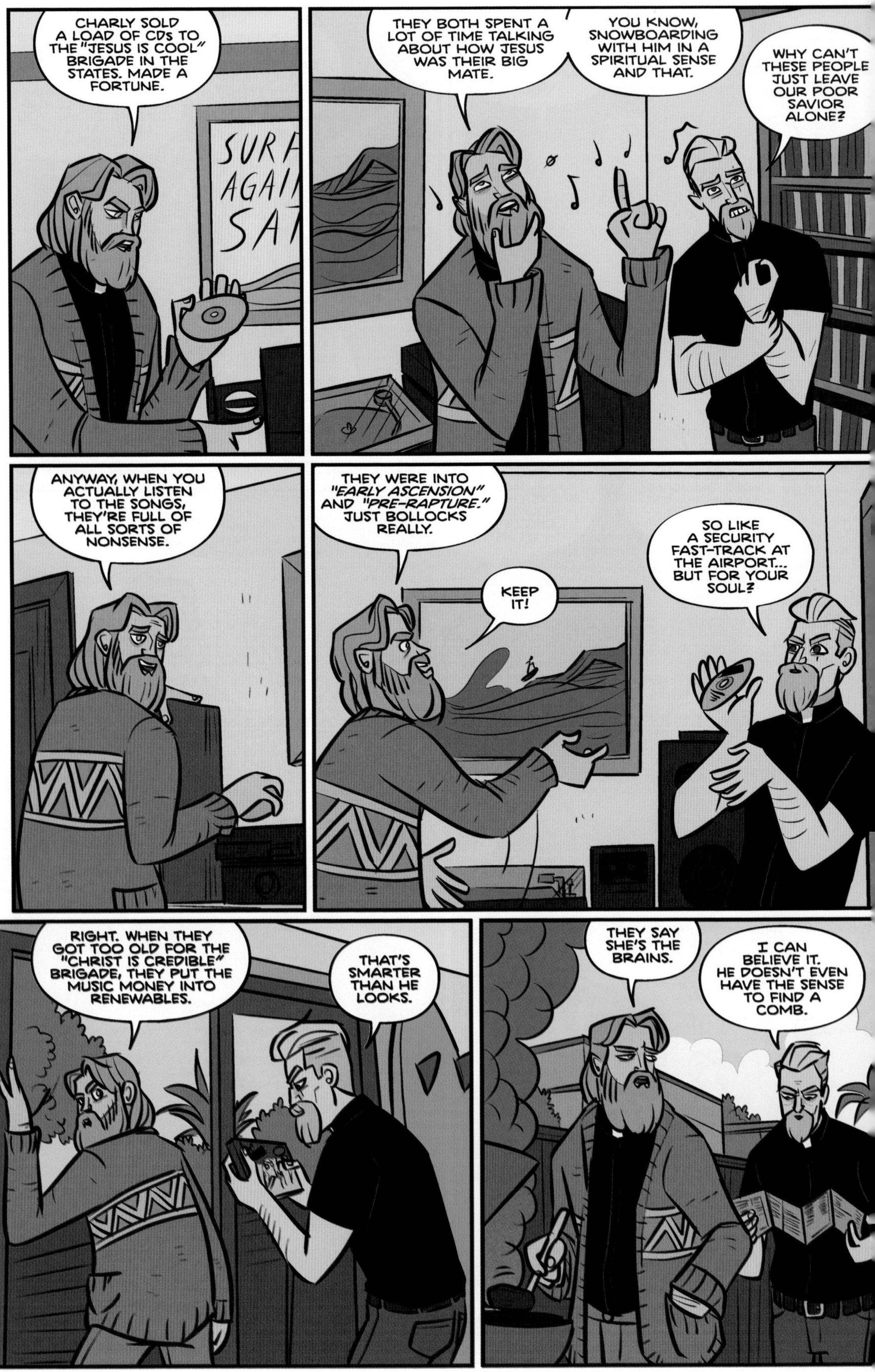
CHARLY SOLD A LOAD OF CDs TO THE "JESUS IS COOL" BRIGADE IN THE STATES. MADE A FORTUNE.
SURF AGAI SAT
THEY BOTH SPENT A LOT OF TIME TALKING ABOUT HOW JESUS WAS THEIR BIG MATE.
YOU KNOW, SNOWBOARDING WITH HIM IN A SPIRITUAL SENSE AND THAT.
WHY CAN'T THESE PEOPLE JUST LEAVE OUR POOR SAVIOR ALONE?
ANYWAY, WHEN YOU ACTUALLY LISTEN TO THE SONGS, THEY'RE FULL OF ALL SORTS OF NONSENSE.
THEY WERE INTO "EARLY ASCENSION" AND "PRE-RAPTURE." JUST BOLLOCKS REALLY.
KEEP IT!
SO LIKE A SECURITY FAST-TRACK AT THE AIRPORT... BUT FOR YOUR SOUL?
RIGHT. WHEN THEY GOT TOO OLD FOR THE "CHRIST IS CREDIBLE" BRIGADE, THEY PUT THE MUSIC MONEY INTO RENEWABLES.
THAT'S SMARTER THAN HE LOOKS.
THEY SAY SHE'S THE BRAINS.
I CAN BELIEVE IT. HE DOESN'T EVEN HAVE THE SENSE TO FIND A COMB.

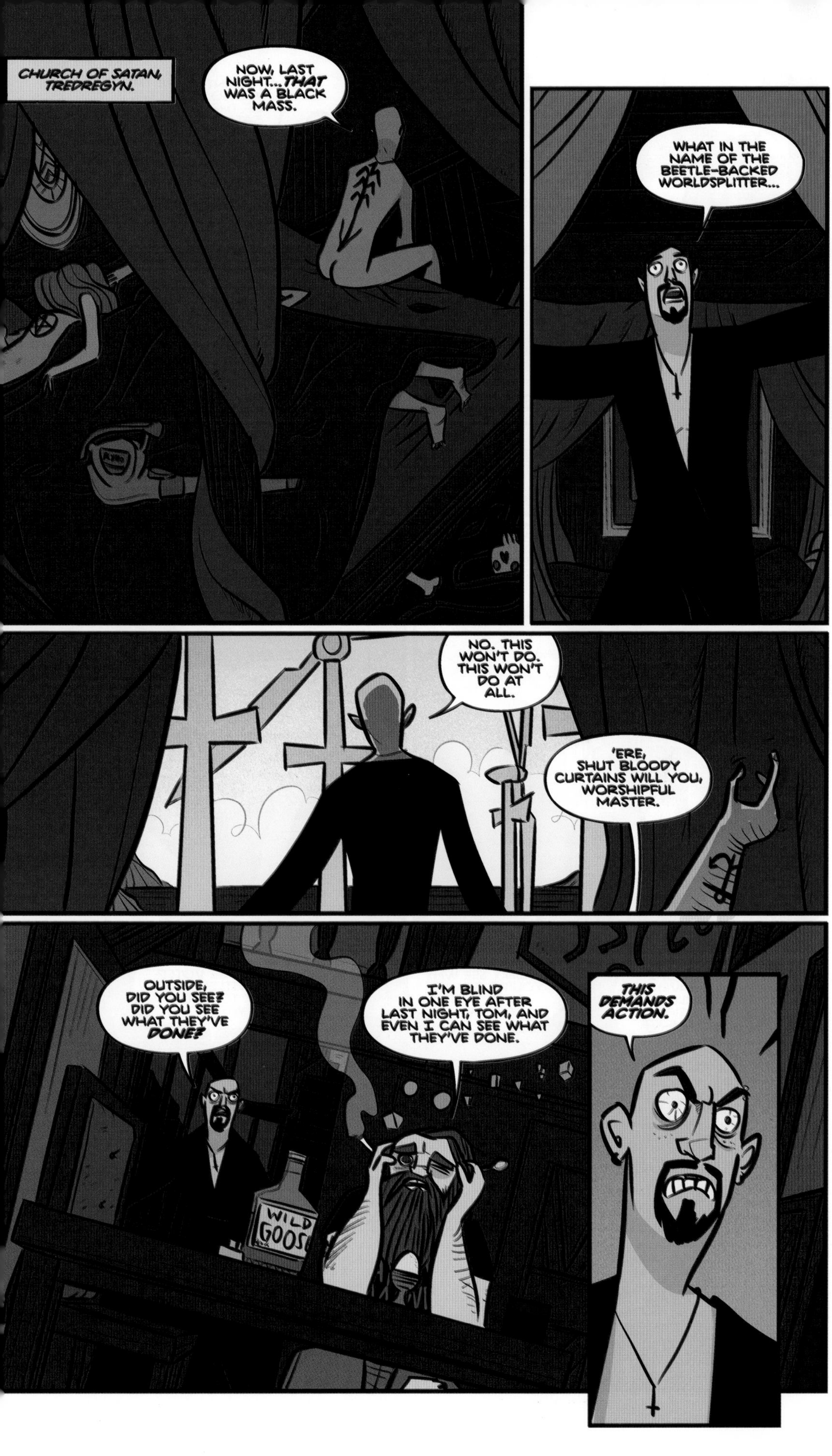
CHURCH OF SATAN, TREDREGYN.
NOW, LAST NIGHT... THAT WAS A BLACK MASS.
WHAT IN THE NAME OF THE BEETLE-BACKED WORLDSPLITTER...
NO. THIS WON'T DO. THIS WON'T DO AT ALL.
'ERE, SHUT BLOODY CURTAINS WILL YOU, WORSHIPFUL MASTER.
OUTSIDE, DID YOU SEE? DID YOU SEE WHAT THEY'VE DONE?
I'M BLIND IN ONE EYE AFTER LAST NIGHT, TOM, AND EVEN I CAN SEE WHAT THEY'VE DONE.
THIS DEMANDS ACTION.
WILD GOOS

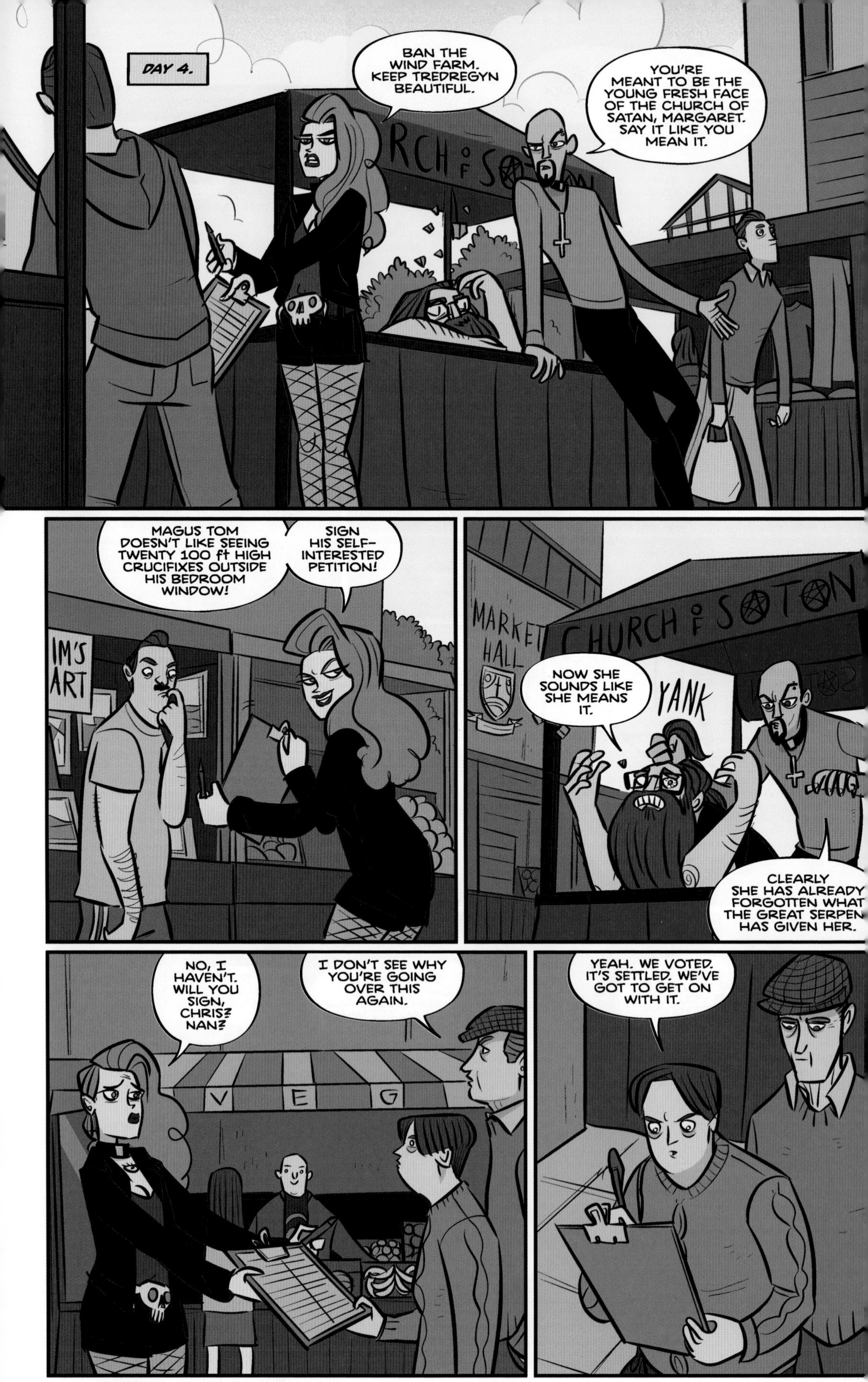
DAY 4.
BAN THE WIND FARM. KEEP TREDREGYN BEAUTIFUL.
CHURCH OF SATAN
YOU'RE MEANT TO BE THE YOUNG FRESH FACE OF THE CHURCH OF SATAN, MARGARET. SAY IT LIKE YOU MEAN IT.
MAGUS TOM DOESN'T LIKE SEEING TWENTY 100 ft HIGH CRUCIFIXES OUTSIDE HIS BEDROOM WINDOW!
SIGN HIS SELF-INTERESTED PETITION!
MARKET HALL
CHURCH OF SATAN
NOW SHE SOUNDS LIKE SHE MEANS IT.
YANK
CLEARLY SHE HAS ALREADY FORGOTTEN WHAT THE GREAT SERPEN HAS GIVEN HER.
NO, I HAVEN'T. WILL YOU SIGN, CHRIS? NAN?
I DON'T SEE WHY YOU'RE GOING OVER THIS AGAIN.
VEG
YEAH. WE VOTED. IT'S SETTLED. WE'VE GOT TO GET ON WITH IT.

NOW THE WIND FARM IS UP, IT'S CLEAR THAT THEY REPRESENT VANDALISM OF OUR AREA'S NATURAL BEAUTY.

I THOUGHT YOU WERE ALWAYS SAYING "DO WHAT THOU WILT," MAGUS TOM. IT'S BEEN WORKING FOR ME.

I FEEL LIKE A YOUNG WOMAN AGAIN.

I'M KNACKERED THOUGH.

AS I SEE IT, IT'S THE MAJESTY OF MAN'S WORKS, IN HARMONY WITH NATURE.

THAT'S CERTAINLY WHAT IT SAYS ON ALL THE BILLBOARDS.

THE MAJES OF MAN'S W IN HARMO WITH NA

that's BEN ARIST

BANA 30P

DUNNO. JUST RINGS TRUE. HAVE A KIWI FRUIT, BEAUTIFUL.

THE OF M IN H WITH

TOMATO'S 6/£1.50

THEY'LL LET ME DAUB THEM WITH GOAT BLOOD, THEY'LL EAT MY COLD BUFFET, BUT WILL THEY DO WHAT I SAY?

SATANISM'S AN EGOISTIC THEOLOGY, TOM. IN NOT DOING WHAT YOU SAY...

...THEY'RE DOING EXACTLY WHAT YOU TOLD THEM TO DO.

WILD COOKE

MY HEAD HURRRRTS.

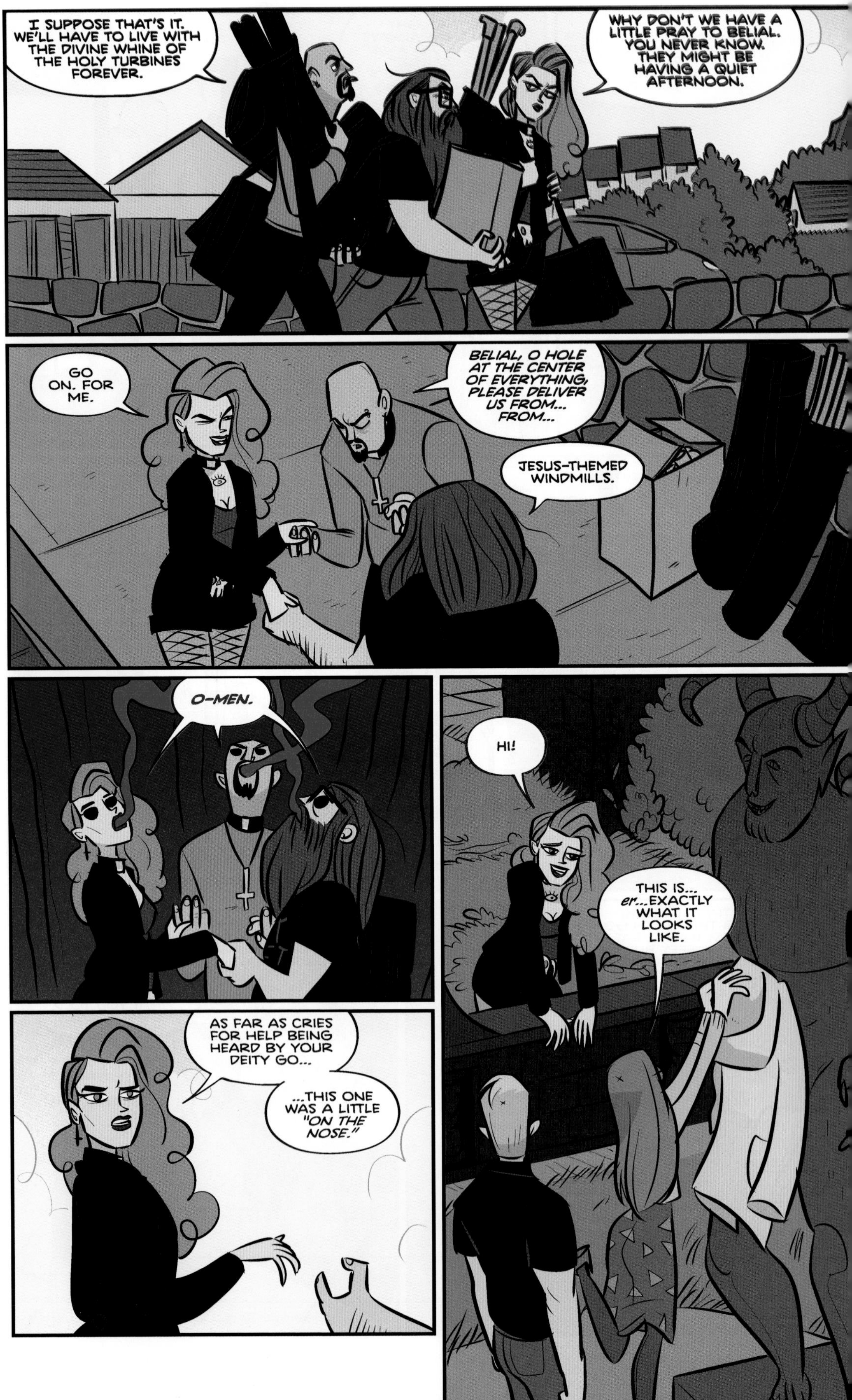
I SUPPOSE THAT'S IT. WE'LL HAVE TO LIVE WITH THE DIVINE WHINE OF THE HOLY TURBINES FOREVER.
WHY DON'T WE HAVE A LITTLE PRAY TO BELIAL. YOU NEVER KNOW. THEY MIGHT BE HAVING A QUIET AFTERNOON.
GO ON. FOR ME.
BELIAL, O HOLE AT THE CENTER OF EVERYTHING, PLEASE DELIVER US FROM... FROM...
JESUS-THEMED WINDMILLS.
O-MEN.
AS FAR AS CRIES FOR HELP BEING HEARD BY YOUR DEITY GO...
...THIS ONE WAS A LITTLE "ON THE NOSE."
HI!
THIS IS... er...EXACTLY WHAT IT LOOKS LIKE.

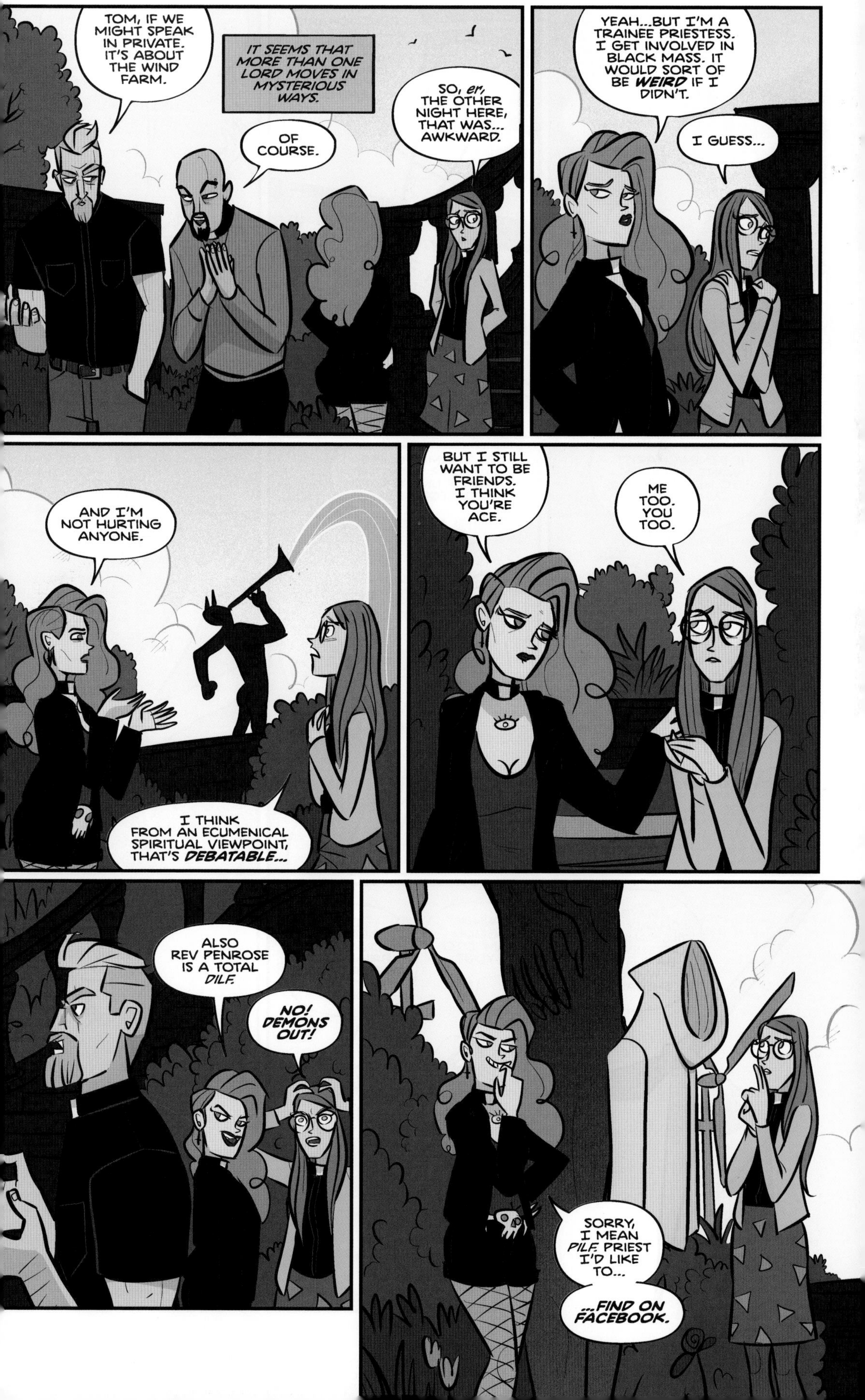
TOM, IF WE MIGHT SPEAK IN PRIVATE. IT'S ABOUT THE WIND FARM.
IT SEEMS THAT MORE THAN ONE LORD MOVES IN MYSTERIOUS WAYS.
OF COURSE.
SO, *er*, THE OTHER NIGHT HERE, THAT WAS... AWKWARD.
YEAH...BUT I'M A TRAINEE PRIESTESS. I GET INVOLVED IN BLACK MASS. IT WOULD SORT OF BE ***WEIRD*** IF I DIDN'T.
I GUESS...
AND I'M NOT HURTING ANYONE.
I THINK FROM AN ECUMENICAL SPIRITUAL VIEWPOINT, THAT'S ***DEBATABLE...***
BUT I STILL WANT TO BE FRIENDS. I THINK YOU'RE ACE.
ME TOO. YOU TOO.
ALSO REV PENROSE IS A TOTAL *DILF.*
NO! DEMONS OUT!
SORRY, I MEAN *PILF.* PRIEST I'D LIKE TO...
...FIND ON FACEBOOK.

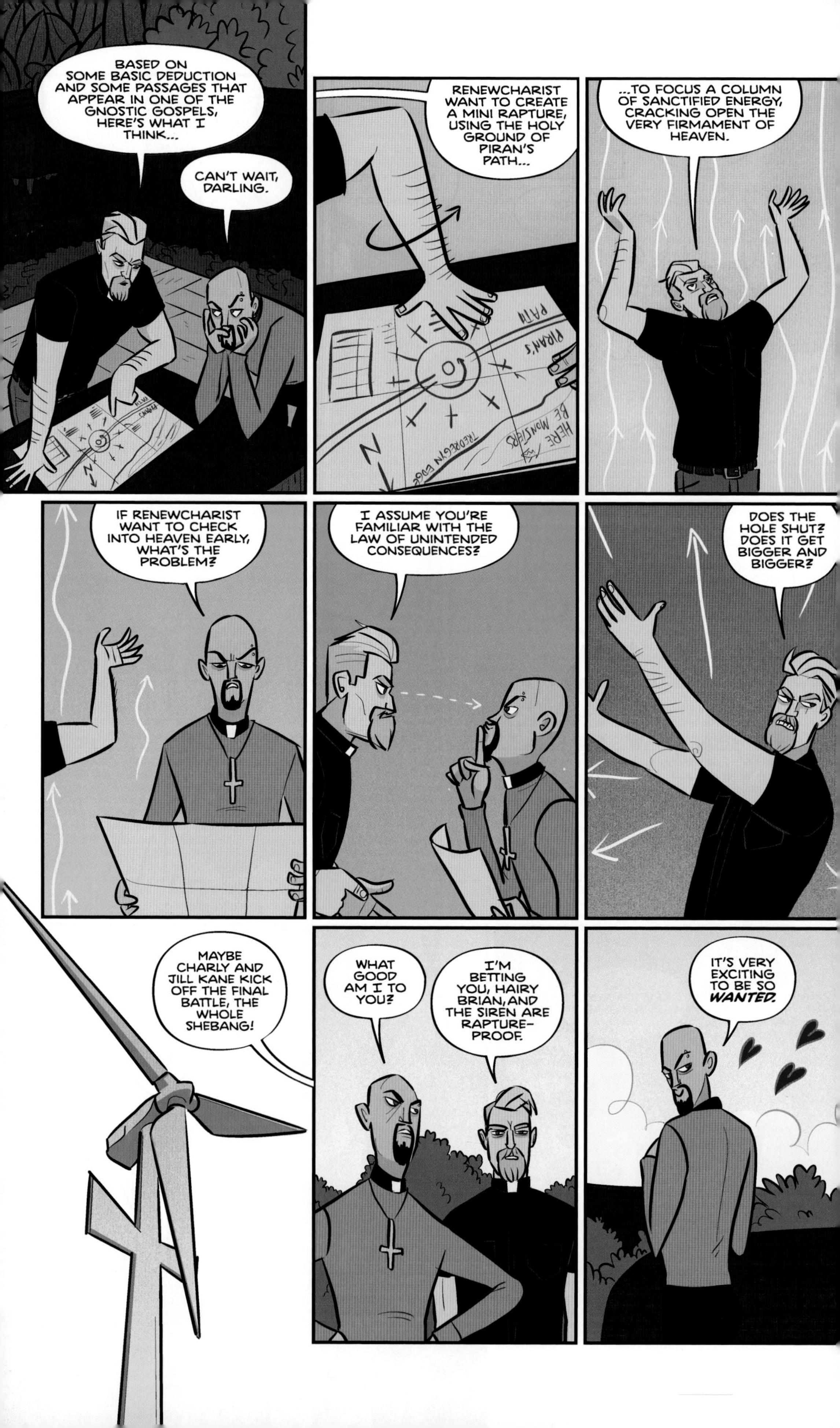
BASED ON SOME BASIC DEDUCTION AND SOME PASSAGES THAT APPEAR IN ONE OF THE GNOSTIC GOSPELS, HERE'S WHAT I THINK...
CAN'T WAIT, DARLING.
RENEWCHARIST WANT TO CREATE A MINI RAPTURE, USING THE HOLY GROUND OF PIRAN'S PATH...
PIRAN'S PATH
HERE BE MONSTERS
TREDEGYN EDGE
...TO FOCUS A COLUMN OF SANCTIFIED ENERGY, CRACKING OPEN THE VERY FIRMAMENT OF HEAVEN.
IF RENEWCHARIST WANT TO CHECK INTO HEAVEN EARLY, WHAT'S THE PROBLEM?
I ASSUME YOU'RE FAMILIAR WITH THE LAW OF UNINTENDED CONSEQUENCES?
DOES THE HOLE SHUT? DOES IT GET BIGGER AND BIGGER?
MAYBE CHARLY AND JILL KANE KICK OFF THE FINAL BATTLE, THE WHOLE SHEBANG!
WHAT GOOD AM I TO YOU?
I'M BETTING YOU, HAIRY BRIAN, AND THE SIREN ARE RAPTURE-PROOF.
IT'S VERY EXCITING TO BE SO *WANTED.*

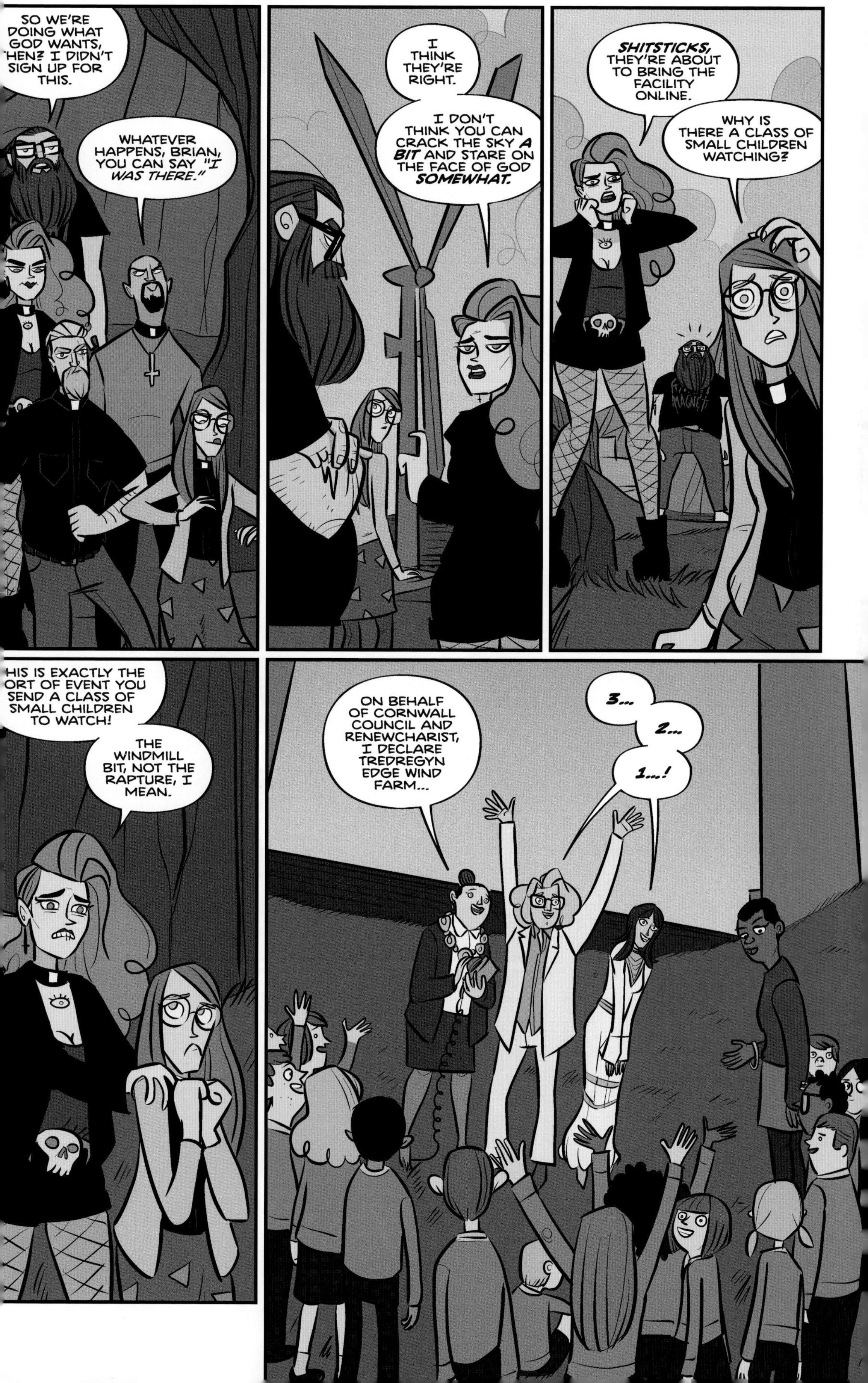
SO WE'RE DOING WHAT GOD WANTS, 'HEN? I DIDN'T SIGN UP FOR THIS.
WHATEVER HAPPENS, BRIAN, YOU CAN SAY "I WAS THERE."
I THINK THEY'RE RIGHT.
I DON'T THINK YOU CAN CRACK THE SKY A BIT AND STARE ON THE FACE OF GOD SOMEWHAT.
SHITSTICKS, THEY'RE ABOUT TO BRING THE FACILITY ONLINE.
WHY IS THERE A CLASS OF SMALL CHILDREN WATCHING?
HIS IS EXACTLY THE ORT OF EVENT YOU SEND A CLASS OF SMALL CHILDREN TO WATCH!
THE WINDMILL BIT, NOT THE RAPTURE, I MEAN.
ON BEHALF OF CORNWALL COUNCIL AND RENEWCHARIST, I DECLARE TREDREGYN EDGE WIND FARM...
3...
2...
1...!

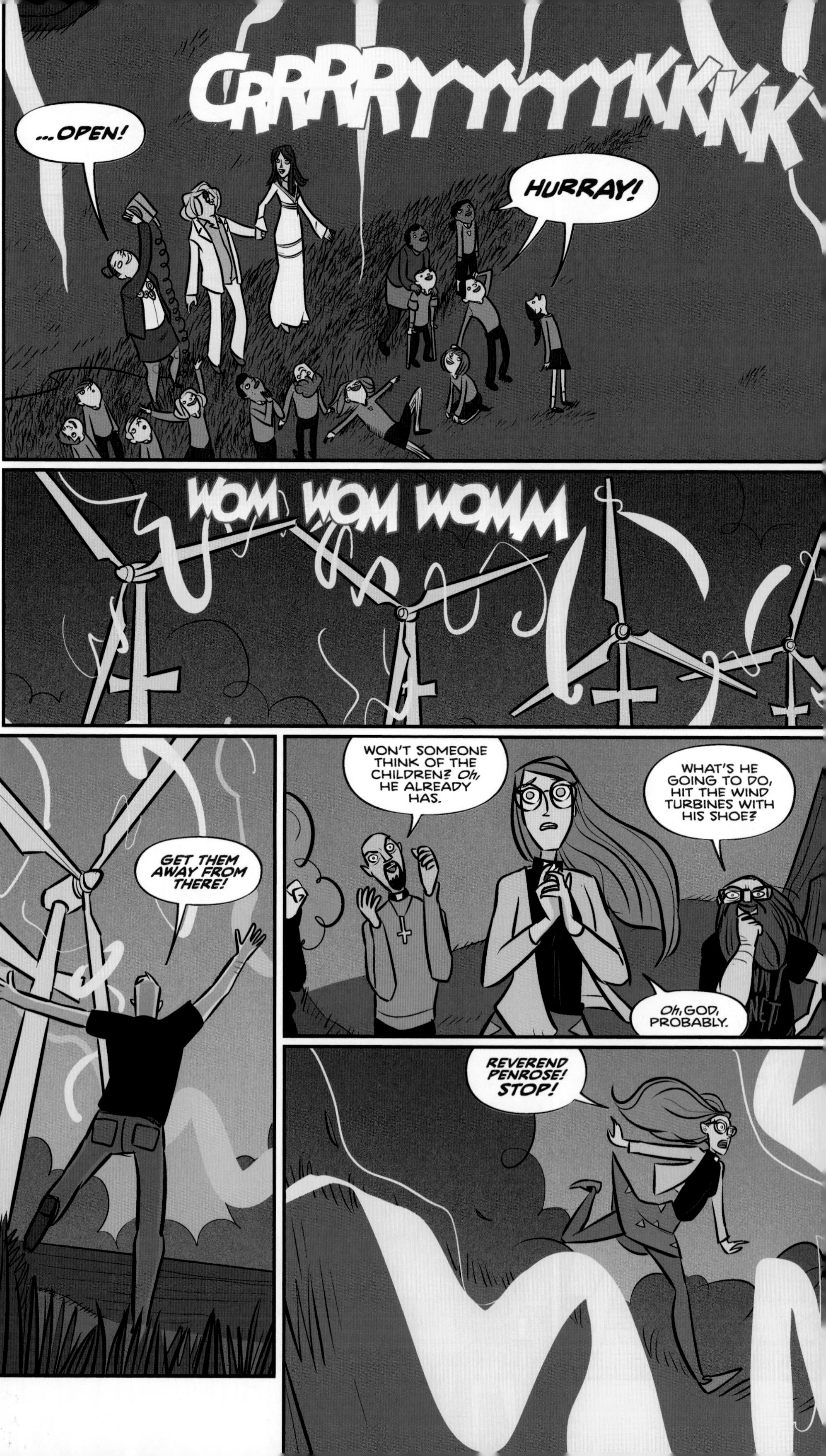

CRRRRYYYYYKKKK
...OPEN!
HURRAY!
WOM WOM WOMM
GET THEM AWAY FROM THERE!
WON'T SOMEONE THINK OF THE CHILDREN? *Oh,* HE ALREADY HAS.
WHAT'S HE GOING TO DO, HIT THE WIND TURBINES WITH HIS SHOE?
Oh, GOD, PROBABLY.
REVEREND PENROSE! STOP!

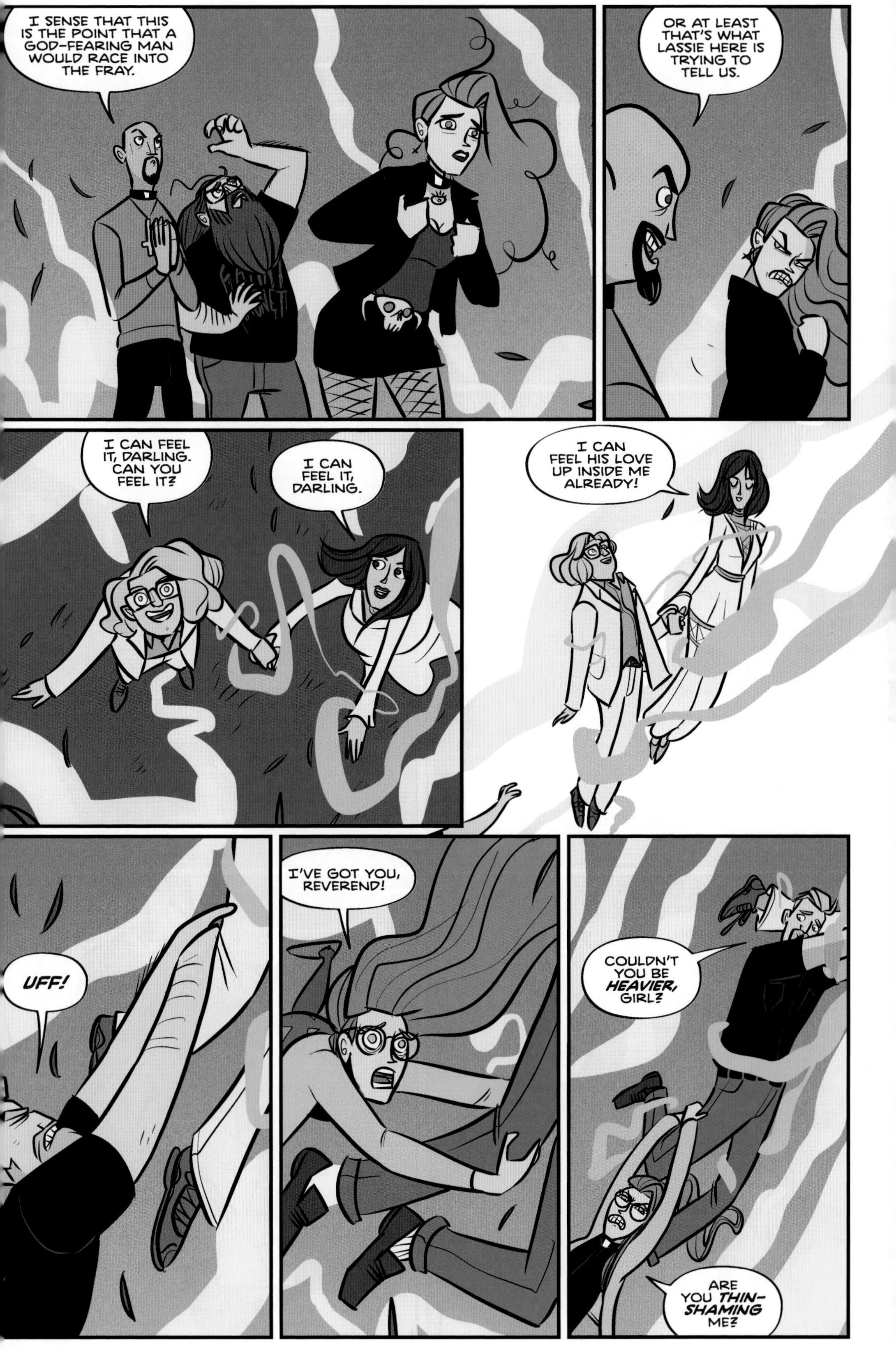
I SENSE THAT THIS IS THE POINT THAT A GOD-FEARING MAN WOULD RACE INTO THE FRAY.
OR AT LEAST THAT'S WHAT LASSIE HERE IS TRYING TO TELL US.
I CAN FEEL IT, DARLING. CAN YOU FEEL IT?
I CAN FEEL IT, DARLING.
I CAN FEEL HIS LOVE UP INSIDE ME ALREADY!
UFF!
I'VE GOT YOU, REVEREND!
COULDN'T YOU BE HEAVIER, GIRL?
ARE YOU THIN-SHAMING ME?

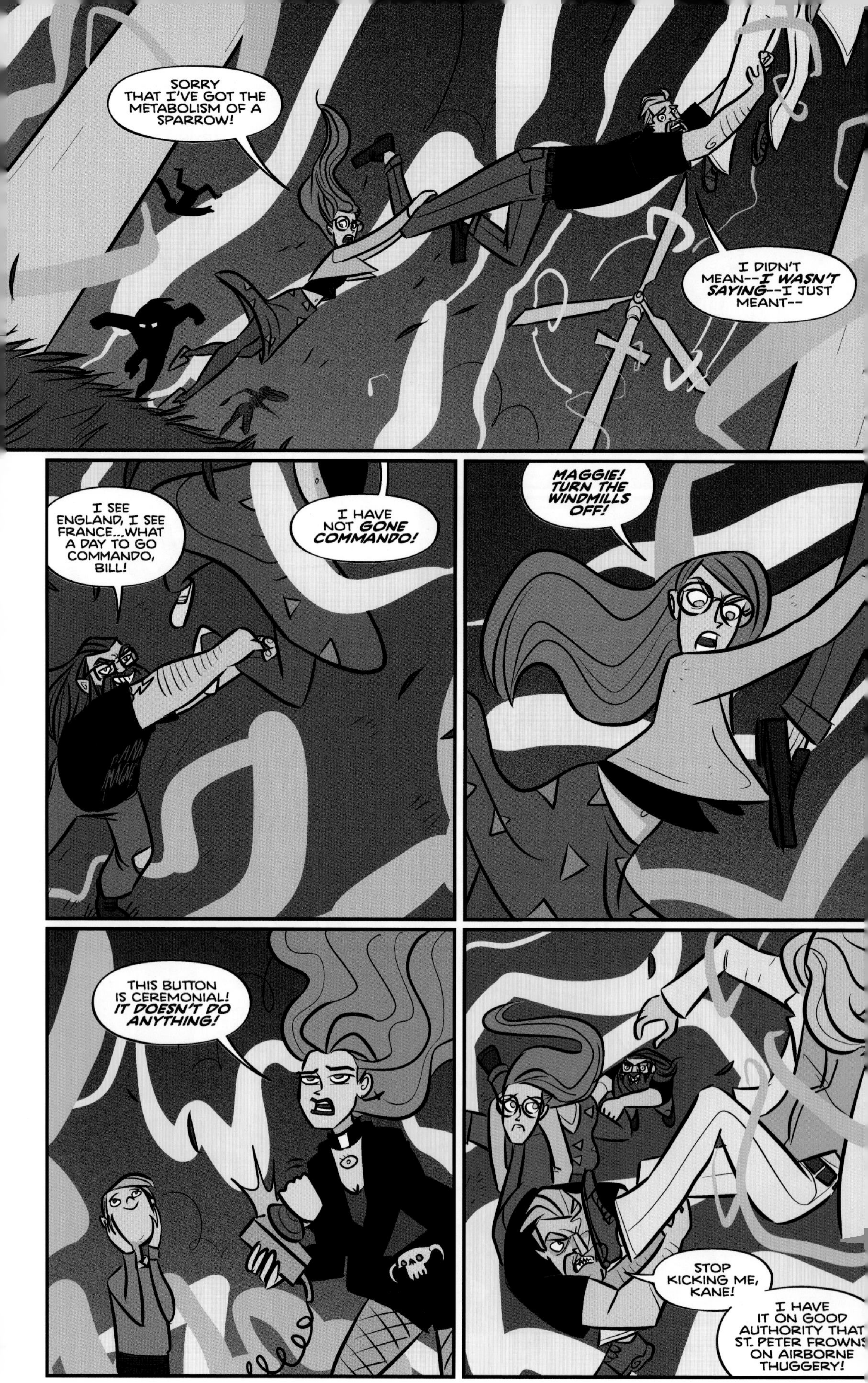
SORRY THAT I'VE GOT THE METABOLISM OF A SPARROW!
I DIDN'T MEAN--*I WASN'T SAYING*--I JUST MEANT--
I SEE ENGLAND, I SEE FRANCE...WHAT A DAY TO GO COMMANDO, BILL!
I HAVE NOT *GONE COMMANDO!*
MAGGIE! TURN THE WINDMILLS OFF!
THIS BUTTON IS CEREMONIAL! *IT DOESN'T DO ANYTHING!*
STOP KICKING ME, KANE!
I HAVE IT ON GOOD AUTHORITY THAT ST. PETER FROWNS ON AIRBORNE THUGGERY!

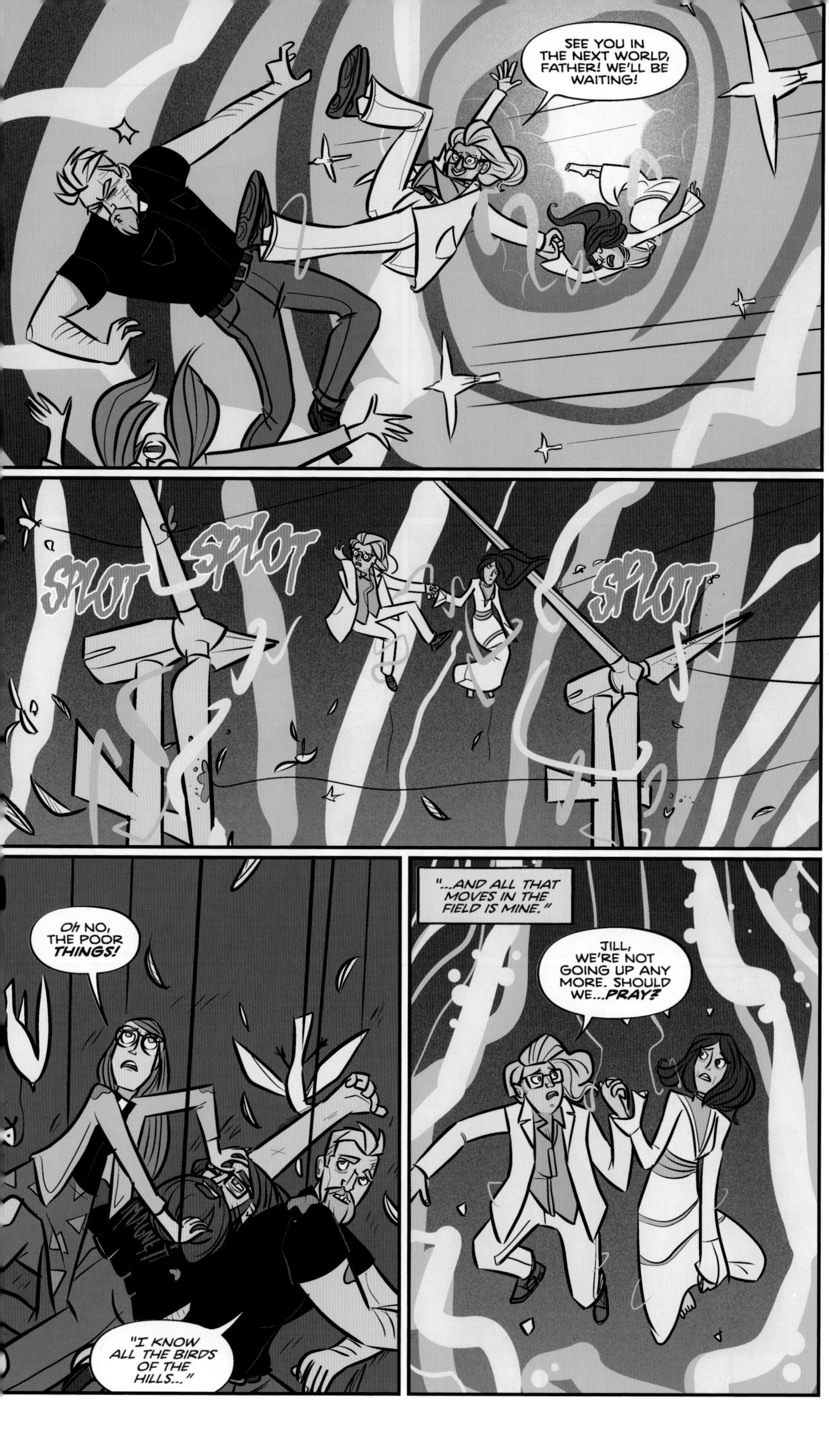

SEE YOU IN THE NEXT WORLD, FATHER! WE'LL BE WAITING!
SPLOT
SPLOT
SPLOT
Oh NO, THE POOR THINGS!
"I KNOW ALL THE BIRDS OF THE HILLS..."
"...AND ALL THAT MOVES IN THE FIELD IS MINE."
JILL, WE'RE NOT GOING UP ANY MORE. SHOULD WE...PRAY?

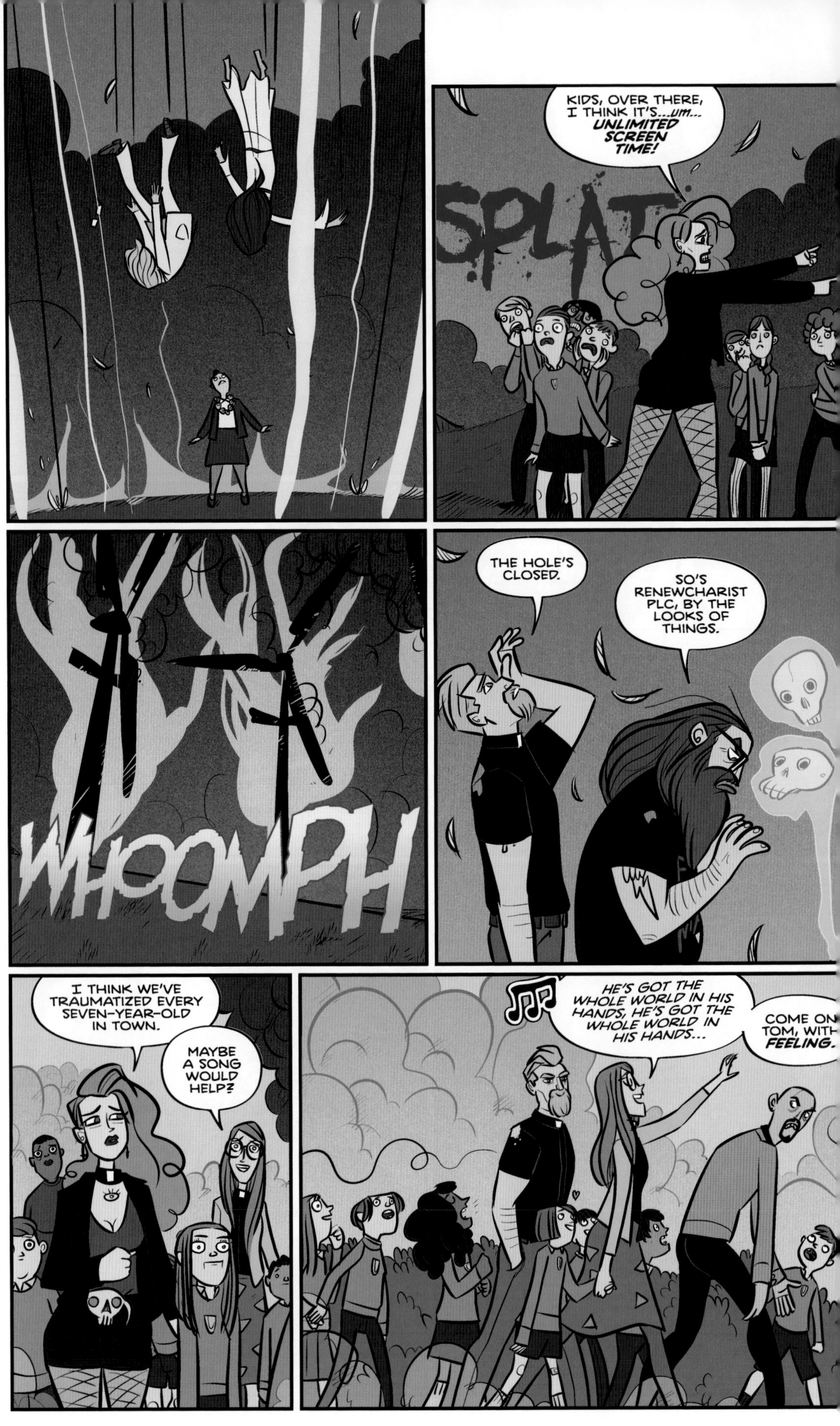
KIDS, OVER THERE, I THINK IT'S...UM... UNLIMITED SCREEN TIME!
SPLAT
WHOOMPH
THE HOLE'S CLOSED.
SO'S RENEWCHARIST PLC, BY THE LOOKS OF THINGS.
I THINK WE'VE TRAUMATIZED EVERY SEVEN-YEAR-OLD IN TOWN.
MAYBE A SONG WOULD HELP?
HE'S GOT THE WHOLE WORLD IN HIS HANDS, HE'S GOT THE WHOLE WORLD IN HIS HANDS...
COME ON TOM, WITH FEELING.

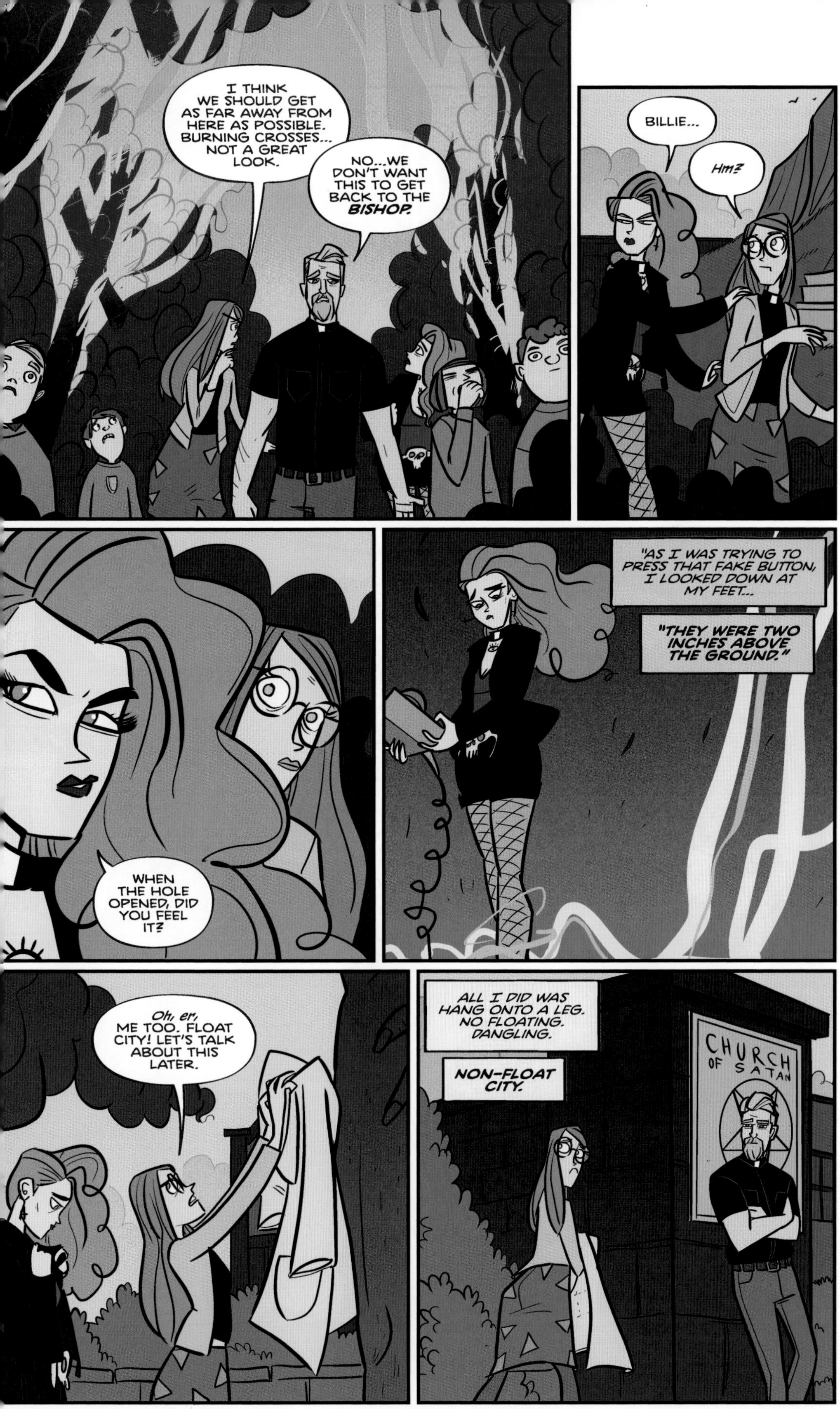
I THINK WE SHOULD GET AS FAR AWAY FROM HERE AS POSSIBLE. BURNING CROSSES... NOT A GREAT LOOK.
NO...WE DON'T WANT THIS TO GET BACK TO THE BISHOP.
BILLIE...
Hm?
WHEN THE HOLE OPENED, DID YOU FEEL IT?
"AS I WAS TRYING TO PRESS THAT FAKE BUTTON, I LOOKED DOWN AT MY FEET...
"THEY WERE TWO INCHES ABOVE THE GROUND."
Oh, er, ME TOO. FLOAT CITY! LET'S TALK ABOUT THIS LATER.
ALL I DID WAS HANG ONTO A LEG. NO FLOATING. DANGLING.
NON-FLOAT CITY.
CHURCH OF SATAN

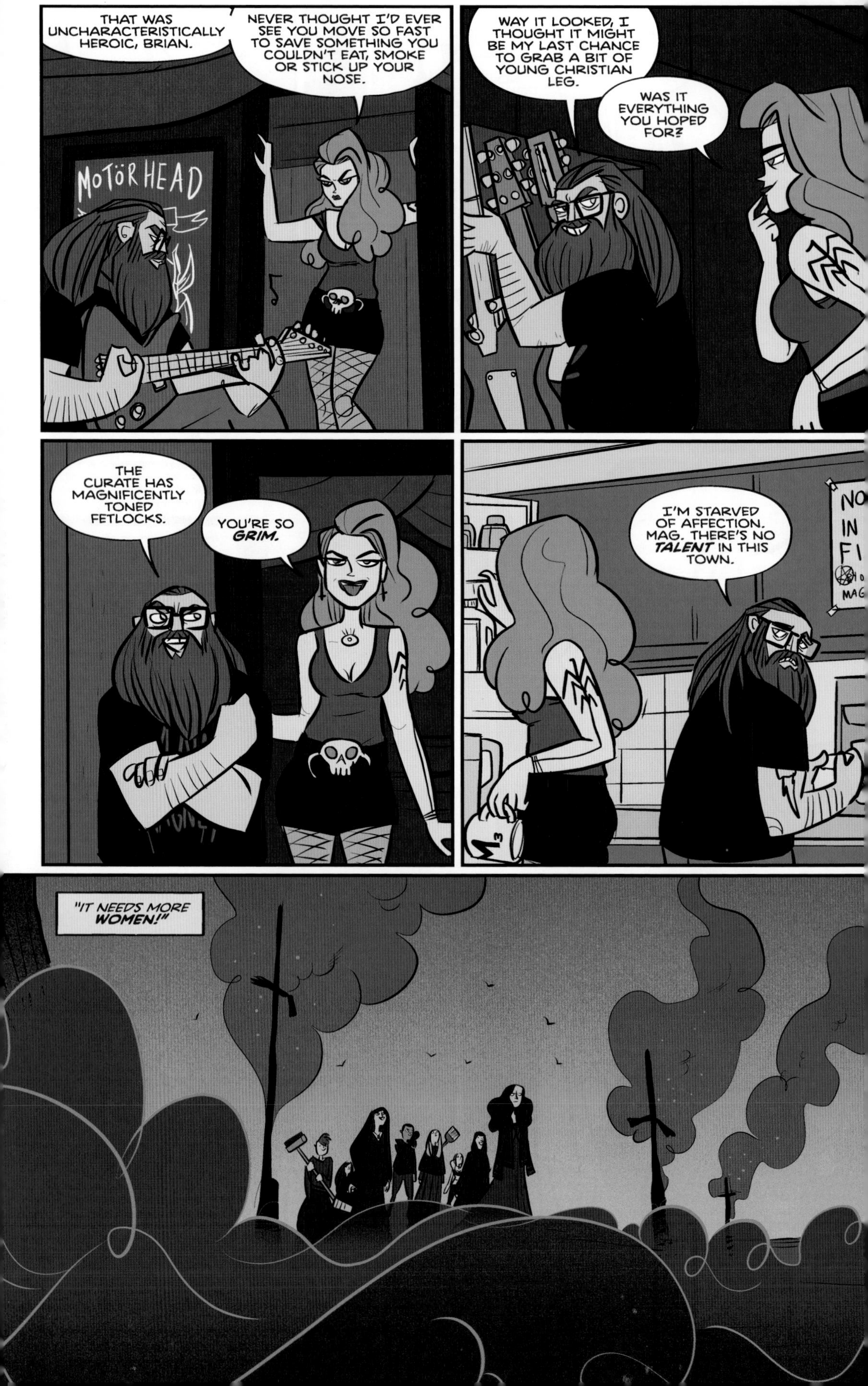
THAT WAS UNCHARACTERISTICALLY HEROIC, BRIAN.
NEVER THOUGHT I'D EVER SEE YOU MOVE SO FAST TO SAVE SOMETHING YOU COULDN'T EAT, SMOKE OR STICK UP YOUR NOSE.
MOTÖRHEAD
WAY IT LOOKED, I THOUGHT IT MIGHT BE MY LAST CHANCE TO GRAB A BIT OF YOUNG CHRISTIAN LEG.
WAS IT EVERYTHING YOU HOPED FOR?
THE CURATE HAS MAGNIFICENTLY TONED FETLOCKS.
YOU'RE SO *GRIM.*
I'M STARVED OF AFFECTION, MAG. THERE'S NO *TALENT* IN THIS TOWN.
"IT NEEDS MORE *WOMEN!*"

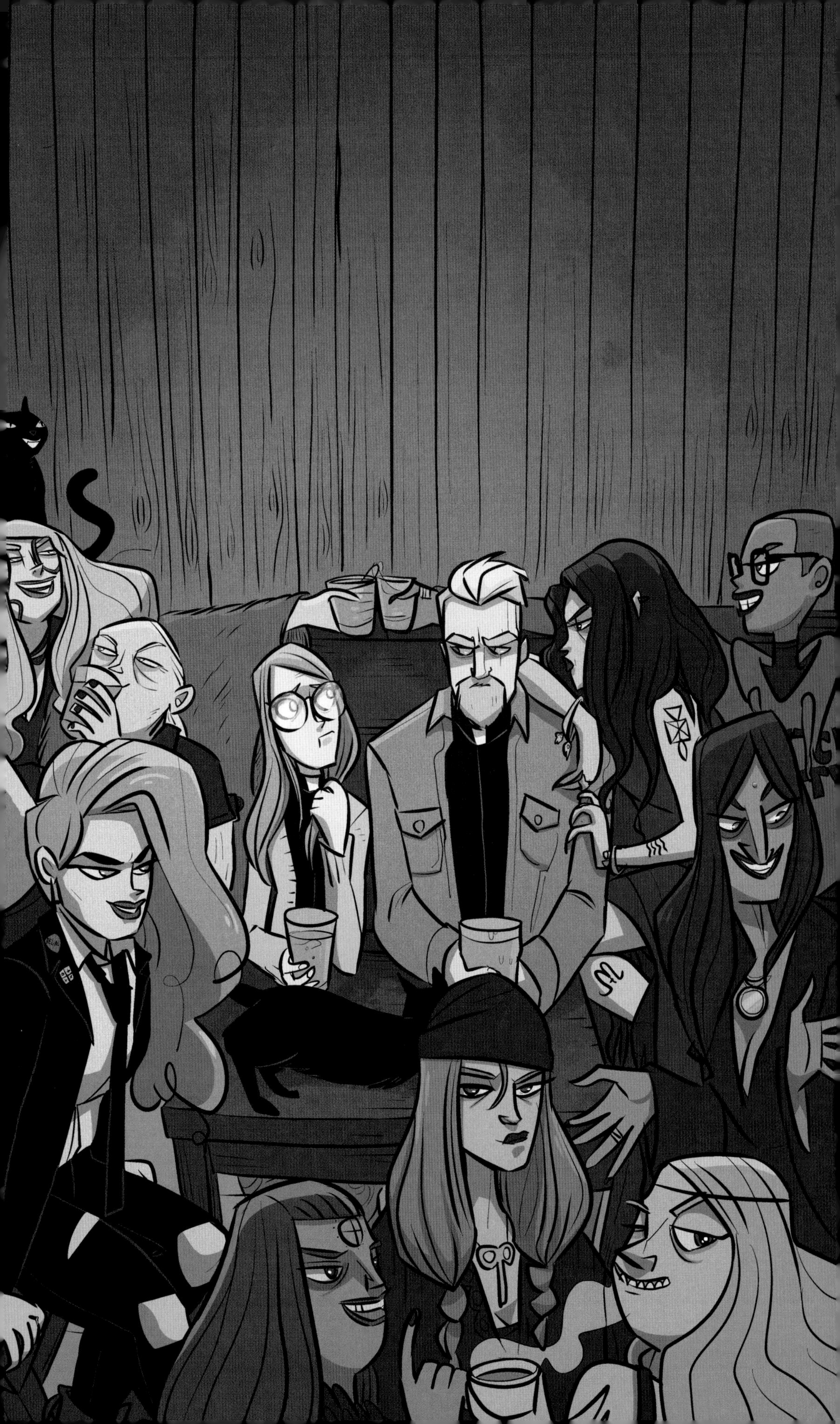

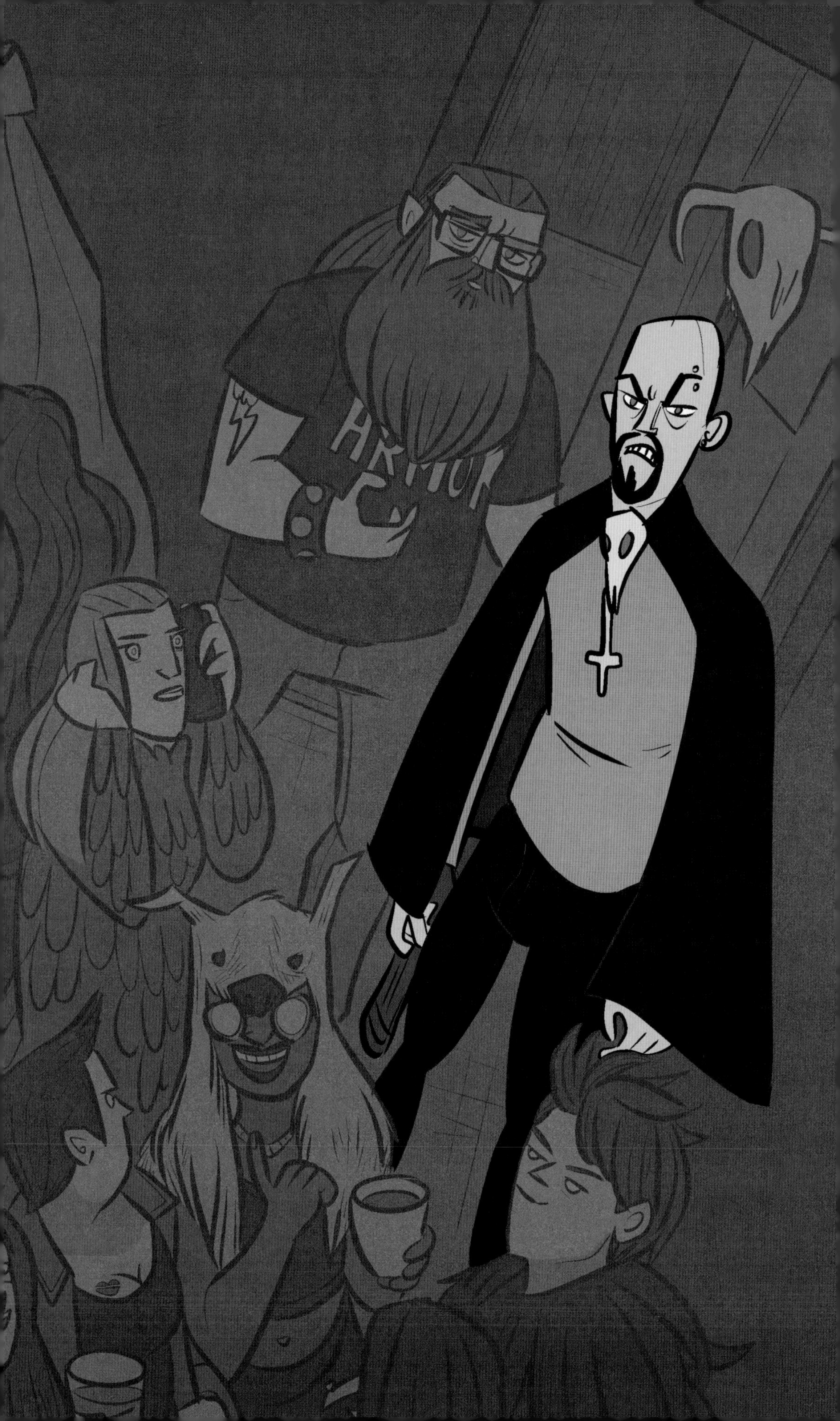

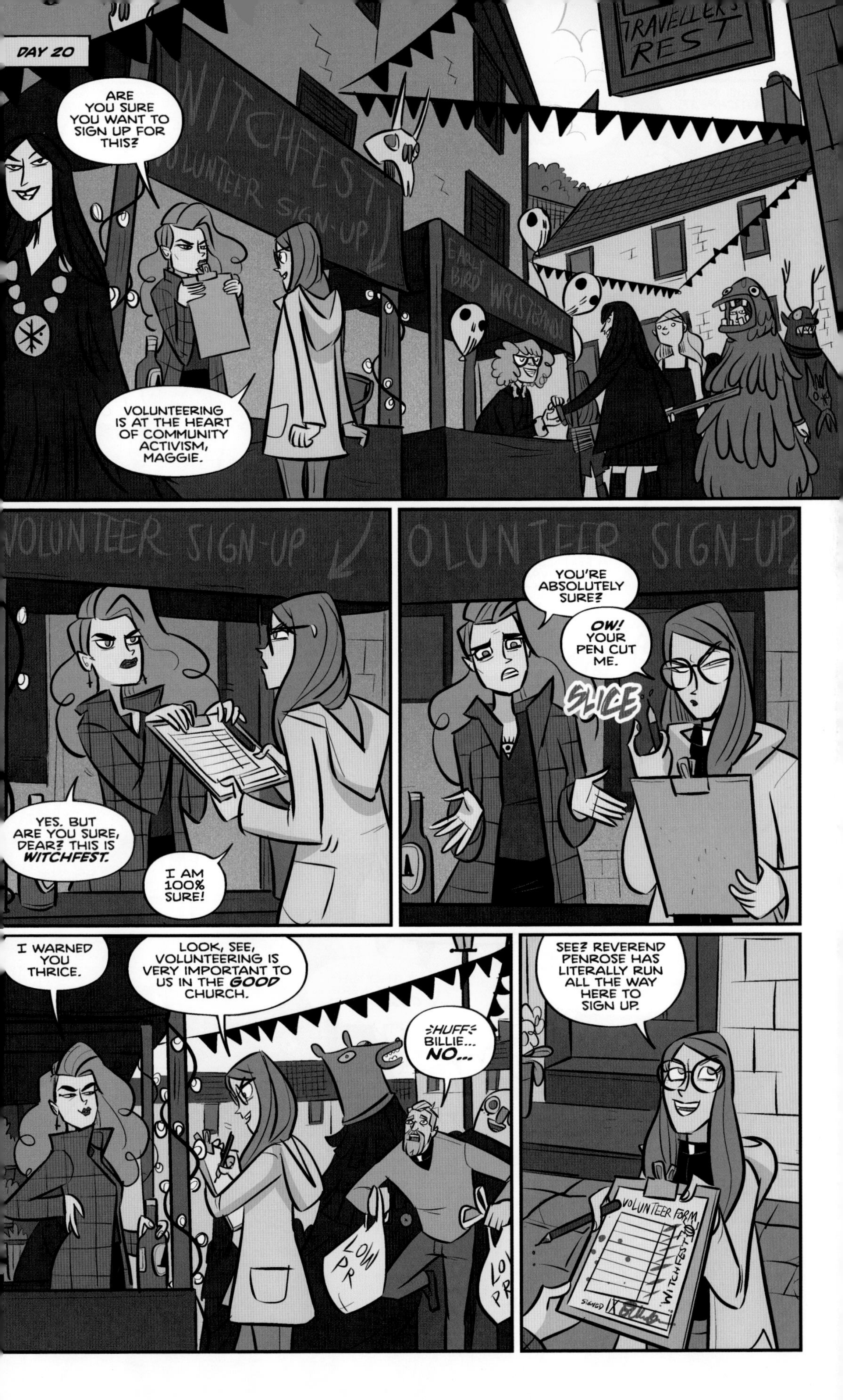

DAY 20
WITCHFEST VOLUNTEER SIGN-UP
TRAVELLERS REST
ARE YOU SURE YOU WANT TO SIGN UP FOR THIS?
VOLUNTEERING IS AT THE HEART OF COMMUNITY ACTIVISM, MAGGIE.
VOLUNTEER SIGN-UP
YES. BUT ARE YOU SURE, DEAR? THIS IS *WITCHFEST.*
I AM 100% SURE!
VOLUNTEER SIGN-UP
YOU'RE ABSOLUTELY SURE?
OW! YOUR PEN CUT ME.
SLICE
I WARNED YOU THRICE.
LOOK, SEE, VOLUNTEERING IS VERY IMPORTANT TO US IN THE *GOOD* CHURCH.
HUFF BILLIE... ***NO...***
SEE? REVEREND PENROSE HAS LITERALLY RUN ALL THE WAY HERE TO SIGN UP.
VOLUNTEER FORM
WITCHFEST
SIGNED X

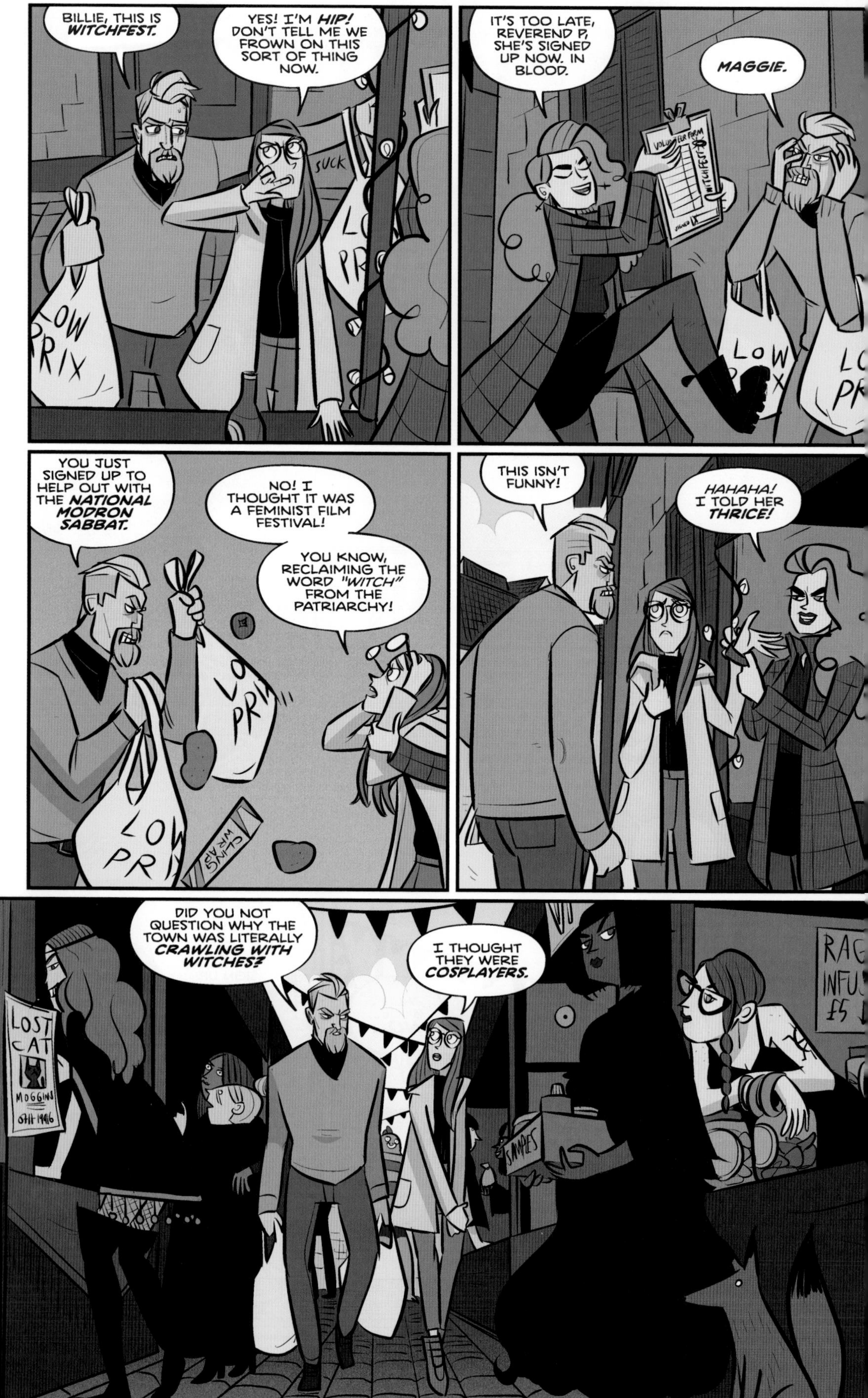
BILLIE, THIS IS WITCHFEST.
YES! I'M HIP! DON'T TELL ME WE FROWN ON THIS SORT OF THING NOW.
SUCK
LOW PRIX
IT'S TOO LATE, REVEREND P, SHE'S SIGNED UP NOW. IN BLOOD.
MAGGIE.
VOLUNTEER FORM
WITCHFEST
LOW PRIX
YOU JUST SIGNED UP TO HELP OUT WITH THE NATIONAL MODRON SABBAT.
NO! I THOUGHT IT WAS A FEMINIST FILM FESTIVAL!
YOU KNOW, RECLAIMING THE WORD "WITCH" FROM THE PATRIARCHY!
CLING WRAP
THIS ISN'T FUNNY!
HAHAHA! I TOLD HER THRICE!
DID YOU NOT QUESTION WHY THE TOWN WAS LITERALLY CRAWLING WITH WITCHES?
I THOUGHT THEY WERE COSPLAYERS.
LOST CAT
MOGGINS
SAMPLES

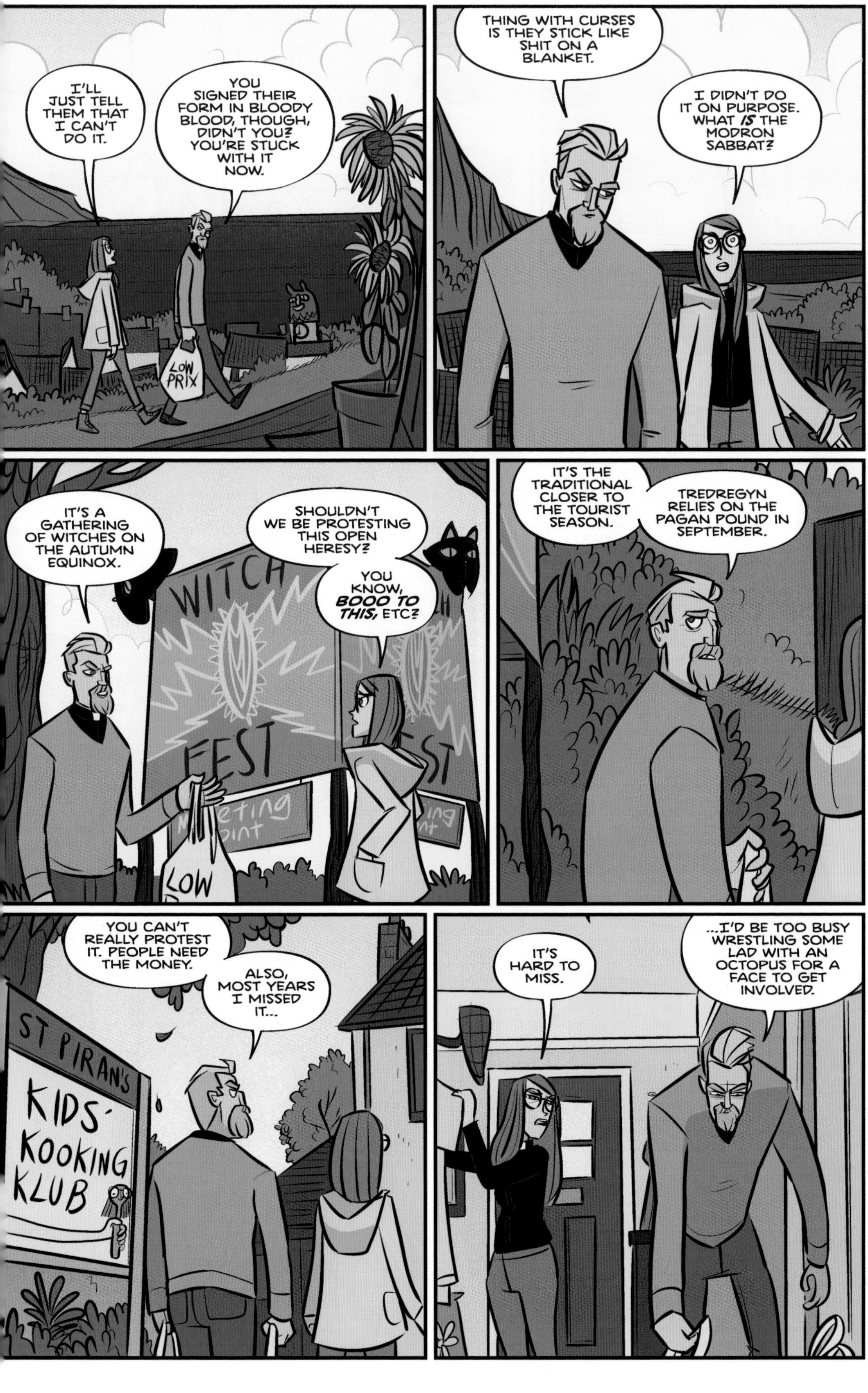
I'LL JUST TELL THEM THAT I CAN'T DO IT.
YOU SIGNED THEIR FORM IN BLOODY BLOOD, THOUGH, DIDN'T YOU? YOU'RE STUCK WITH IT NOW.
LOW PRIX
THING WITH CURSES IS THEY STICK LIKE SHIT ON A BLANKET.
I DIDN'T DO IT ON PURPOSE. WHAT *IS* THE MODRON SABBAT?
IT'S A GATHERING OF WITCHES ON THE AUTUMN EQUINOX.
SHOULDN'T WE BE PROTESTING THIS OPEN HERESY?
YOU KNOW, ***BOOO TO THIS,*** ETC?
IT'S THE TRADITIONAL CLOSER TO THE TOURIST SEASON.
TREDREGYN RELIES ON THE PAGAN POUND IN SEPTEMBER.
YOU CAN'T REALLY PROTEST IT. PEOPLE NEED THE MONEY.
ALSO, MOST YEARS I MISSED IT...
ST PIRAN'S
KIDS' KOOKING KLUB
IT'S HARD TO MISS.
...I'D BE TOO BUSY WRESTLING SOME LAD WITH AN OCTOPUS FOR A FACE TO GET INVOLVED.

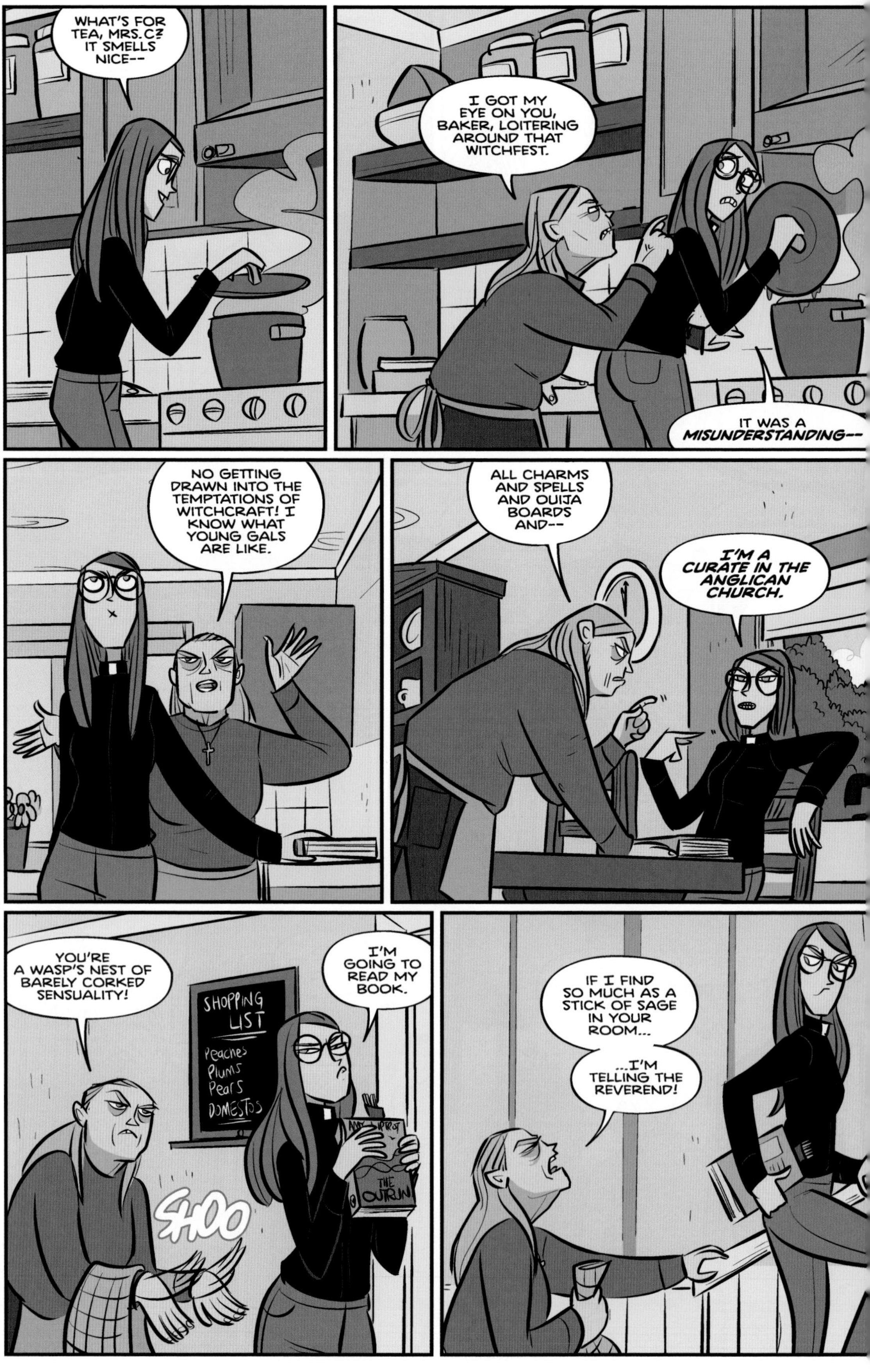
WHAT'S FOR TEA, MRS. C? IT SMELLS NICE--
I GOT MY EYE ON YOU, BAKER, LOITERING AROUND THAT WITCHFEST.
IT WAS A MISUNDERSTANDING--
NO GETTING DRAWN INTO THE TEMPTATIONS OF WITCHCRAFT! I KNOW WHAT YOUNG GALS ARE LIKE.
ALL CHARMS AND SPELLS AND OUIJA BOARDS AND--
I'M A CURATE IN THE ANGLICAN CHURCH.
YOU'RE A WASP'S NEST OF BARELY CORKED SENSUALITY!
SHOPPING LIST
Peaches
Plums
Pears
DOMESTOS
I'M GOING TO READ MY BOOK.
THE OUTRUN
SHOO
IF I FIND SO MUCH AS A STICK OF SAGE IN YOUR ROOM...
...I'M TELLING THE REVEREND!

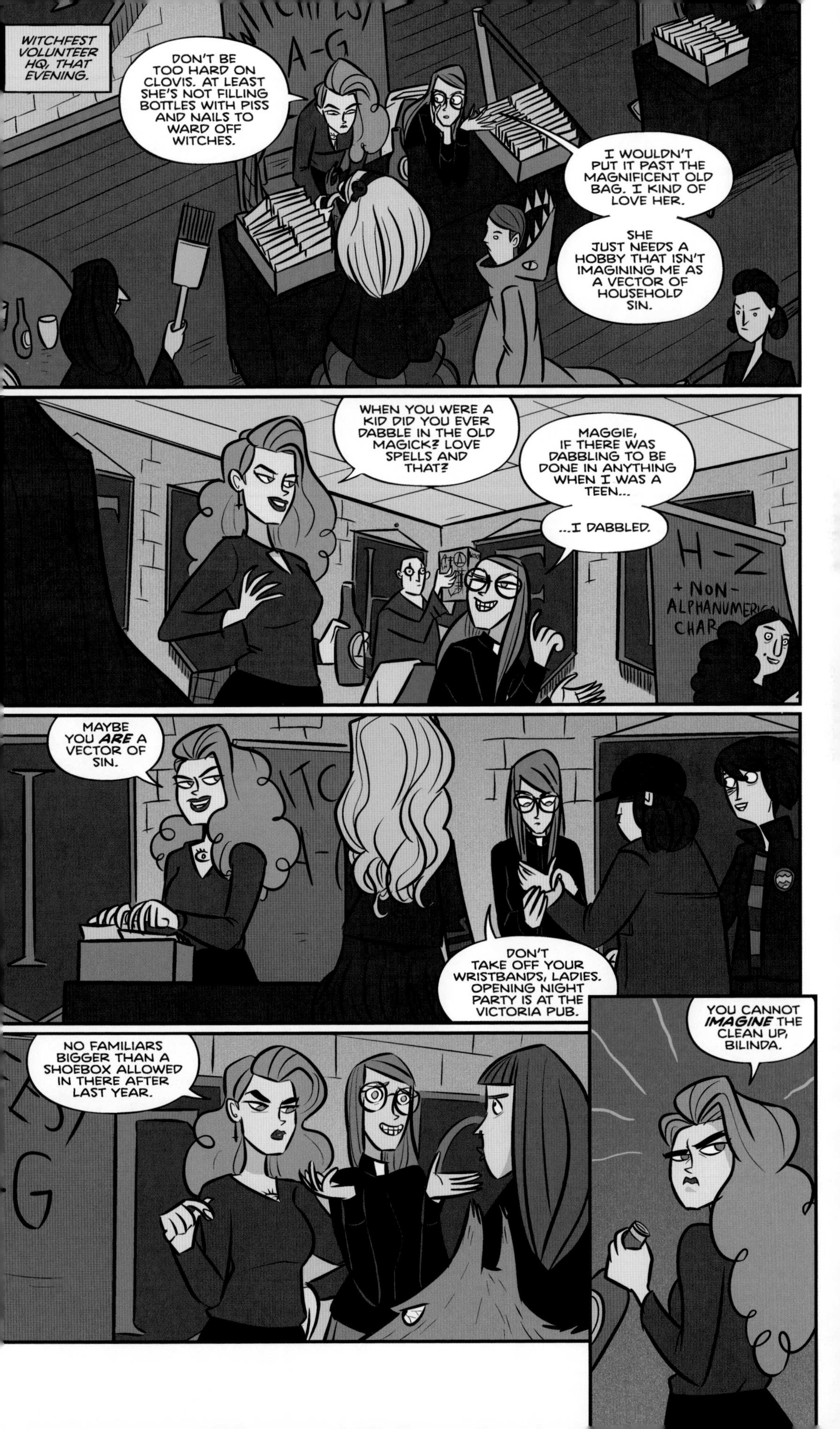
WITCHFEST VOLUNTEER HQ, THAT EVENING.
DON'T BE TOO HARD ON CLOVIS. AT LEAST SHE'S NOT FILLING BOTTLES WITH PISS AND NAILS TO WARD OFF WITCHES.
I WOULDN'T PUT IT PAST THE MAGNIFICENT OLD BAG. I KIND OF LOVE HER.
SHE JUST NEEDS A HOBBY THAT ISN'T IMAGINING ME AS A VECTOR OF HOUSEHOLD SIN.
WHEN YOU WERE A KID DID YOU EVER DABBLE IN THE OLD MAGICK? LOVE SPELLS AND THAT?
MAGGIE, IF THERE WAS DABBLING TO BE DONE IN ANYTHING WHEN I WAS A TEEN...
...I DABBLED.
H-Z + NON-ALPHANUMERICAL CHAR
MAYBE YOU *ARE* A VECTOR OF SIN.
DON'T TAKE OFF YOUR WRISTBANDS, LADIES. OPENING NIGHT PARTY IS AT THE VICTORIA PUB.
NO FAMILIARS BIGGER THAN A SHOEBOX ALLOWED IN THERE AFTER LAST YEAR.
YOU CANNOT *IMAGINE* THE CLEAN UP, BILINDA.

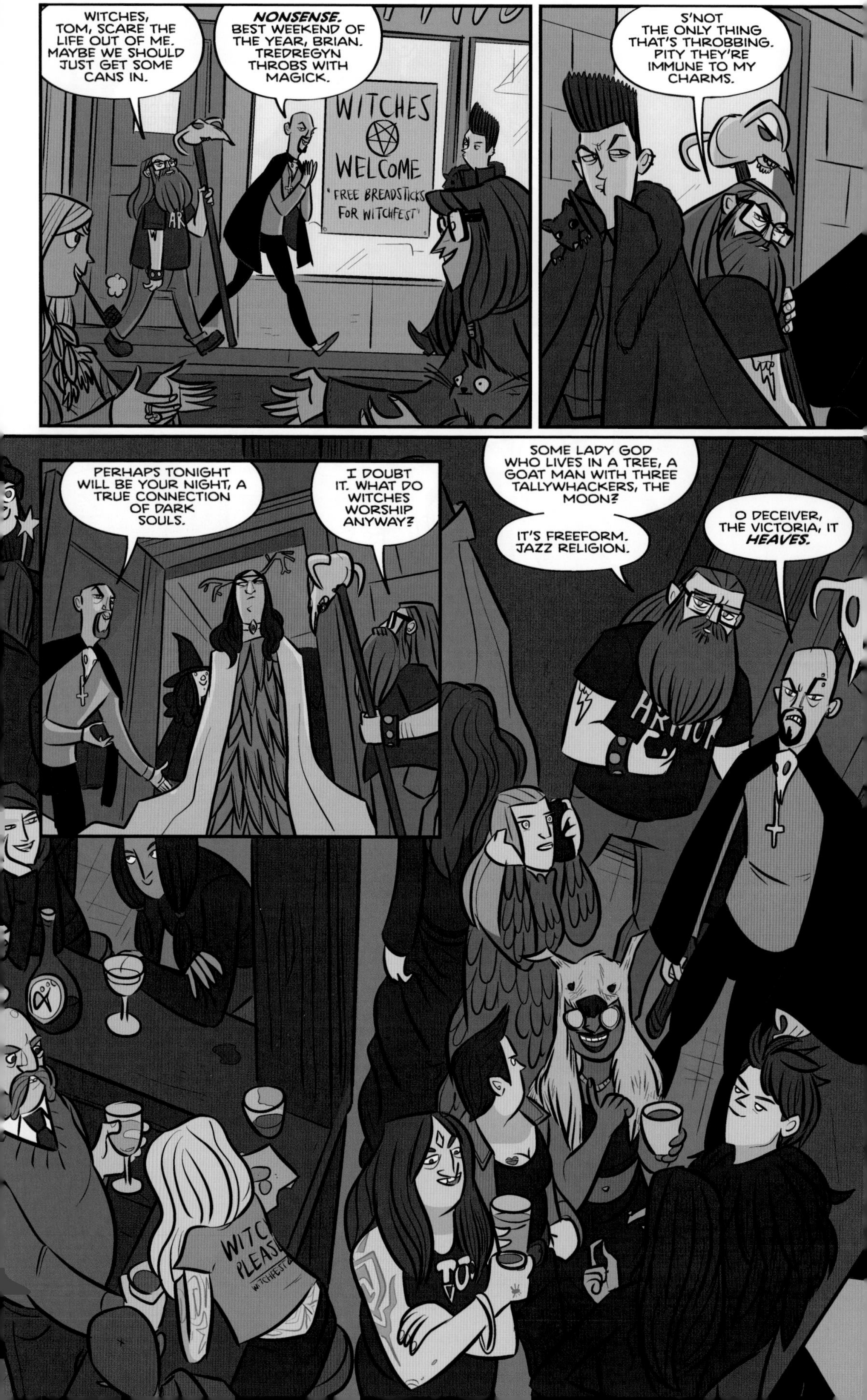
WITCHES, TOM, SCARE THE LIFE OUT OF ME. MAYBE WE SHOULD JUST GET SOME CANS IN.
NONSENSE. BEST WEEKEND OF THE YEAR, BRIAN. TREDREGYN THROBS WITH MAGICK.
WITCHES WELCOME "FREE BREADSTICKS FOR WITCHFEST"
S'NOT THE ONLY THING THAT'S THROBBING. PITY THEY'RE IMMUNE TO MY CHARMS.
PERHAPS TONIGHT WILL BE YOUR NIGHT, A TRUE CONNECTION OF DARK SOULS.
I DOUBT IT. WHAT DO WITCHES WORSHIP ANYWAY?
SOME LADY GOD WHO LIVES IN A TREE, A GOAT MAN WITH THREE TALLYWHACKERS, THE MOON?
IT'S FREEFORM. JAZZ RELIGION.
O DECEIVER, THE VICTORIA, IT HEAVES.
WITCH PLEASE WITCHFEST

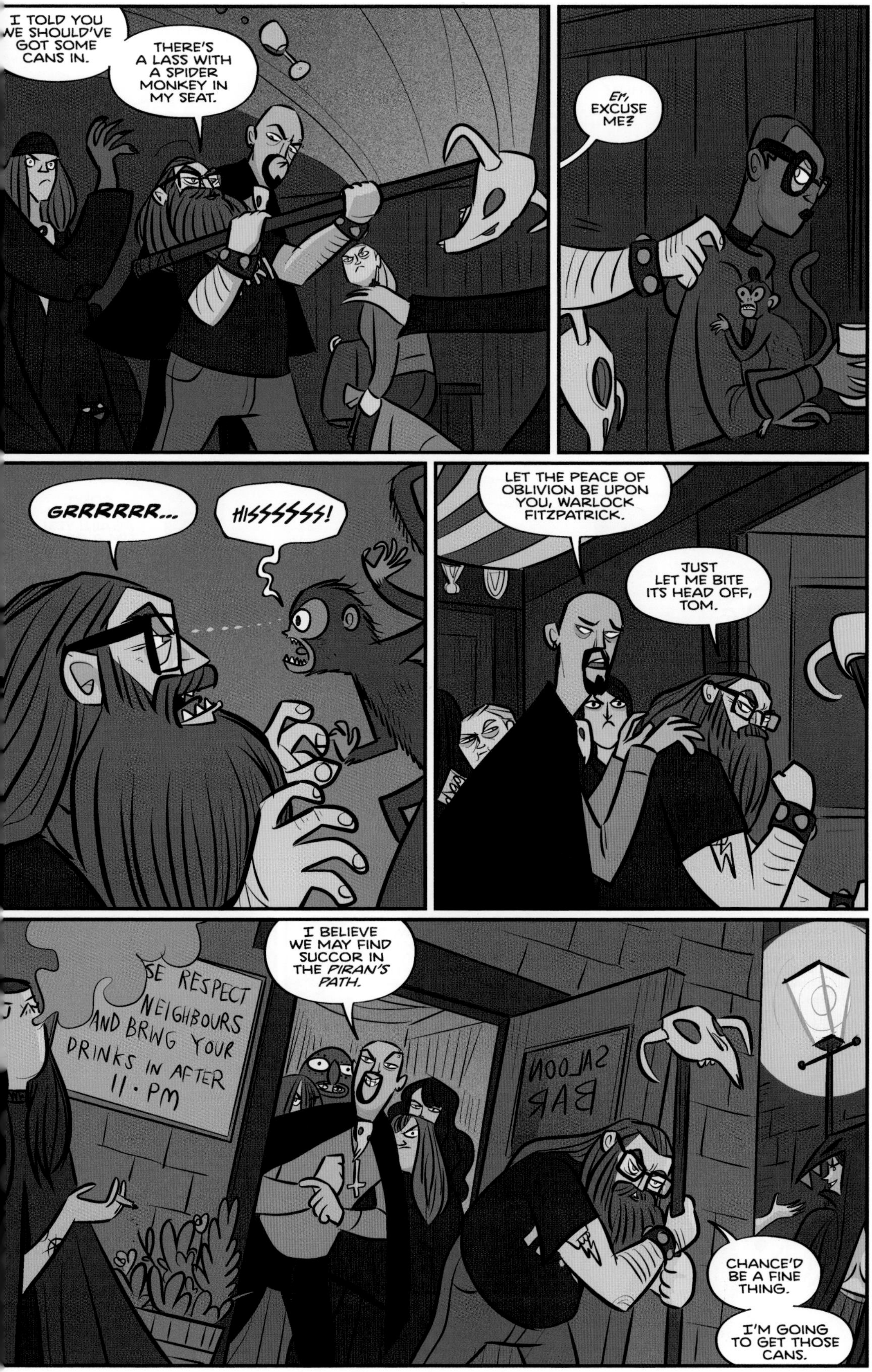
I TOLD YOU WE SHOULD'VE GOT SOME CANS IN.
THERE'S A LASS WITH A SPIDER MONKEY IN MY SEAT.
Er, EXCUSE ME?
GRRRRRR...
HISSSSSS!
LET THE PEACE OF OBLIVION BE UPON YOU, WARLOCK FITZPATRICK.
JUST LET ME BITE ITS HEAD OFF, TOM.
SE RESPECT NEIGHBOURS AND BRING YOUR DRINKS IN AFTER 11.PM
I BELIEVE WE MAY FIND SUCCOR IN THE *PIRAN'S PATH.*
SALOON BAR
CHANCE'D BE A FINE THING.
I'M GOING TO GET THOSE CANS.

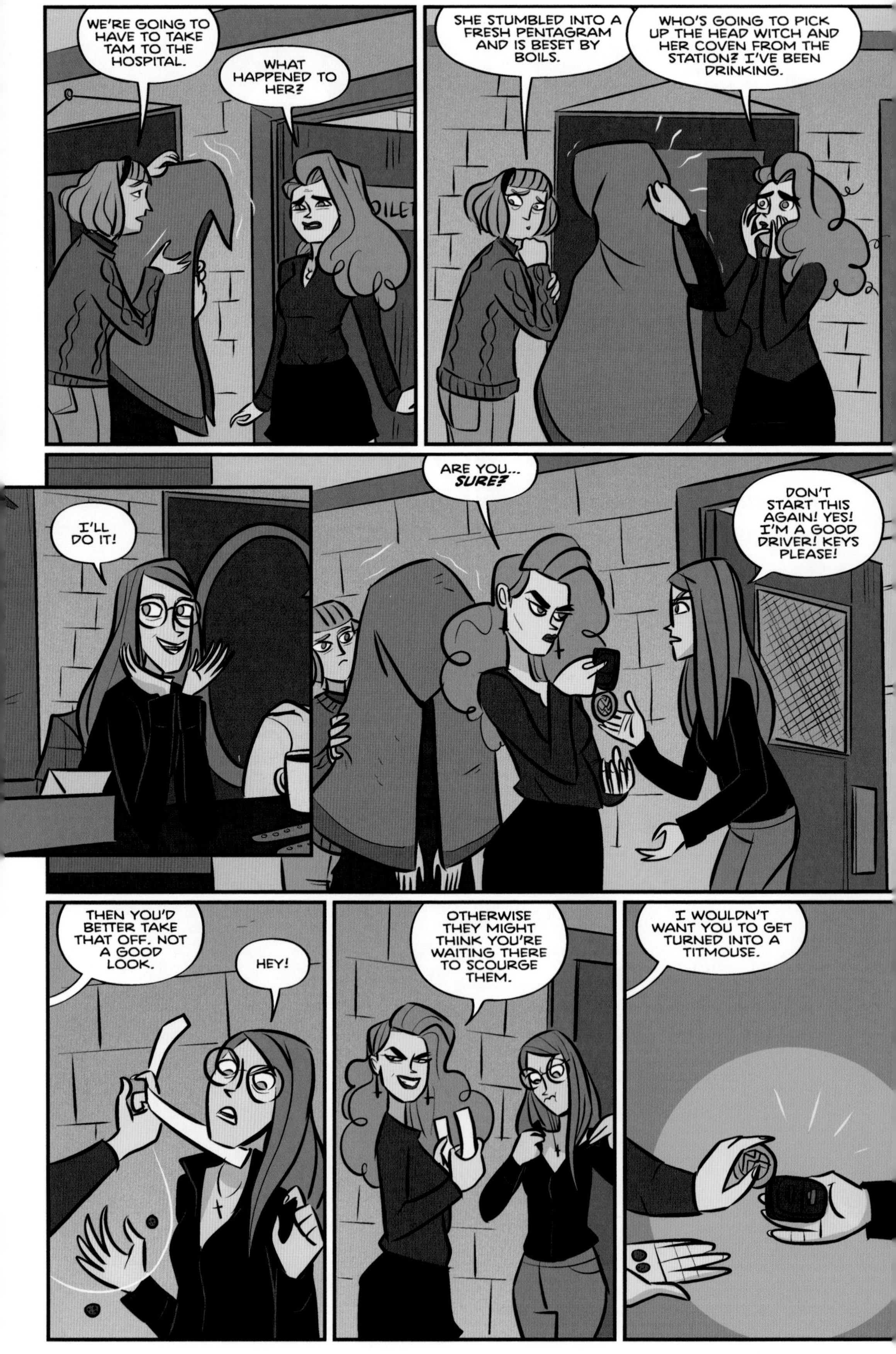
WE'RE GOING TO HAVE TO TAKE TAM TO THE HOSPITAL.
WHAT HAPPENED TO HER?
SHE STUMBLED INTO A FRESH PENTAGRAM AND IS BESET BY BOILS.
WHO'S GOING TO PICK UP THE HEAD WITCH AND HER COVEN FROM THE STATION? I'VE BEEN DRINKING.
I'LL DO IT!
ARE YOU... *SURE?*
DON'T START THIS AGAIN! YES! I'M A GOOD DRIVER! KEYS PLEASE!
THEN YOU'D BETTER TAKE THAT OFF. NOT A GOOD LOOK.
HEY!
OTHERWISE THEY MIGHT THINK YOU'RE WAITING THERE TO SCOURGE THEM.
I WOULDN'T WANT YOU TO GET TURNED INTO A TITMOUSE.

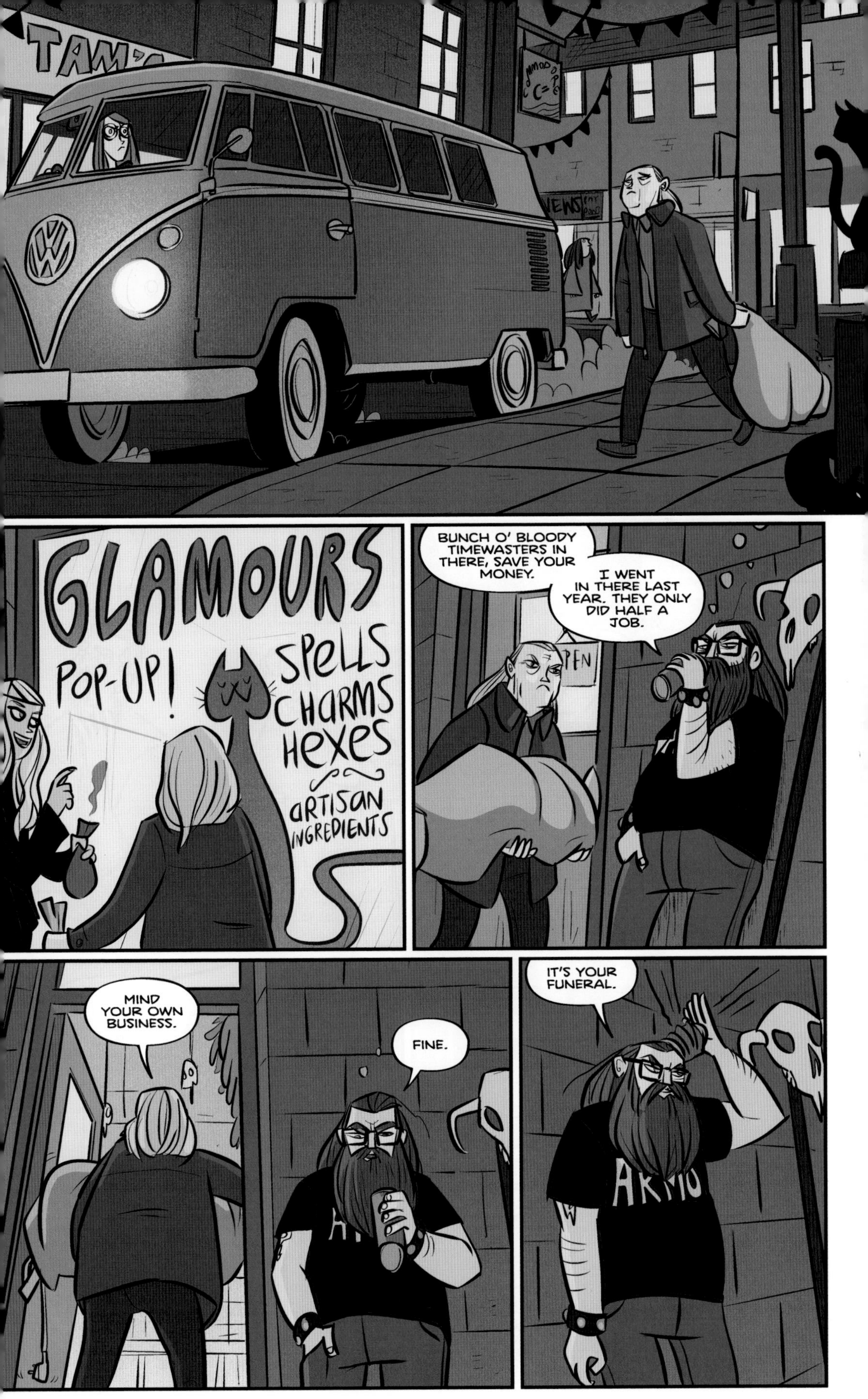
GLAMOURS
POP-UP!
SPELLS
CHARMS
HEXES
ARTISAN INGREDIENTS
BUNCH O' BLOODY TIMEWASTERS IN THERE, SAVE YOUR MONEY.
I WENT IN THERE LAST YEAR. THEY ONLY DID HALF A JOB.
MIND YOUR OWN BUSINESS.
FINE.
IT'S YOUR FUNERAL.

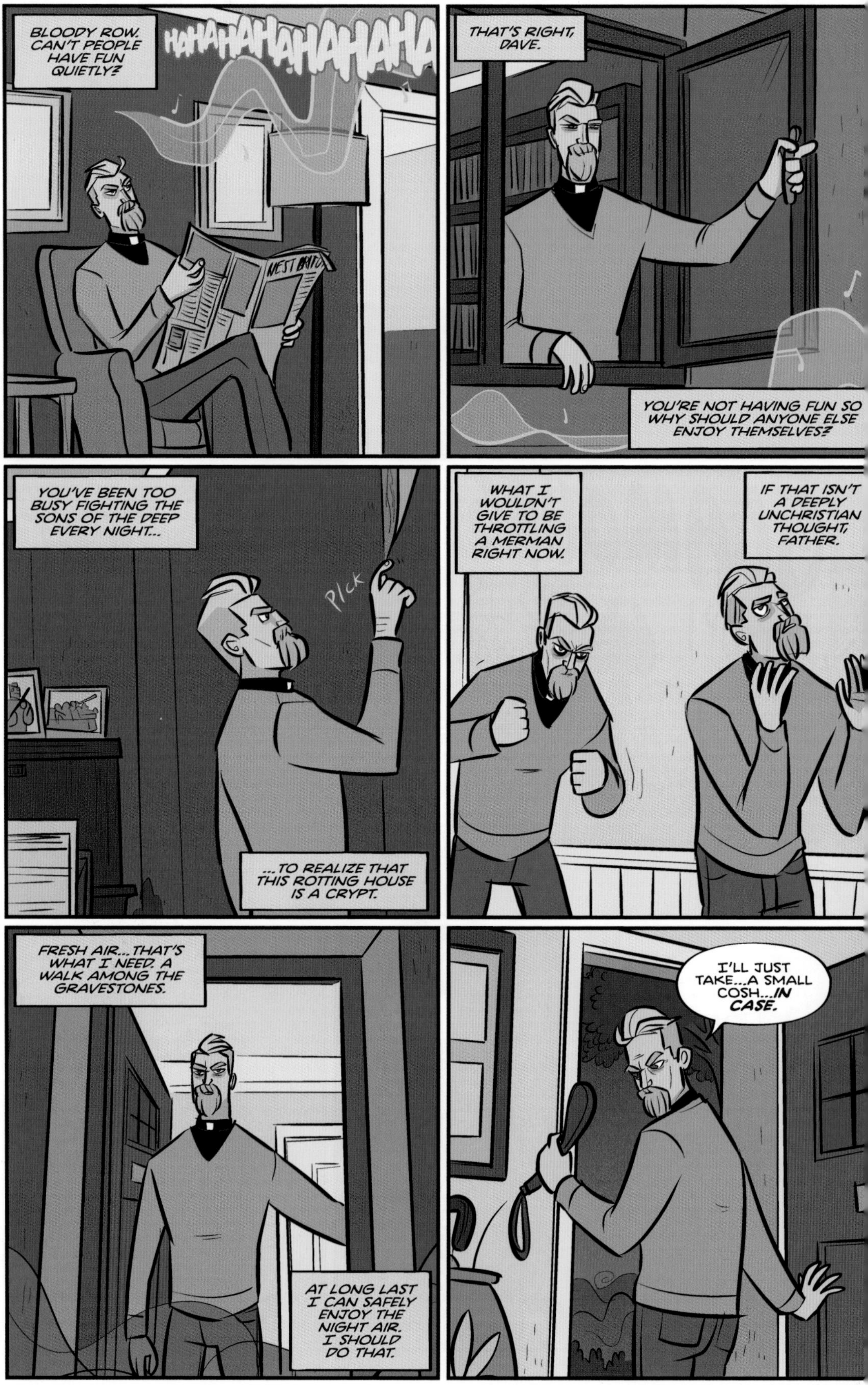
BLOODY ROW. CAN'T PEOPLE HAVE FUN QUIETLY?
HAHAHAHAHAHAHAHA
THAT'S RIGHT, DAVE.
YOU'RE NOT HAVING FUN SO WHY SHOULD ANYONE ELSE ENJOY THEMSELVES?
YOU'VE BEEN TOO BUSY FIGHTING THE SONS OF THE DEEP EVERY NIGHT...
PICK
...TO REALIZE THAT THIS ROTTING HOUSE IS A CRYPT.
WHAT I WOULDN'T GIVE TO BE THROTTLING A MERMAN RIGHT NOW.
IF THAT ISN'T A DEEPLY UNCHRISTIAN THOUGHT, FATHER.
FRESH AIR... THAT'S WHAT I NEED. A WALK AMONG THE GRAVESTONES.
AT LONG LAST I CAN SAFELY ENJOY THE NIGHT AIR. I SHOULD DO THAT.
I'LL JUST TAKE... A SMALL COSH... ***IN CASE.***

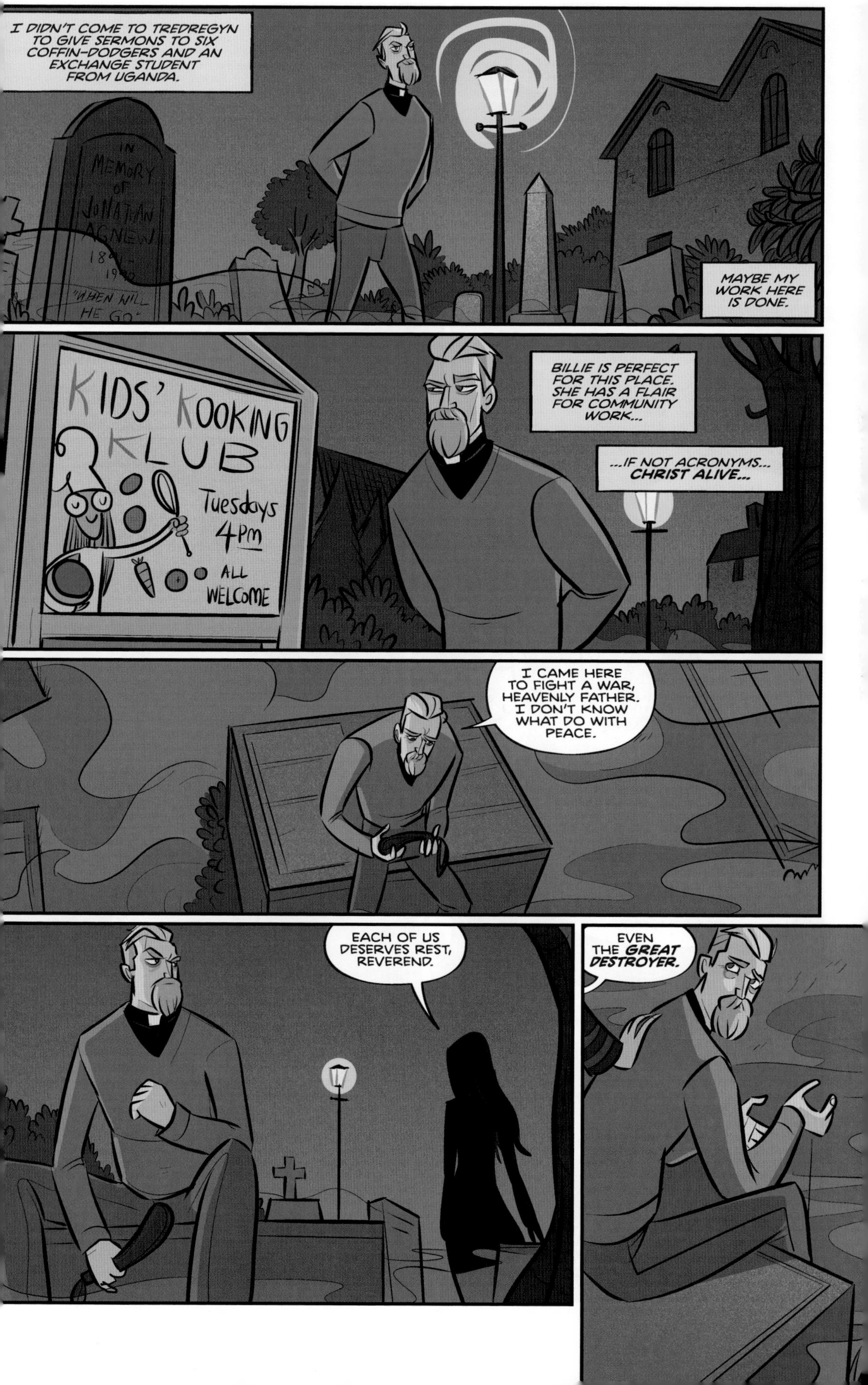
I DIDN'T COME TO TREDREGYN TO GIVE SERMONS TO SIX COFFIN-DODGERS AND AN EXCHANGE STUDENT FROM UGANDA.
IN MEMORY OF JONATHAN AGNEW
MAYBE MY WORK HERE IS DONE.
KIDS' KOOKING KLUB
Tuesdays 4pm
ALL WELCOME
BILLIE IS PERFECT FOR THIS PLACE. SHE HAS A FLAIR FOR COMMUNITY WORK...
...IF NOT ACRONYMS... **CHRIST ALIVE...**
I CAME HERE TO FIGHT A WAR, HEAVENLY FATHER. I DON'T KNOW WHAT DO WITH PEACE.
EACH OF US DESERVES REST, REVEREND.
EVEN THE ***GREAT DESTROYER.***

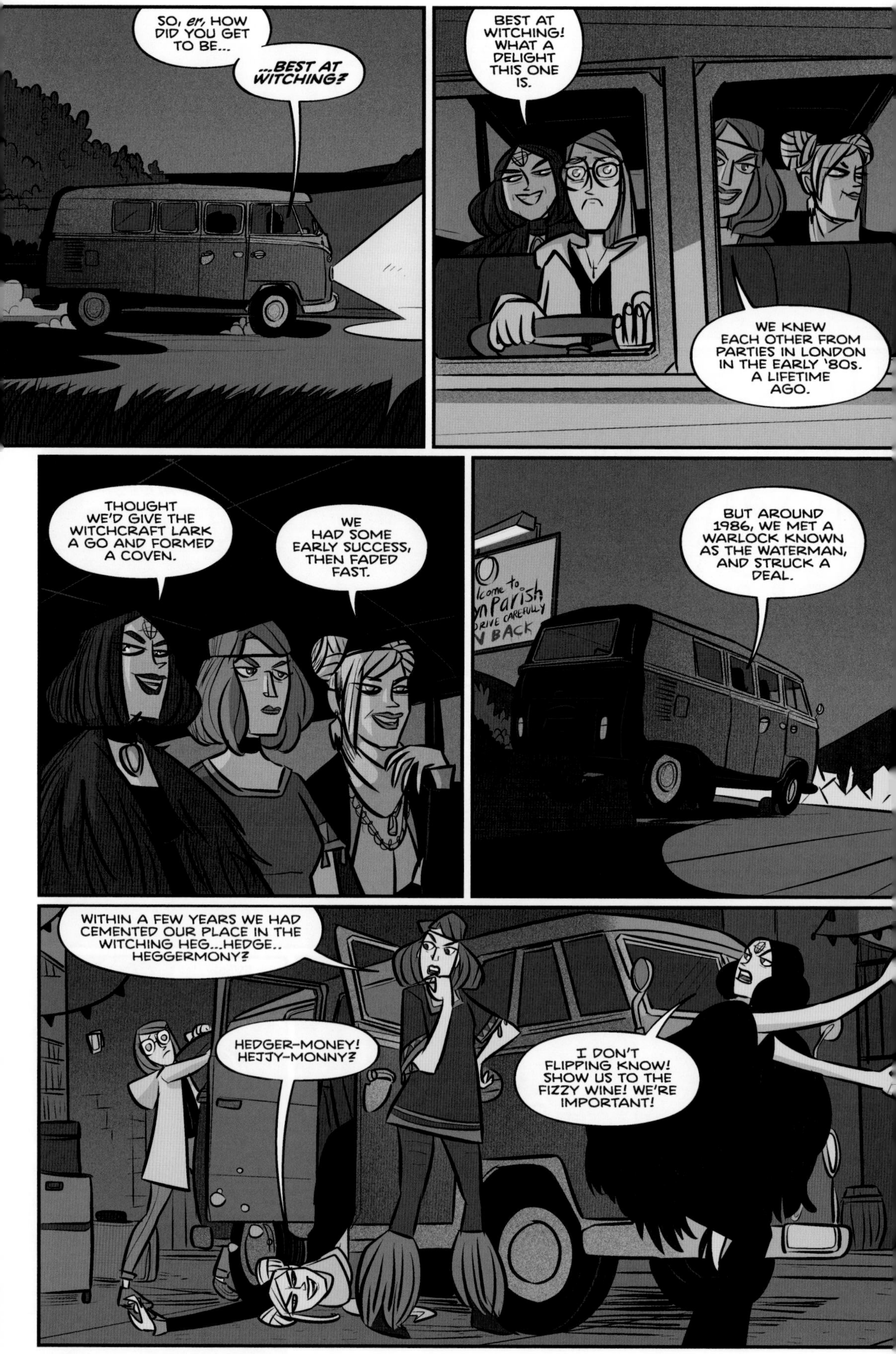
SO, *er,* HOW DID YOU GET TO BE...
...BEST AT WITCHING?
BEST AT WITCHING! WHAT A DELIGHT THIS ONE IS.
WE KNEW EACH OTHER FROM PARTIES IN LONDON IN THE EARLY '80s. A LIFETIME AGO.
THOUGHT WE'D GIVE THE WITCHCRAFT LARK A GO AND FORMED A COVEN.
WE HAD SOME EARLY SUCCESS, THEN FADED FAST.
BUT AROUND 1986, WE MET A WARLOCK KNOWN AS THE WATERMAN, AND STRUCK A DEAL.
WITHIN A FEW YEARS WE HAD CEMENTED OUR PLACE IN THE WITCHING HEG...HEDGE.. HEGGERMONY?
HEDGER-MONEY! HEJJY-MONNY?
I DON'T FLIPPING KNOW! SHOW US TO THE FIZZY WINE! WE'RE IMPORTANT!

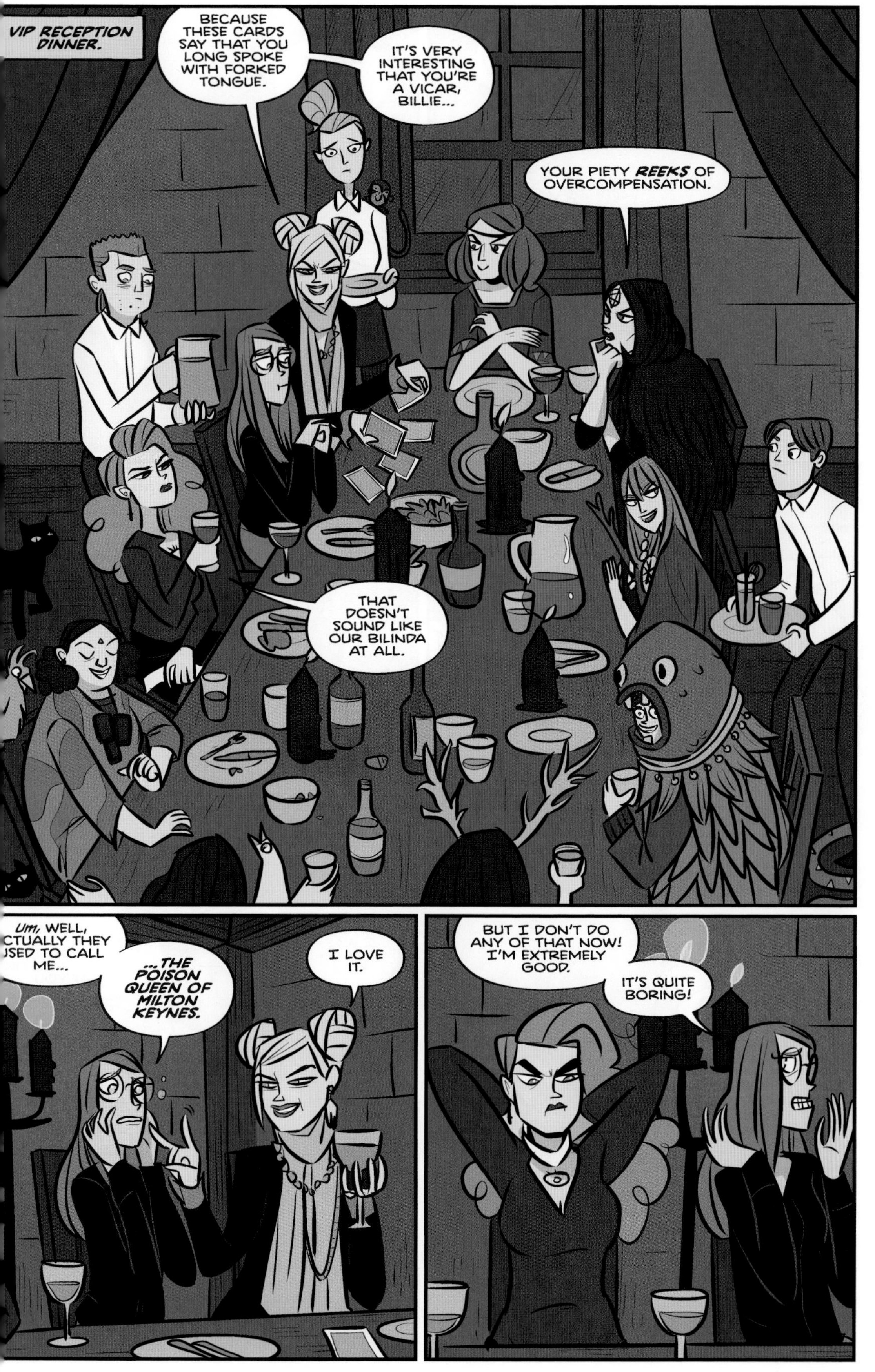
VIP RECEPTION DINNER.
IT'S VERY INTERESTING THAT YOU'RE A VICAR, BILLIE...
BECAUSE THESE CARDS SAY THAT YOU LONG SPOKE WITH FORKED TONGUE.
YOUR PIETY REEKS OF OVERCOMPENSATION.
THAT DOESN'T SOUND LIKE OUR BILINDA AT ALL.
Um, WELL, CTUALLY THEY USED TO CALL ME...
...THE POISON QUEEN OF MILTON KEYNES.
I LOVE IT.
BUT I DON'T DO ANY OF THAT NOW! I'M EXTREMELY GOOD.
IT'S QUITE BORING!

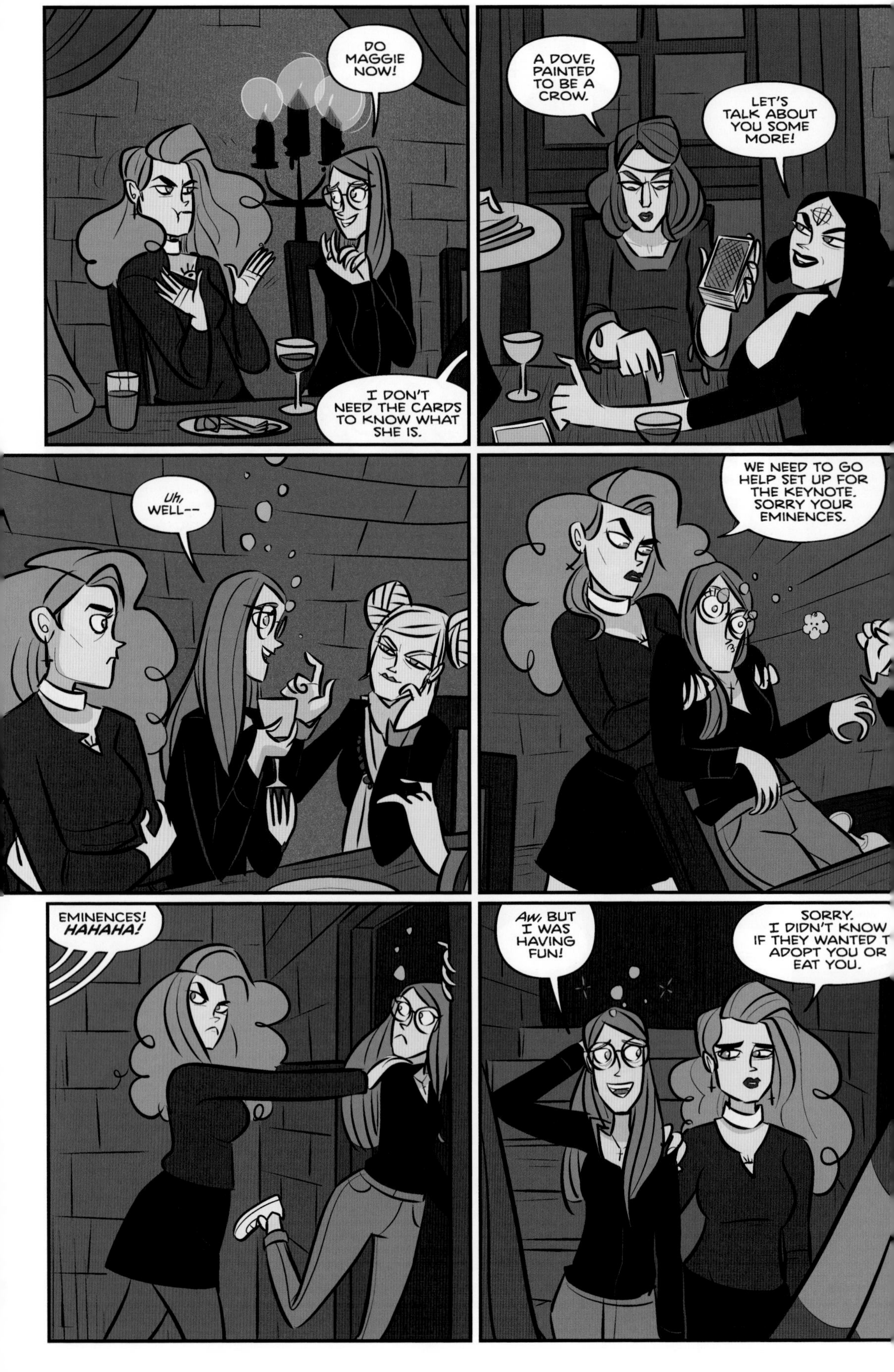
DO MAGGIE NOW!
I DON'T NEED THE CARDS TO KNOW WHAT SHE IS.
A DOVE, PAINTED TO BE A CROW.
LET'S TALK ABOUT YOU SOME MORE!
Uh, WELL--
WE NEED TO GO HELP SET UP FOR THE KEYNOTE. SORRY YOUR EMINENCES.
EMINENCES! ***HAHAHA!***
Aw, BUT I WAS HAVING FUN!
SORRY. I DIDN'T KNOW IF THEY WANTED T ADOPT YOU OR EAT YOU.

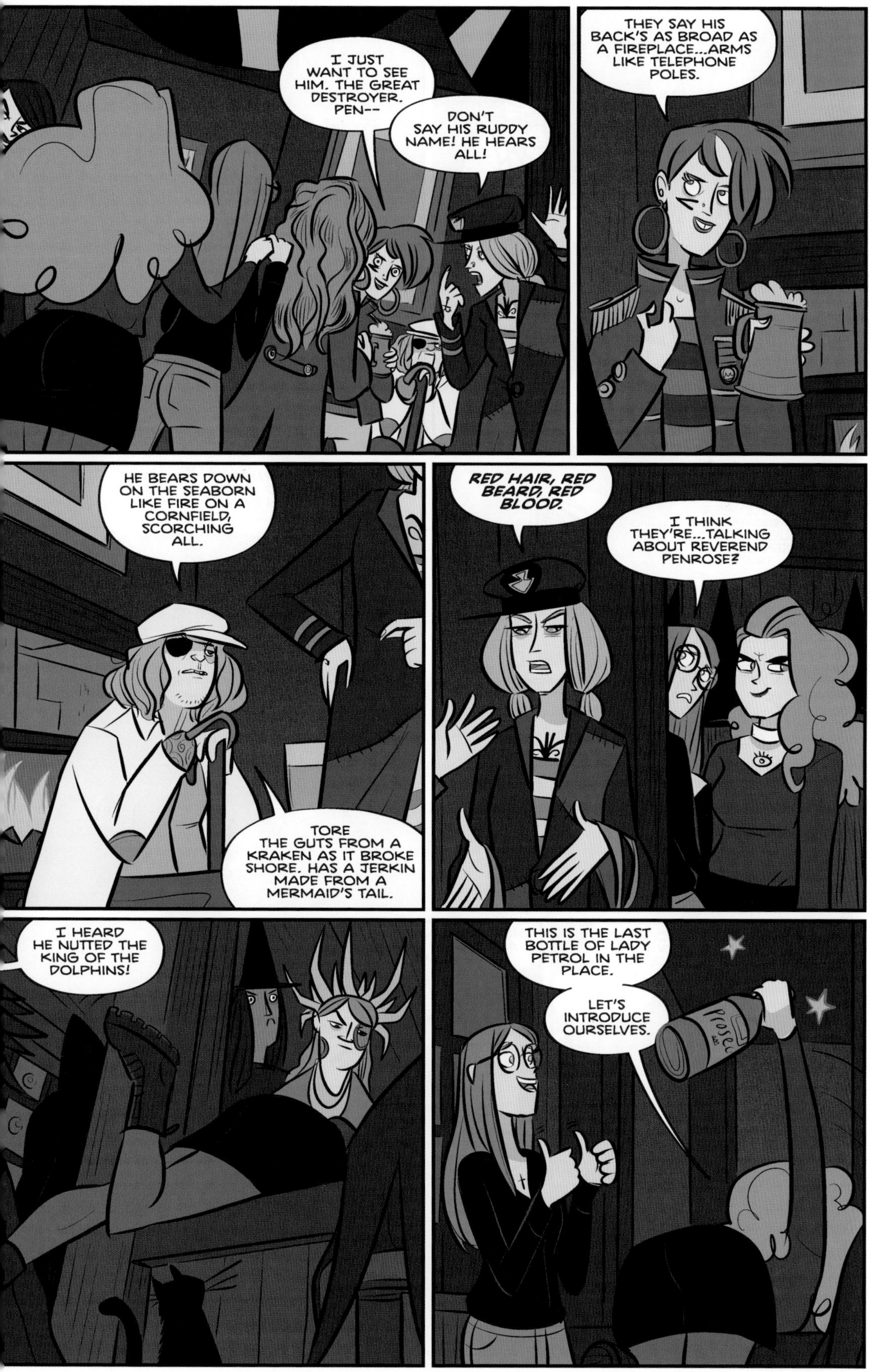
I JUST WANT TO SEE HIM. THE GREAT DESTROYER. PEN--
DON'T SAY HIS RUDDY NAME! HE HEARS ALL!
THEY SAY HIS BACK'S AS BROAD AS A FIREPLACE...ARMS LIKE TELEPHONE POLES.
HE BEARS DOWN ON THE SEABORN LIKE FIRE ON A CORNFIELD, SCORCHING ALL.
TORE THE GUTS FROM A KRAKEN AS IT BROKE SHORE. HAS A JERKIN MADE FROM A MERMAID'S TAIL.
RED HAIR, RED BEARD, RED BLOOD.
I THINK THEY'RE...TALKING ABOUT REVEREND PENROSE?
I HEARD HE NUTTED THE KING OF THE DOLPHINS!
THIS IS THE LAST BOTTLE OF LADY PETROL IN THE PLACE.
LET'S INTRODUCE OURSELVES.

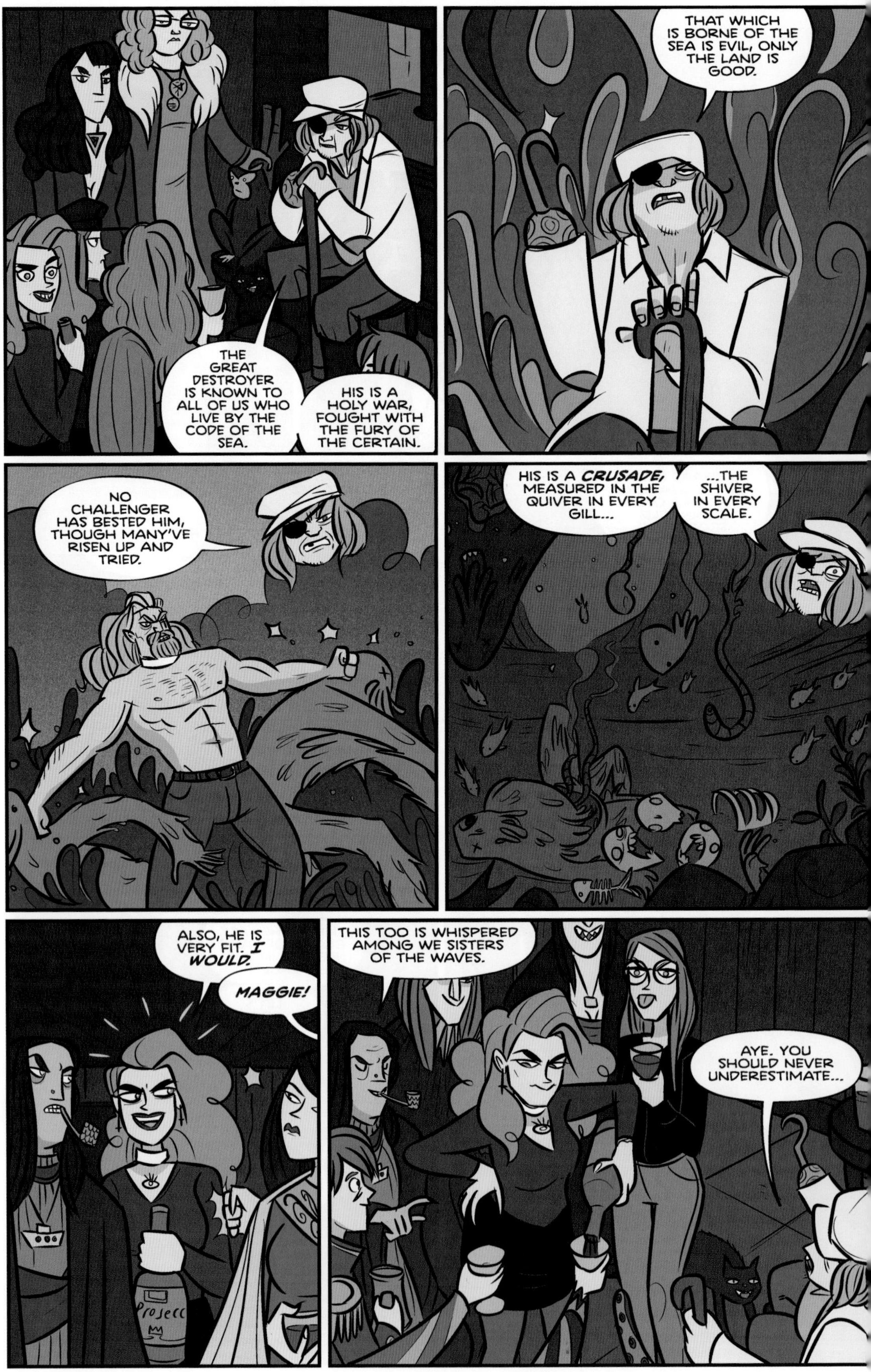
THE GREAT DESTROYER IS KNOWN TO ALL OF US WHO LIVE BY THE CODE OF THE SEA.
HIS IS A HOLY WAR, FOUGHT WITH THE FURY OF THE CERTAIN.
THAT WHICH IS BORNE OF THE SEA IS EVIL, ONLY THE LAND IS GOOD.
NO CHALLENGER HAS BESTED HIM, THOUGH MANY'VE RISEN UP AND TRIED.
HIS IS A *CRUSADE,* MEASURED IN THE QUIVER IN EVERY GILL...
...THE SHIVER IN EVERY SCALE.
ALSO, HE IS VERY FIT. *I WOULD.*
MAGGIE!
THIS TOO IS WHISPERED AMONG WE SISTERS OF THE WAVES.
AYE. YOU SHOULD NEVER UNDERESTIMATE...

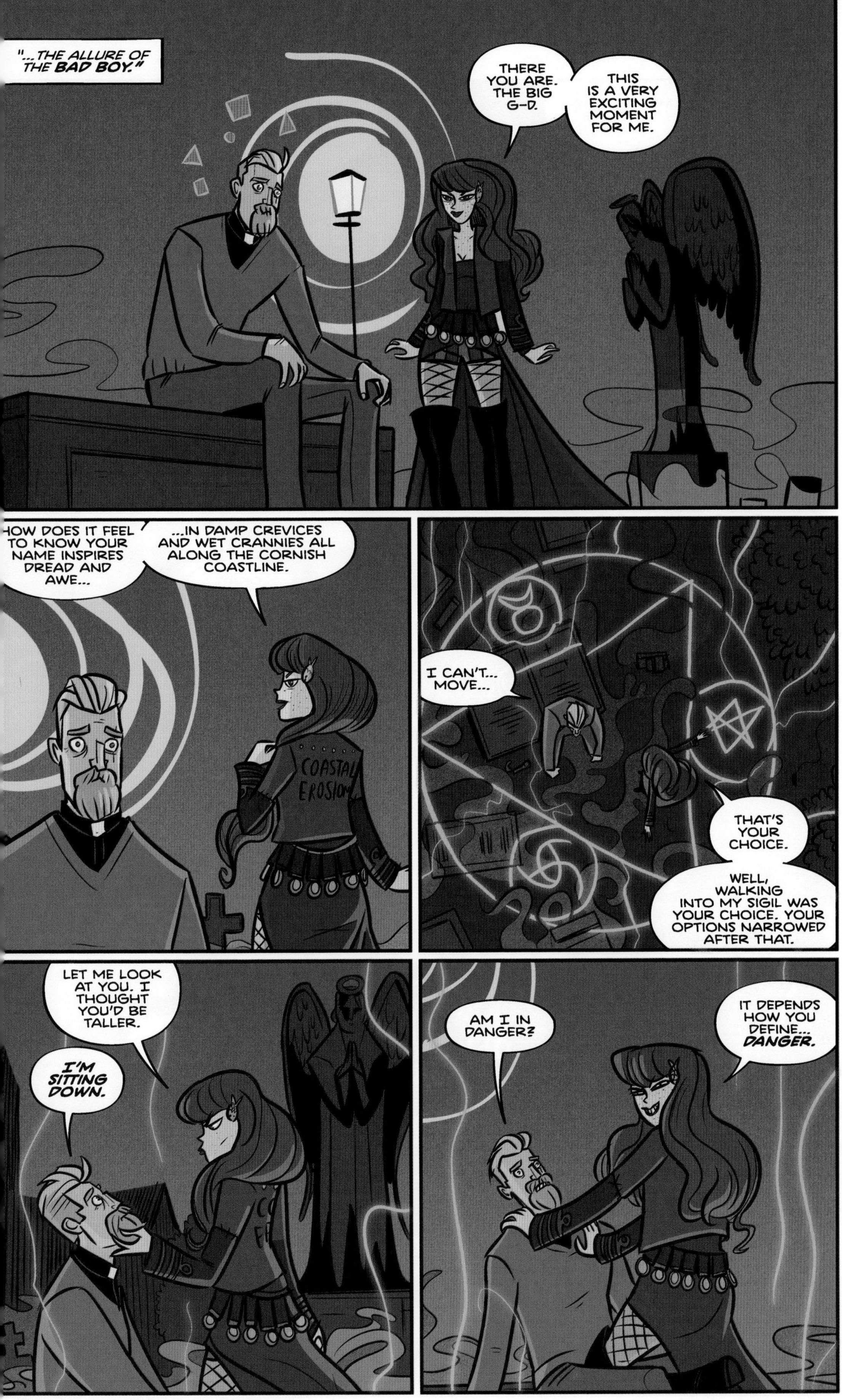
"...THE ALLURE OF THE BAD BOY."
THERE YOU ARE. THE BIG G-D.
THIS IS A VERY EXCITING MOMENT FOR ME.
HOW DOES IT FEEL TO KNOW YOUR NAME INSPIRES DREAD AND AWE...
...IN DAMP CREVICES AND WET CRANNIES ALL ALONG THE CORNISH COASTLINE.
COASTAL EROSION
I CAN'T... MOVE...
THAT'S YOUR CHOICE.
WELL, WALKING INTO MY SIGIL WAS YOUR CHOICE. YOUR OPTIONS NARROWED AFTER THAT.
LET ME LOOK AT YOU. I THOUGHT YOU'D BE TALLER.
I'M SITTING DOWN.
AM I IN DANGER?
IT DEPENDS HOW YOU DEFINE... DANGER.

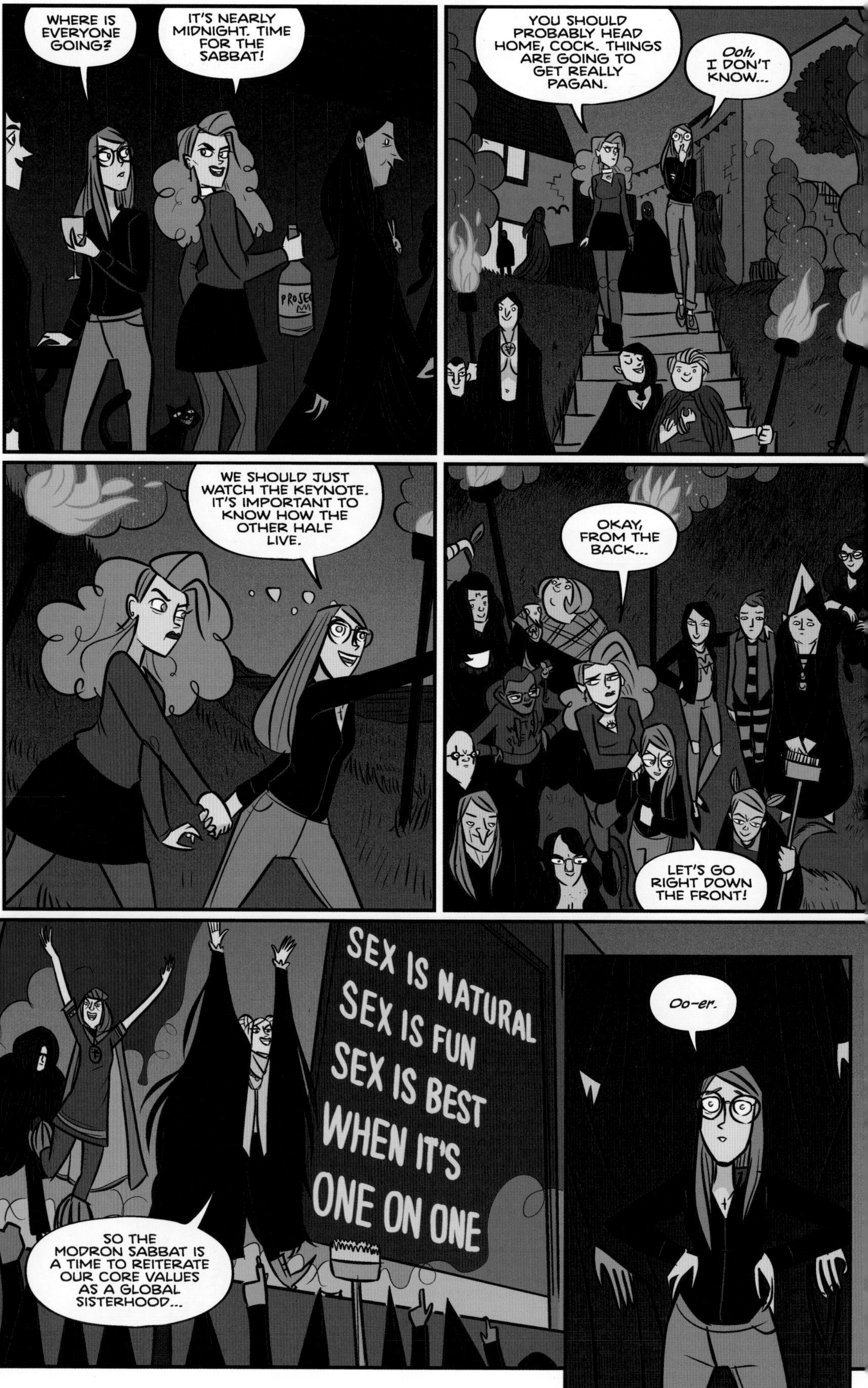
WHERE IS EVERYONE GOING?
IT'S NEARLY MIDNIGHT. TIME FOR THE SABBAT!
PROSECCO
YOU SHOULD PROBABLY HEAD HOME, COCK. THINGS ARE GOING TO GET REALLY PAGAN.
Ooh, I DON'T KNOW...
WE SHOULD JUST WATCH THE KEYNOTE. IT'S IMPORTANT TO KNOW HOW THE OTHER HALF LIVE.
OKAY, FROM THE BACK...
LET'S GO RIGHT DOWN THE FRONT!
SEX IS NATURAL
SEX IS FUN
SEX IS BEST
WHEN IT'S
ONE ON ONE
SO THE MODRON SABBAT IS A TIME TO REITERATE OUR CORE VALUES AS A GLOBAL SISTERHOOD...
Oo-er.

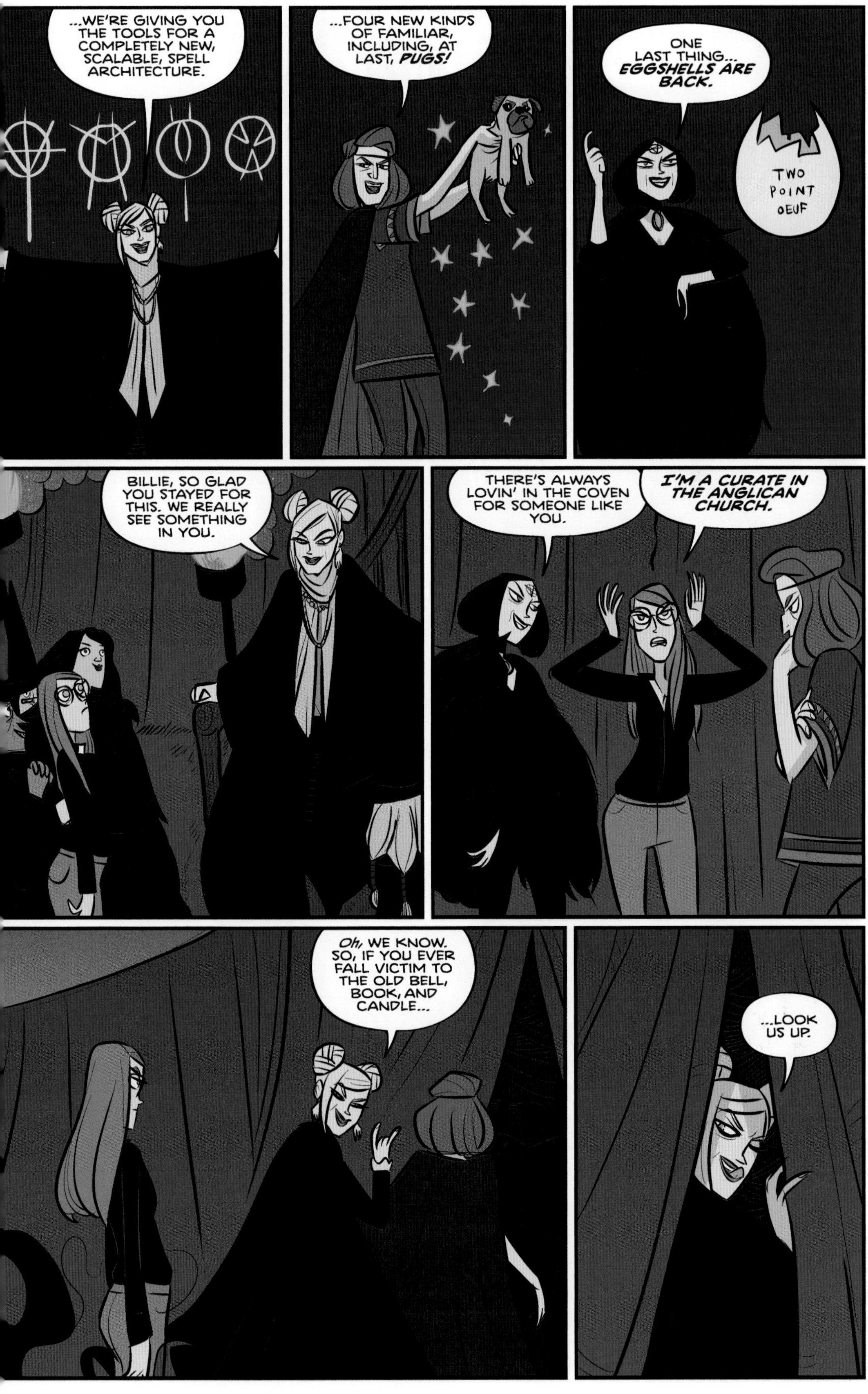

...WE'RE GIVING YOU THE TOOLS FOR A COMPLETELY NEW, SCALABLE, SPELL ARCHITECTURE.
...FOUR NEW KINDS OF FAMILIAR, INCLUDING, AT LAST, PUGS!
ONE LAST THING... EGGSHELLS ARE BACK.
TWO POINT OEUF
BILLIE, SO GLAD YOU STAYED FOR THIS. WE REALLY SEE SOMETHING IN YOU.
THERE'S ALWAYS LOVIN' IN THE COVEN FOR SOMEONE LIKE YOU.
I'M A CURATE IN THE ANGLICAN CHURCH.
Oh, WE KNOW. SO, IF YOU EVER FALL VICTIM TO THE OLD BELL, BOOK, AND CANDLE...
...LOOK US UP.

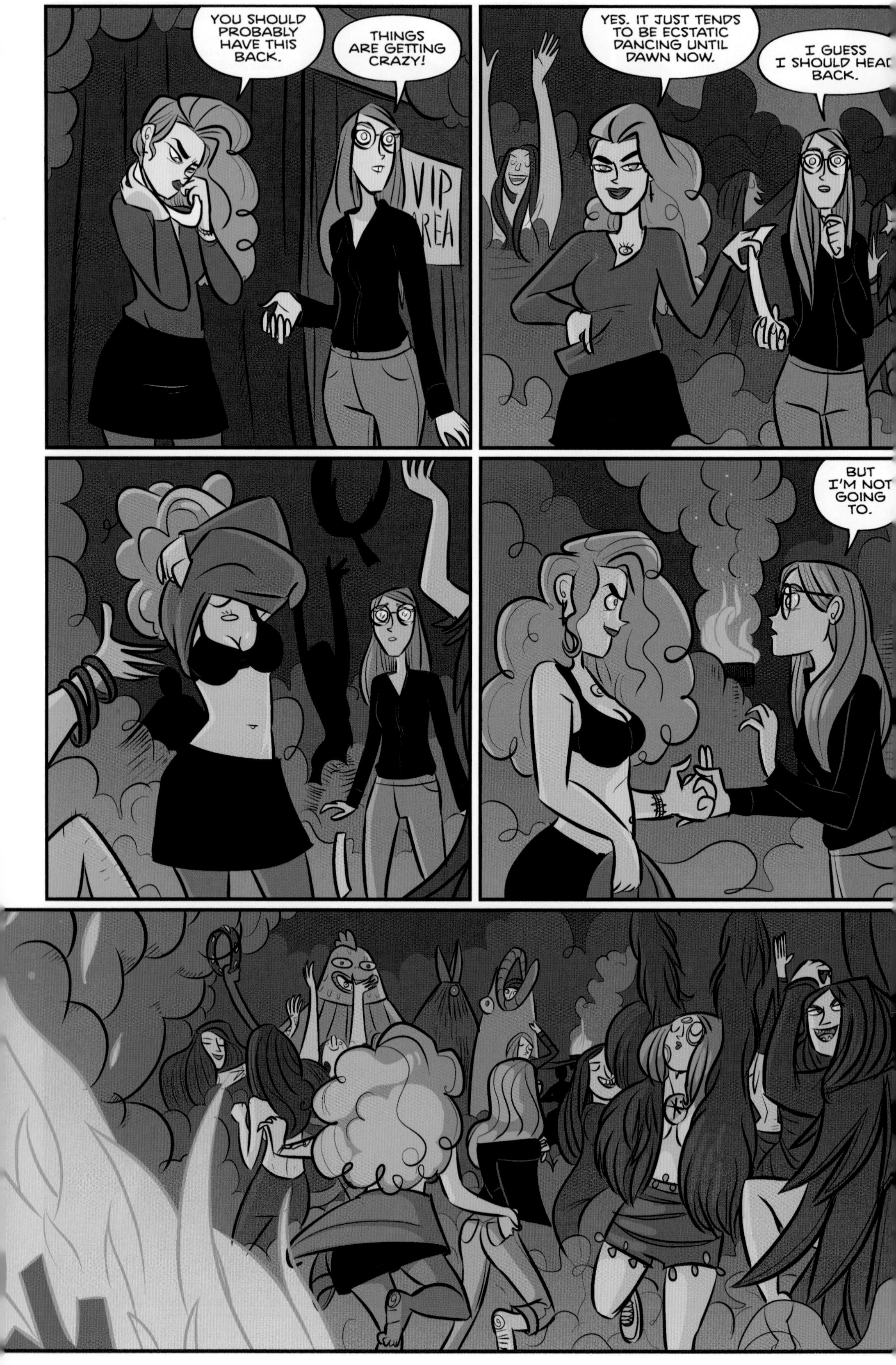
YOU SHOULD PROBABLY HAVE THIS BACK.
THINGS ARE GETTING CRAZY!
VIP AREA
YES. IT JUST TENDS TO BE ECSTATIC DANCING UNTIL DAWN NOW.
I GUESS I SHOULD HEAD BACK.
BUT I'M NOT GOING TO.

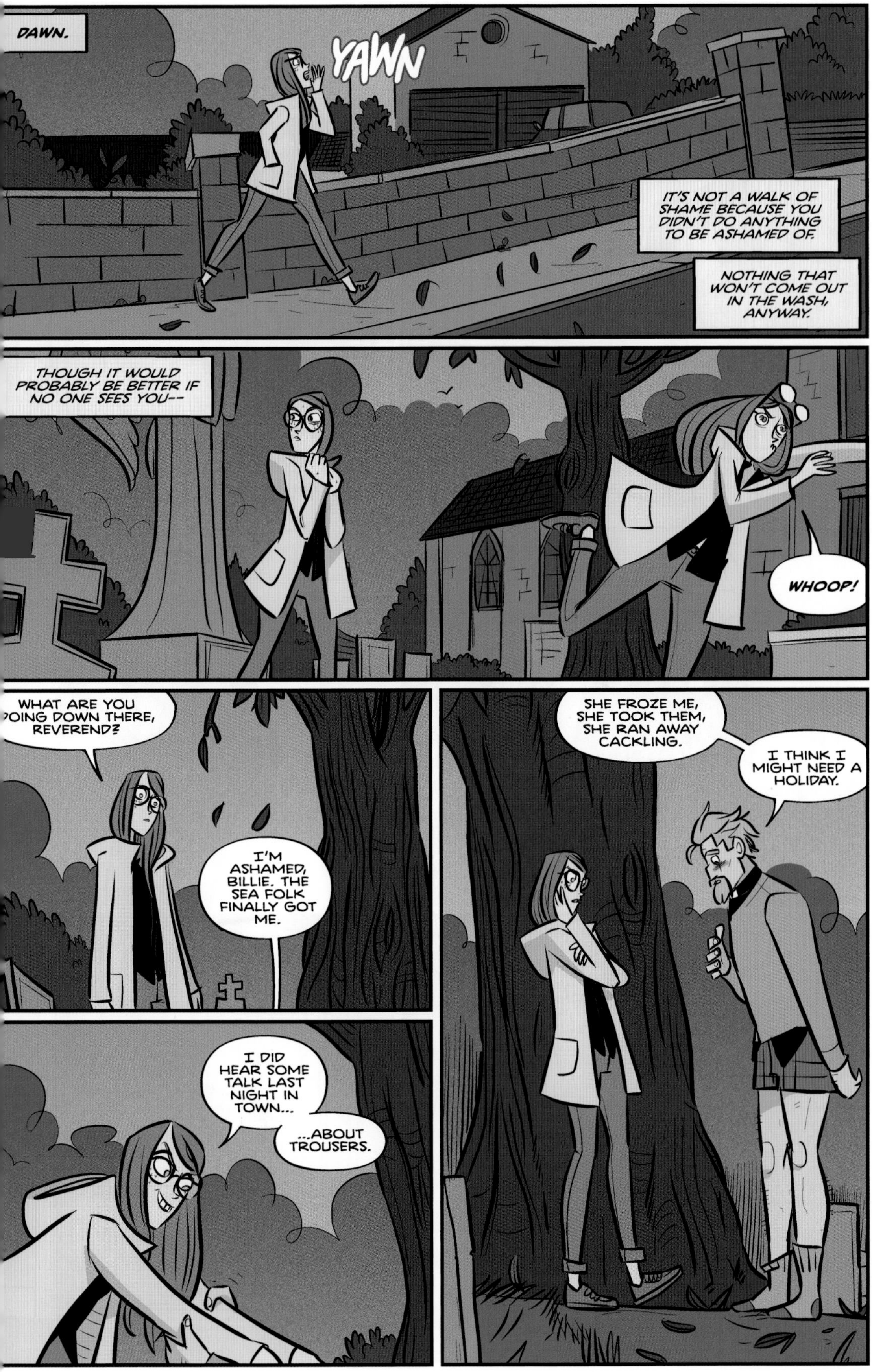
DAWN.
YAWN
IT'S NOT A WALK OF SHAME BECAUSE YOU DIDN'T DO ANYTHING TO BE ASHAMED OF.
NOTHING THAT WON'T COME OUT IN THE WASH, ANYWAY.
THOUGH IT WOULD PROBABLY BE BETTER IF NO ONE SEES YOU--
WHOOP!
WHAT ARE YOU DOING DOWN THERE, REVEREND?
I'M ASHAMED, BILLIE. THE SEA FOLK FINALLY GOT ME.
I DID HEAR SOME TALK LAST NIGHT IN TOWN...
...ABOUT TROUSERS.
SHE FROZE ME, SHE TOOK THEM, SHE RAN AWAY CACKLING.
I THINK I MIGHT NEED A HOLIDAY.

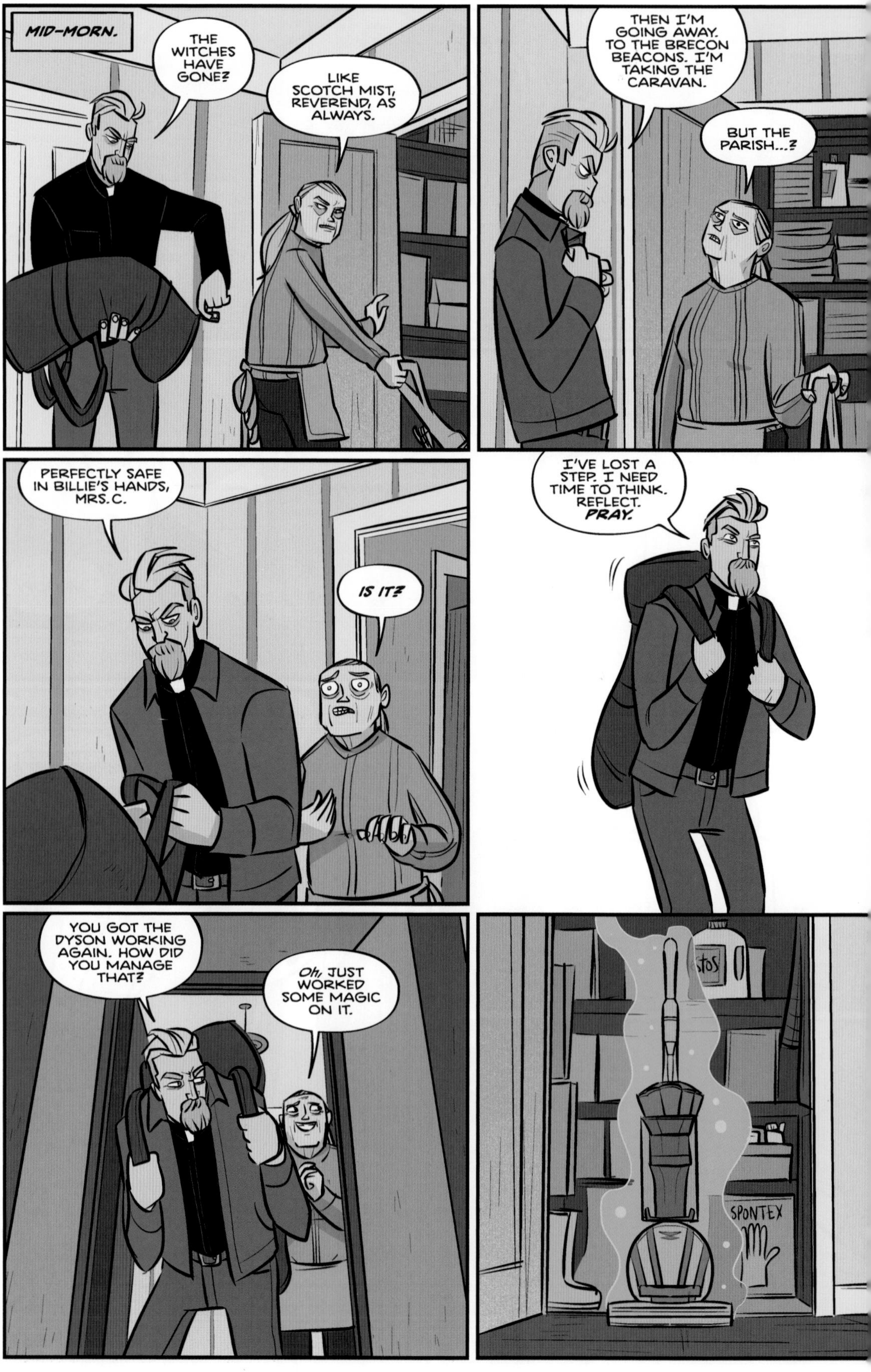
MID-MORN.
THE WITCHES HAVE GONE?
LIKE SCOTCH MIST, REVEREND, AS ALWAYS.
THEN I'M GOING AWAY. TO THE BRECON BEACONS. I'M TAKING THE CARAVAN.
BUT THE PARISH...?
PERFECTLY SAFE IN BILLIE'S HANDS, MRS. C.
IS IT?
I'VE LOST A STEP. I NEED TIME TO THINK. REFLECT. PRAY.
YOU GOT THE DYSON WORKING AGAIN. HOW DID YOU MANAGE THAT?
Oh, JUST WORKED SOME MAGIC ON IT.
SPONTEX

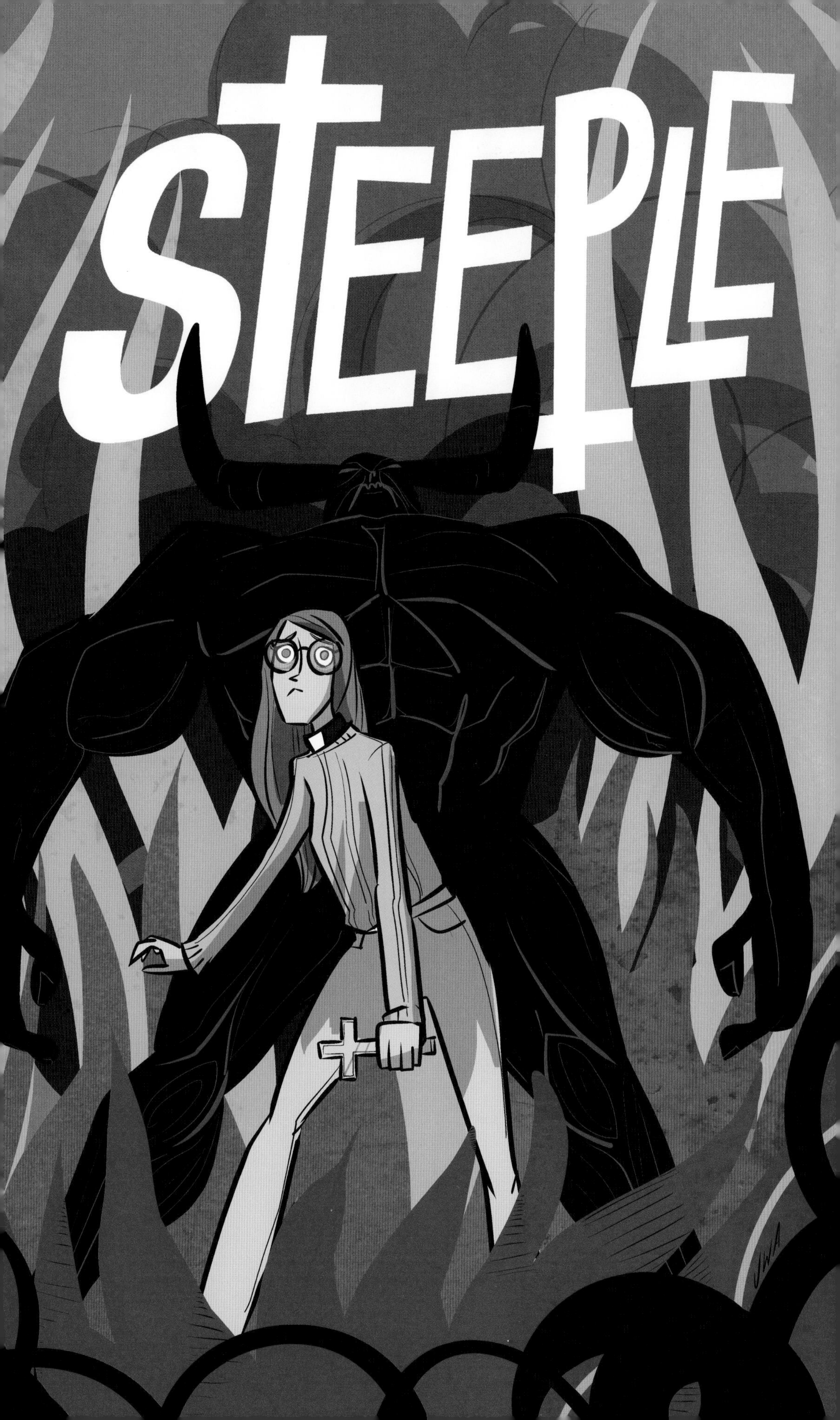
STEEPLE
JWA

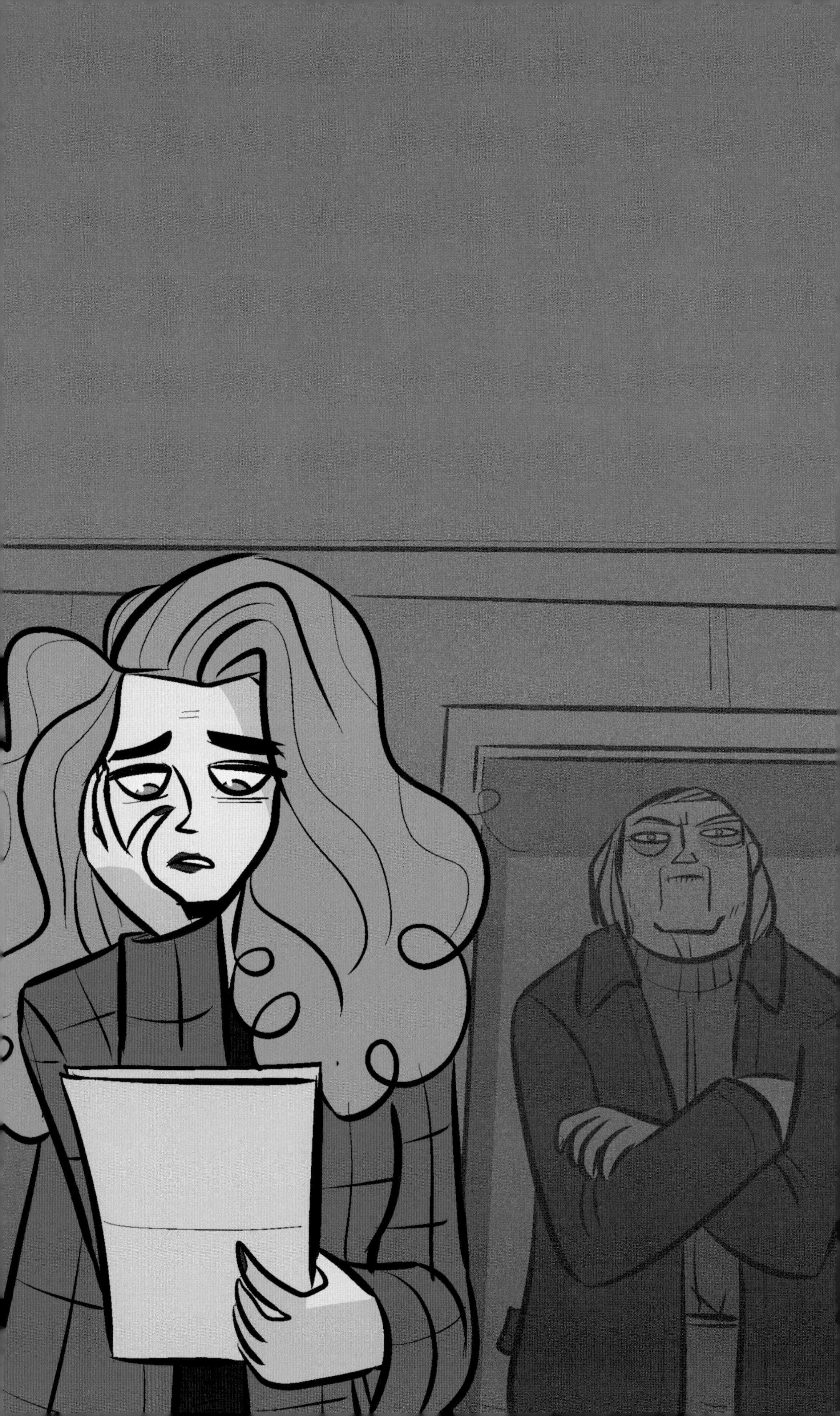

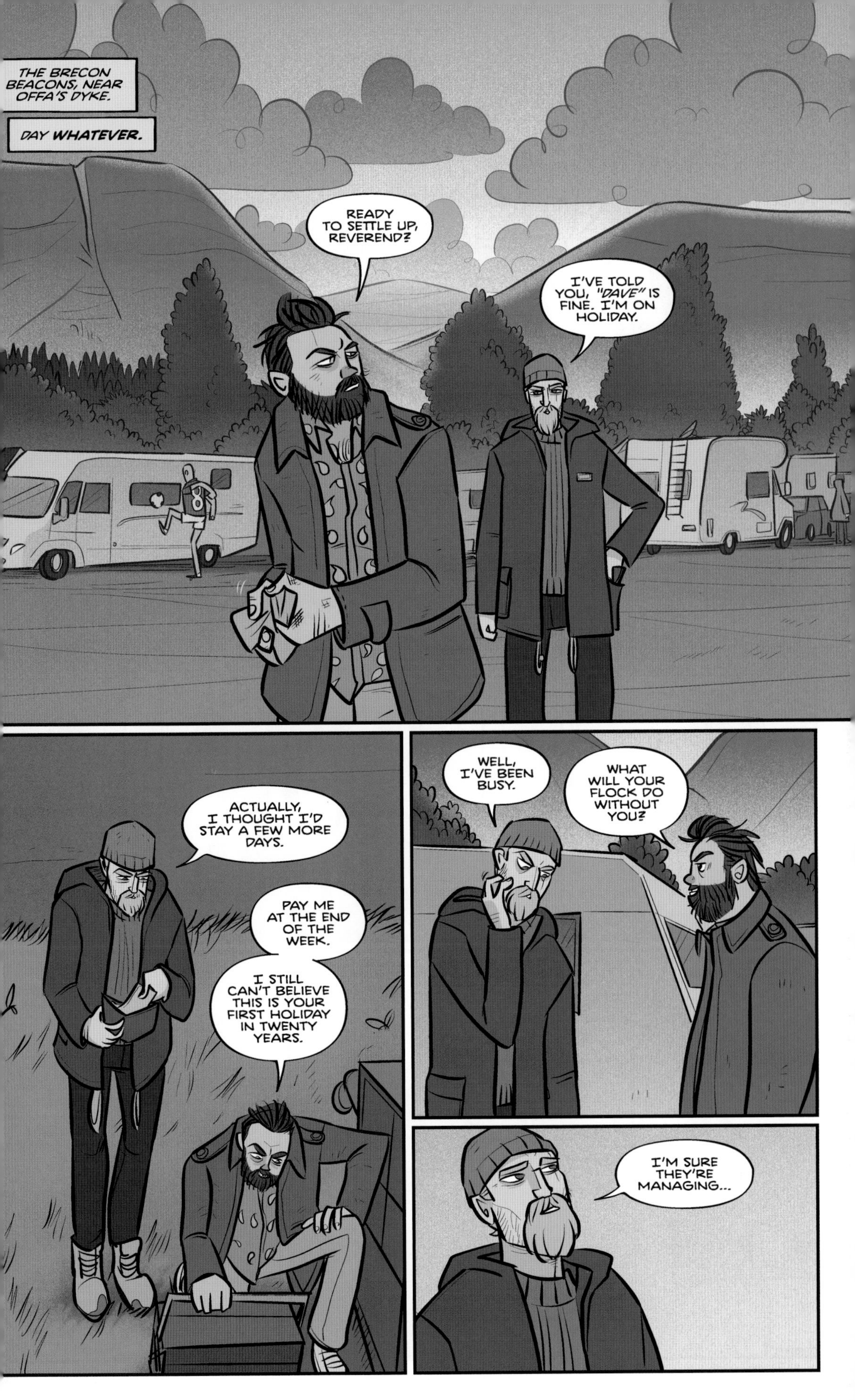
THE BRECON BEACONS, NEAR OFFA'S DYKE.
DAY WHATEVER.
READY TO SETTLE UP, REVEREND?
I'VE TOLD YOU, "DAVE" IS FINE. I'M ON HOLIDAY.
ACTUALLY, I THOUGHT I'D STAY A FEW MORE DAYS.
PAY ME AT THE END OF THE WEEK.
I STILL CAN'T BELIEVE THIS IS YOUR FIRST HOLIDAY IN TWENTY YEARS.
WELL, I'VE BEEN BUSY.
WHAT WILL YOUR FLOCK DO WITHOUT YOU?
I'M SURE THEY'RE MANAGING...

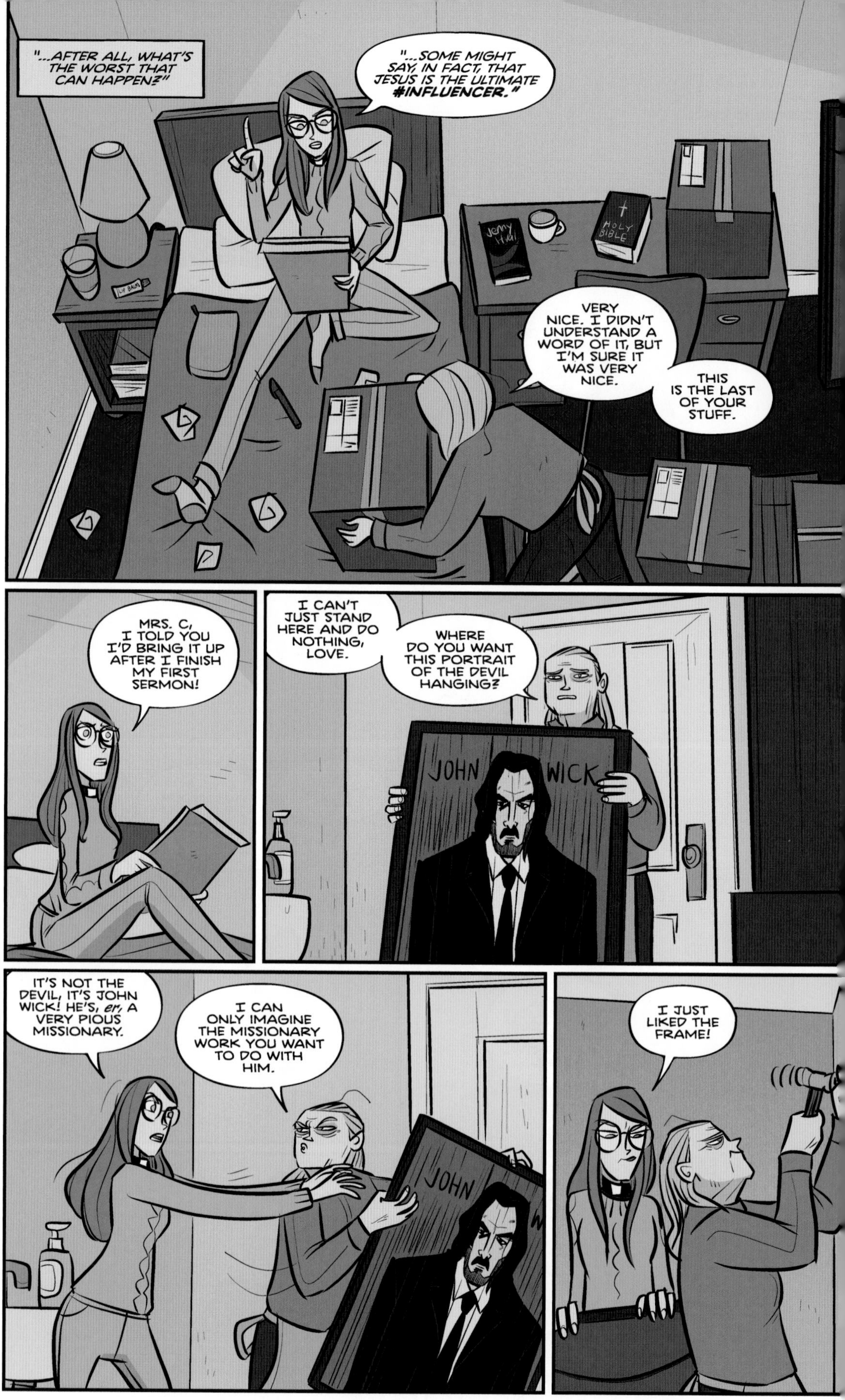
"...AFTER ALL, WHAT'S THE WORST THAT CAN HAPPEN?"
"...SOME MIGHT SAY, IN FACT, THAT JESUS IS THE ULTIMATE #INFLUENCER."
HOLY BIBLE
VERY NICE. I DIDN'T UNDERSTAND A WORD OF IT, BUT I'M SURE IT WAS VERY NICE.
THIS IS THE LAST OF YOUR STUFF.
MRS. C, I TOLD YOU I'D BRING IT UP AFTER I FINISH MY FIRST SERMON!
I CAN'T JUST STAND HERE AND DO NOTHING, LOVE.
WHERE DO YOU WANT THIS PORTRAIT OF THE DEVIL HANGING?
JOHN WICK
IT'S NOT THE DEVIL, IT'S JOHN WICK! HE'S, *er*, A VERY PIOUS MISSIONARY.
I CAN ONLY IMAGINE THE MISSIONARY WORK YOU WANT TO DO WITH HIM.
JOHN
I JUST LIKED THE FRAME!

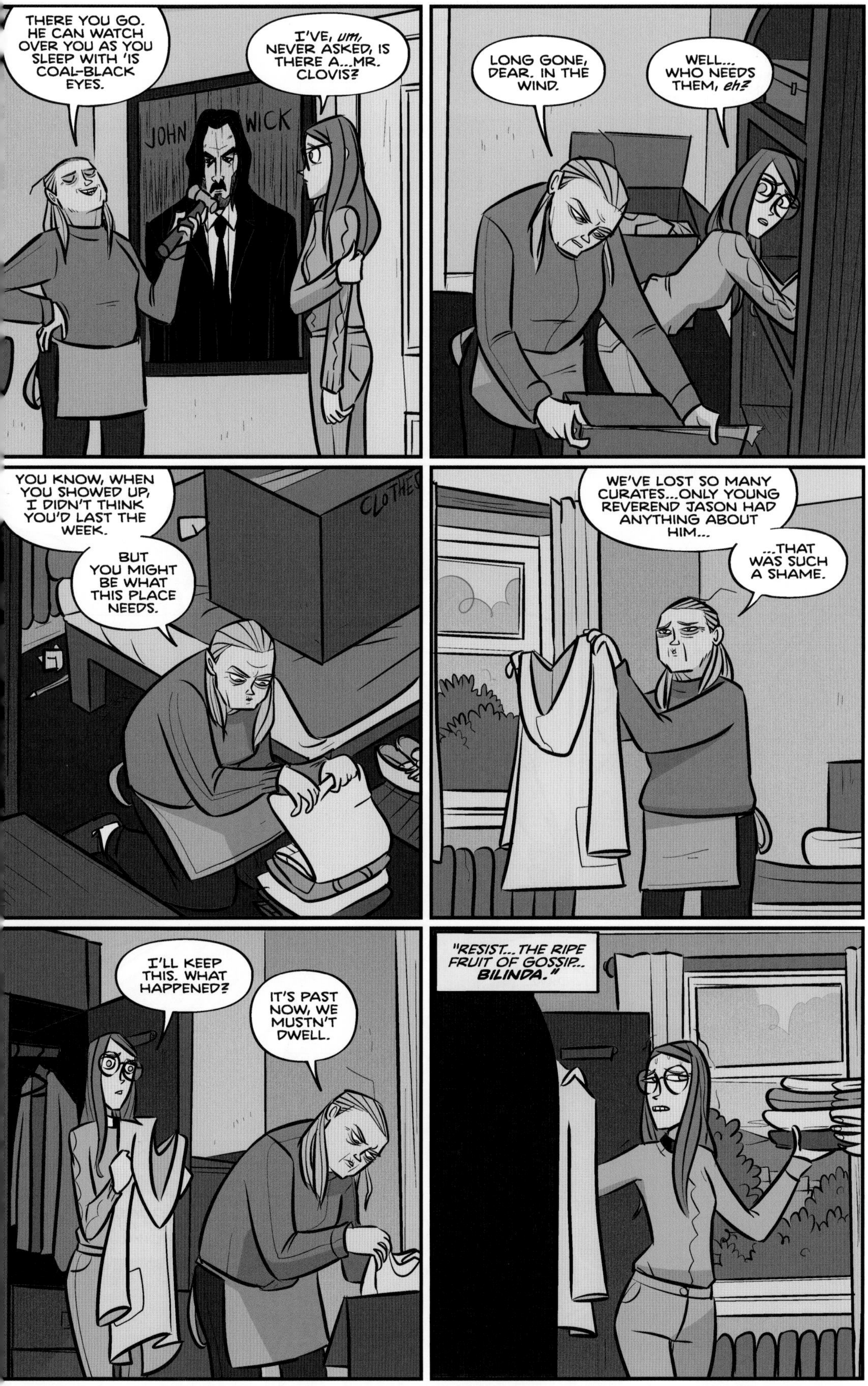
THERE YOU GO. HE CAN WATCH OVER YOU AS YOU SLEEP WITH 'IS COAL-BLACK EYES.
I'VE, *um,* NEVER ASKED, IS THERE A...MR. CLOVIS?
JOHN WICK
LONG GONE, DEAR. IN THE WIND.
WELL... WHO NEEDS THEM, *eh?*
YOU KNOW, WHEN YOU SHOWED UP, I DIDN'T THINK YOU'D LAST THE WEEK.
BUT YOU MIGHT BE WHAT THIS PLACE NEEDS.
CLOTHES
WE'VE LOST SO MANY CURATES...ONLY YOUNG REVEREND JASON HAD ANYTHING ABOUT HIM...
...THAT WAS SUCH A SHAME.
I'LL KEEP THIS. WHAT HAPPENED?
IT'S PAST NOW, WE MUSTN'T DWELL.
*"RESIST... THE RIPE FRUIT OF GOSSIP... **BILINDA.**"*

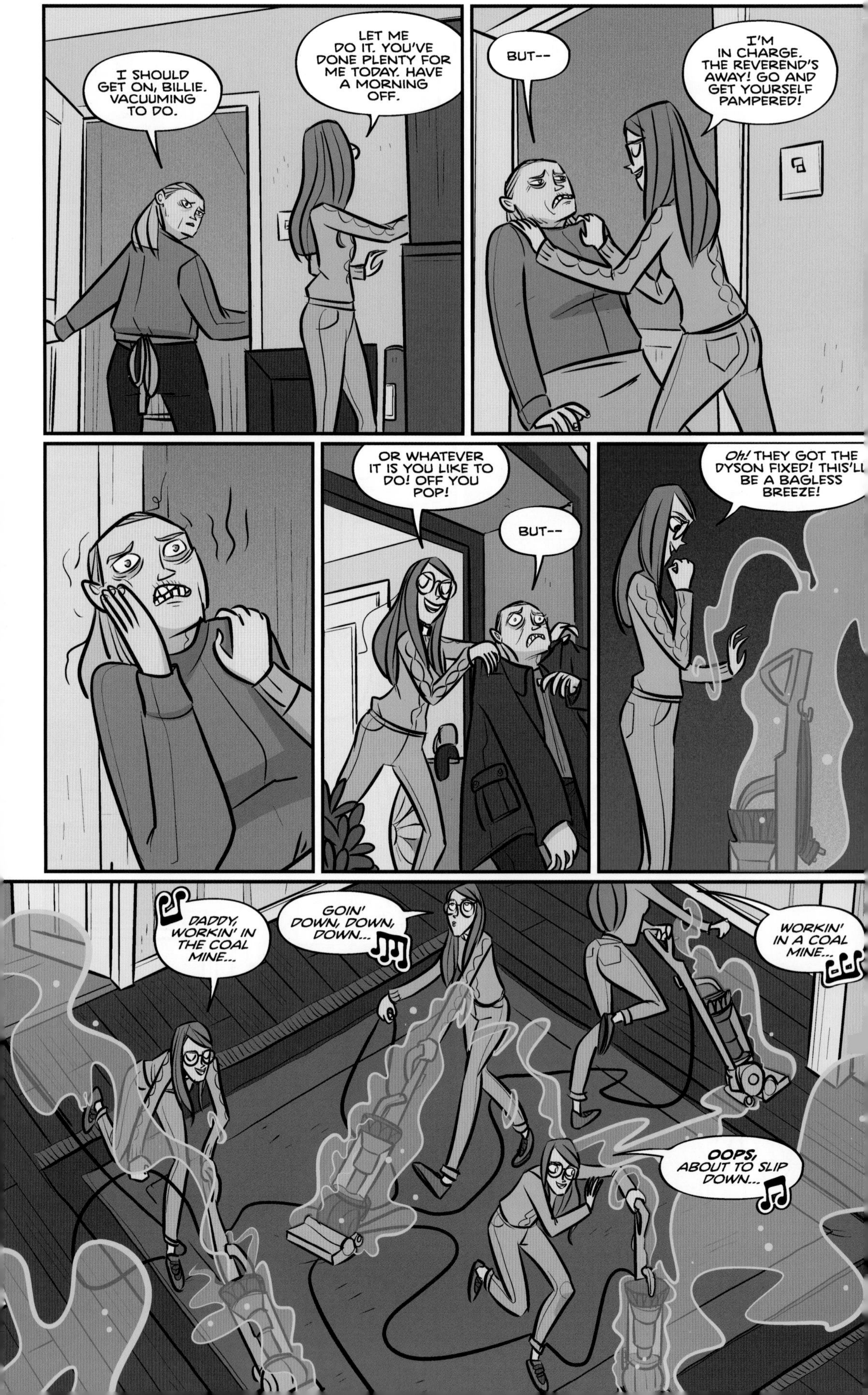
I SHOULD GET ON, BILLIE. VACUUMING TO DO.
LET ME DO IT. YOU'VE DONE PLENTY FOR ME TODAY. HAVE A MORNING OFF.
BUT--
I'M IN CHARGE. THE REVEREND'S AWAY! GO AND GET YOURSELF PAMPERED!
OR WHATEVER IT IS YOU LIKE TO DO! OFF YOU POP!
BUT--
Oh! THEY GOT THE DYSON FIXED! THIS'LL BE A BAGLESS BREEZE!
DADDY, WORKIN' IN THE COAL MINE...
GOIN' DOWN, DOWN, DOWN...
WORKIN' IN A COAL MINE...
OOPS, ABOUT TO SLIP DOWN...

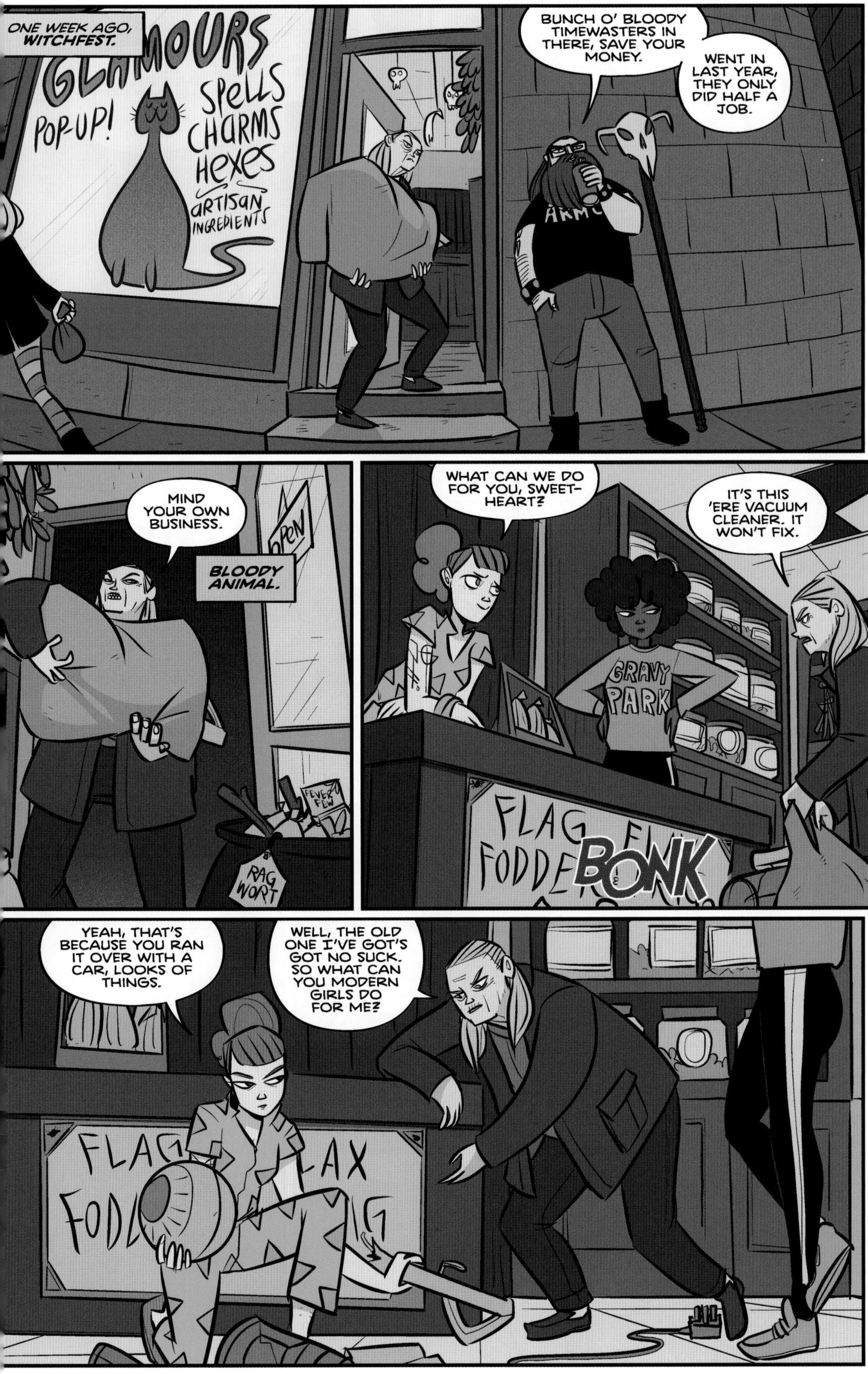
ONE WEEK AGO, WITCHFEST.
GLAMOURS
POP-UP!
SPELLS CHARMS HEXES ARTISAN INGREDIENTS
BUNCH O' BLOODY TIMEWASTERS IN THERE, SAVE YOUR MONEY.
WENT IN LAST YEAR, THEY ONLY DID HALF A JOB.
MIND YOUR OWN BUSINESS.
BLOODY ANIMAL.
OPEN
FEVERFEW
RAGWORT
WHAT CAN WE DO FOR YOU, SWEET-HEART?
IT'S THIS 'ERE VACUUM CLEANER. IT WON'T FIX.
GRAVY PARK
FLAG FODDE
BONK
YEAH, THAT'S BECAUSE YOU RAN IT OVER WITH A CAR, LOOKS OF THINGS.
WELL, THE OLD ONE I'VE GOT'S GOT NO SUCK. SO WHAT CAN YOU MODERN GIRLS DO FOR ME?

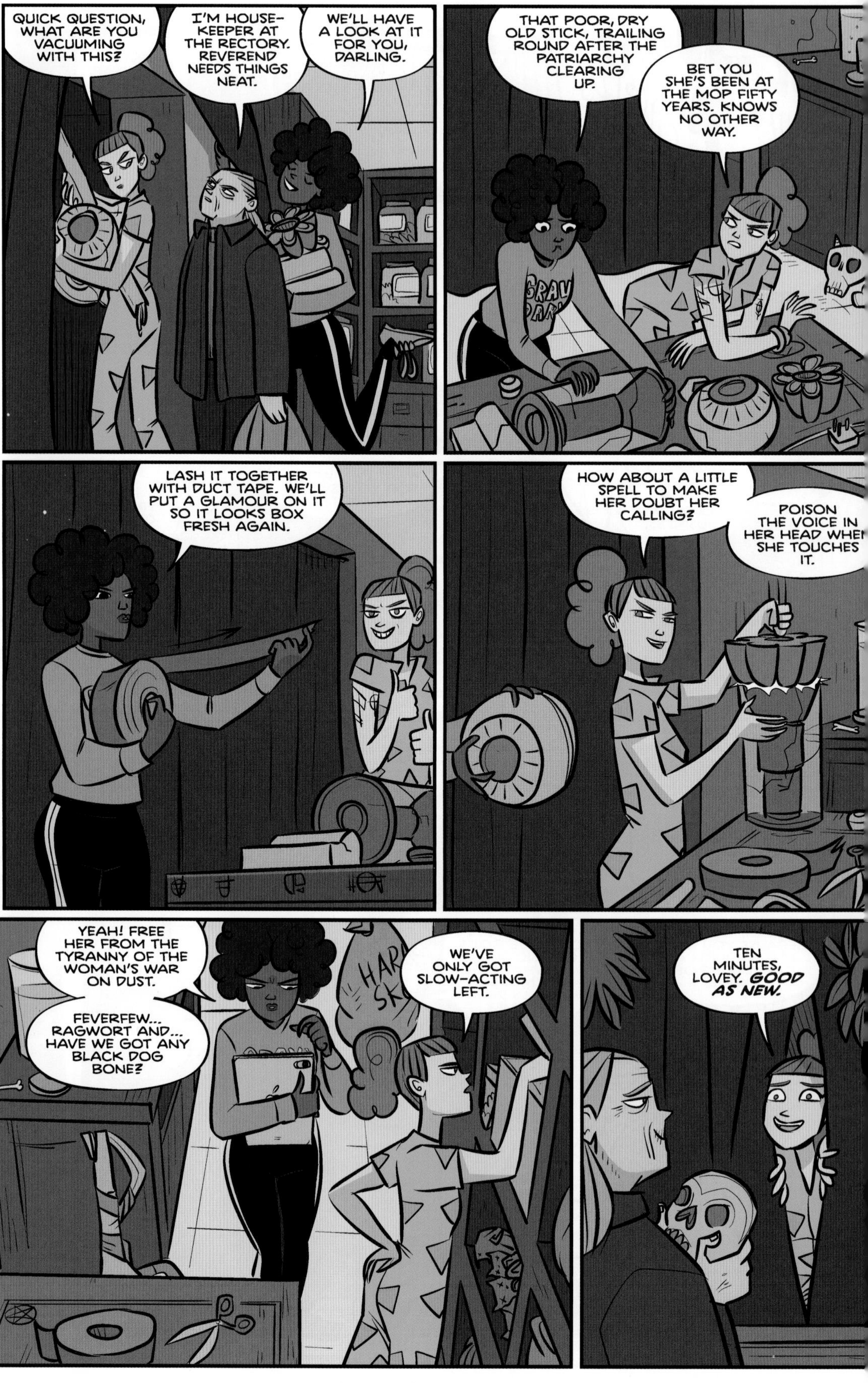

QUICK QUESTION, WHAT ARE YOU VACUUMING WITH THIS?
I'M HOUSE-KEEPER AT THE RECTORY. REVEREND NEEDS THINGS NEAT.
WE'LL HAVE A LOOK AT IT FOR YOU, DARLING.
THAT POOR, DRY OLD STICK, TRAILING ROUND AFTER THE PATRIARCHY CLEARING UP.
BET YOU SHE'S BEEN AT THE MOP FIFTY YEARS. KNOWS NO OTHER WAY.
LASH IT TOGETHER WITH DUCT TAPE. WE'LL PUT A GLAMOUR ON IT SO IT LOOKS BOX FRESH AGAIN.
HOW ABOUT A LITTLE SPELL TO MAKE HER DOUBT HER CALLING?
POISON THE VOICE IN HER HEAD WHEN SHE TOUCHES IT.
YEAH! FREE HER FROM THE TYRANNY OF THE WOMAN'S WAR ON DUST.
FEVERFEW... RAGWORT AND... HAVE WE GOT ANY BLACK DOG BONE?
WE'VE ONLY GOT SLOW-ACTING LEFT.
TEN MINUTES, LOVEY. ***GOOD AS NEW.***

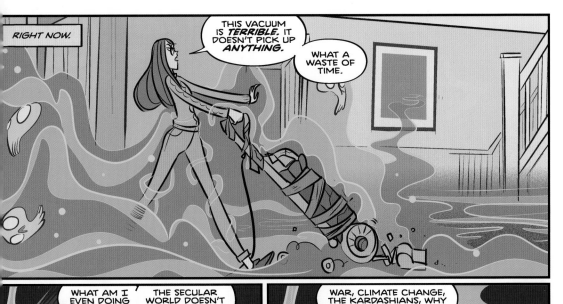

RIGHT NOW.

THIS VACUUM IS *TERRIBLE*. IT DOESN'T PICK UP *ANYTHING*.

WHAT A WASTE OF TIME.

WHAT AM I EVEN DOING HERE?

THE SECULAR WORLD DOESN'T NEED PRIESTS ANY MORE.

WAR, CLIMATE CHANGE, THE KARDASHIANS, WHY NOT JUST GIVE IN TO IT ALL?

GRAB A HANDFUL OF SOMETHING. TREAD ON SOMEONE TO GET IT.

Oh, JUST TO BE *EVIL* FOR A DAY.

PIECE OF SHIT! PICK SHIT UP!

EEP!

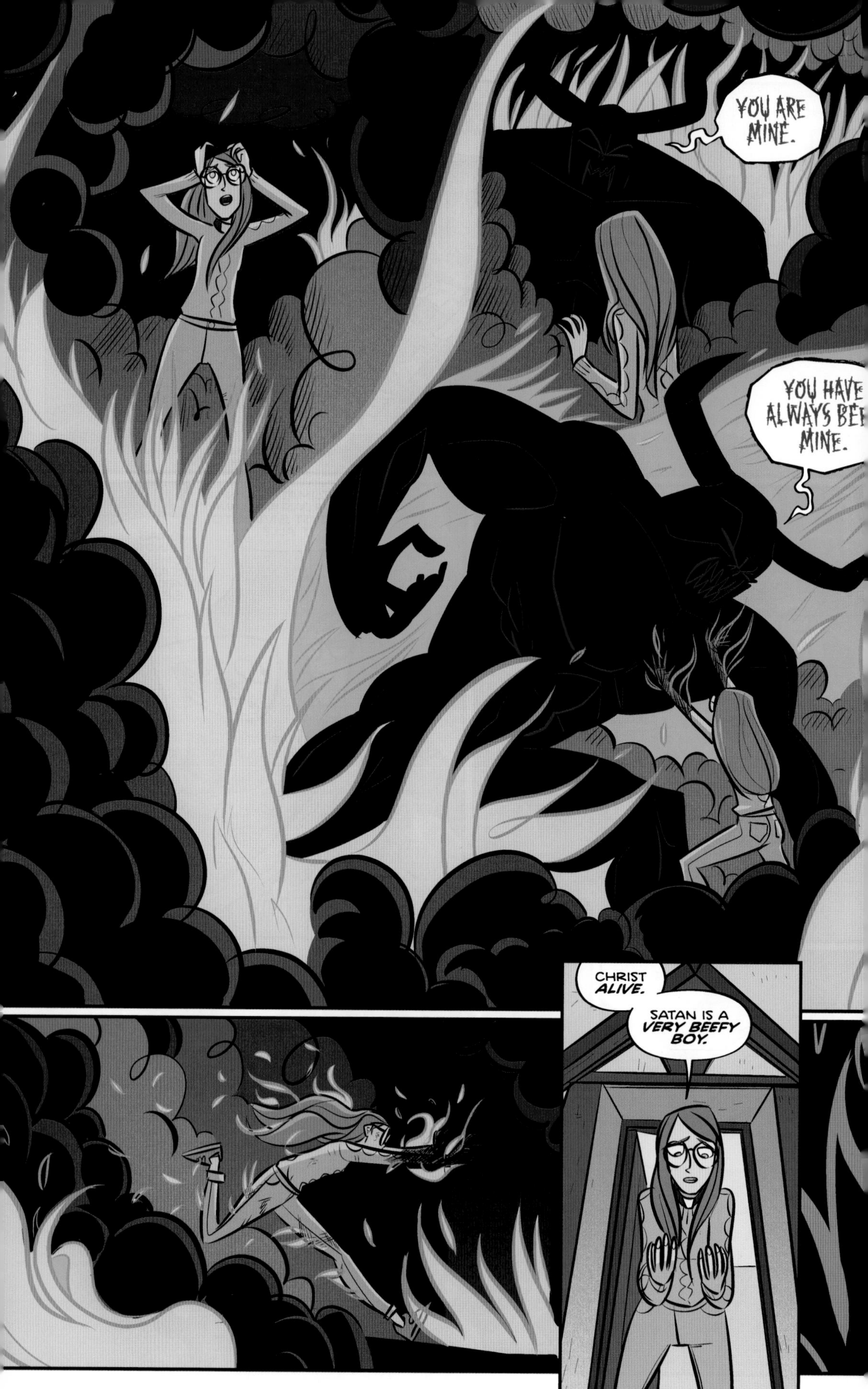
YOU ARE MINE.
YOU HAVE ALWAYS BE
MINE.
CHRIST ALIVE.
SATAN IS A VERY BEEFY BOY.

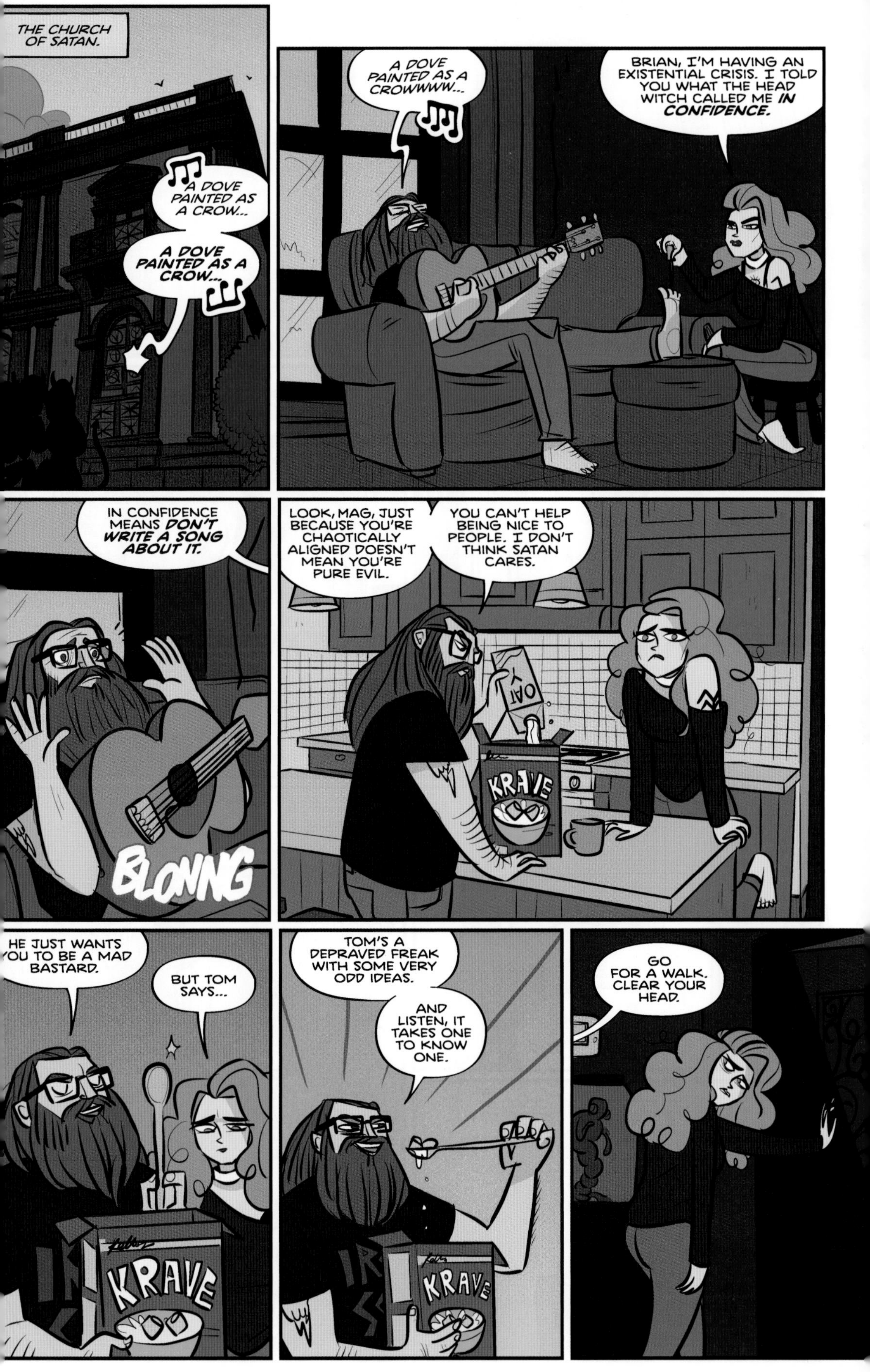
THE CHURCH OF SATAN.
A DOVE PAINTED AS A CROW...
A DOVE PAINTED AS A CROW...
A DOVE PAINTED AS A CROWWWW...
BRIAN, I'M HAVING AN EXISTENTIAL CRISIS. I TOLD YOU WHAT THE HEAD WITCH CALLED ME IN CONFIDENCE.
IN CONFIDENCE MEANS DON'T WRITE A SONG ABOUT IT.
BLONNG
LOOK, MAG, JUST BECAUSE YOU'RE CHAOTICALLY ALIGNED DOESN'T MEAN YOU'RE PURE EVIL.
YOU CAN'T HELP BEING NICE TO PEOPLE. I DON'T THINK SATAN CARES.
KRAVE
HE JUST WANTS YOU TO BE A MAD BASTARD.
BUT TOM SAYS...
KRAVE
TOM'S A DEPRAVED FREAK WITH SOME VERY ODD IDEAS.
AND LISTEN, IT TAKES ONE TO KNOW ONE.
KRAVE
GO FOR A WALK. CLEAR YOUR HEAD.

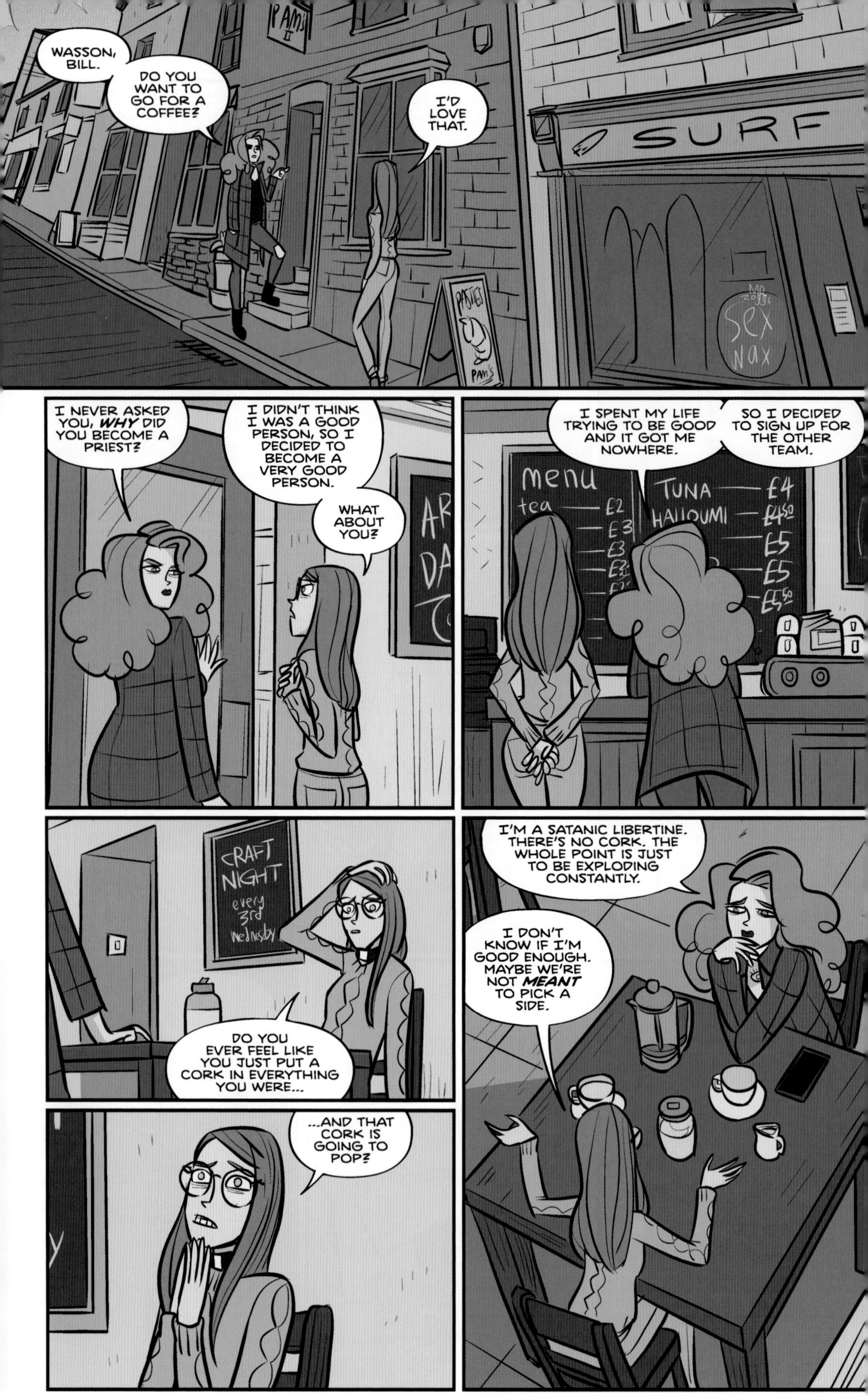
WASSON, BILL.
DO YOU WANT TO GO FOR A COFFEE?
I'D LOVE THAT.
SURF
PASTIES
PAM'S
SEX WAX
I NEVER ASKED YOU, ***WHY*** DID YOU BECOME A PRIEST?
I DIDN'T THINK I WAS A GOOD PERSON, SO I DECIDED TO BECOME A VERY GOOD PERSON.
WHAT ABOUT YOU?
I SPENT MY LIFE TRYING TO BE GOOD AND IT GOT ME NOWHERE.
SO I DECIDED TO SIGN UP FOR THE OTHER TEAM.
menu
tea — £2
TUNA — £4
HALLOUMI — £4.50
CRAFT NIGHT every 3rd wednesday
DO YOU EVER FEEL LIKE YOU JUST PUT A CORK IN EVERYTHING YOU WERE...
...AND THAT CORK IS GOING TO POP?
I'M A SATANIC LIBERTINE. THERE'S NO CORK. THE WHOLE POINT IS JUST TO BE EXPLODING CONSTANTLY.
I DON'T KNOW IF I'M GOOD ENOUGH. MAYBE WE'RE NOT ***MEANT*** TO PICK A SIDE.

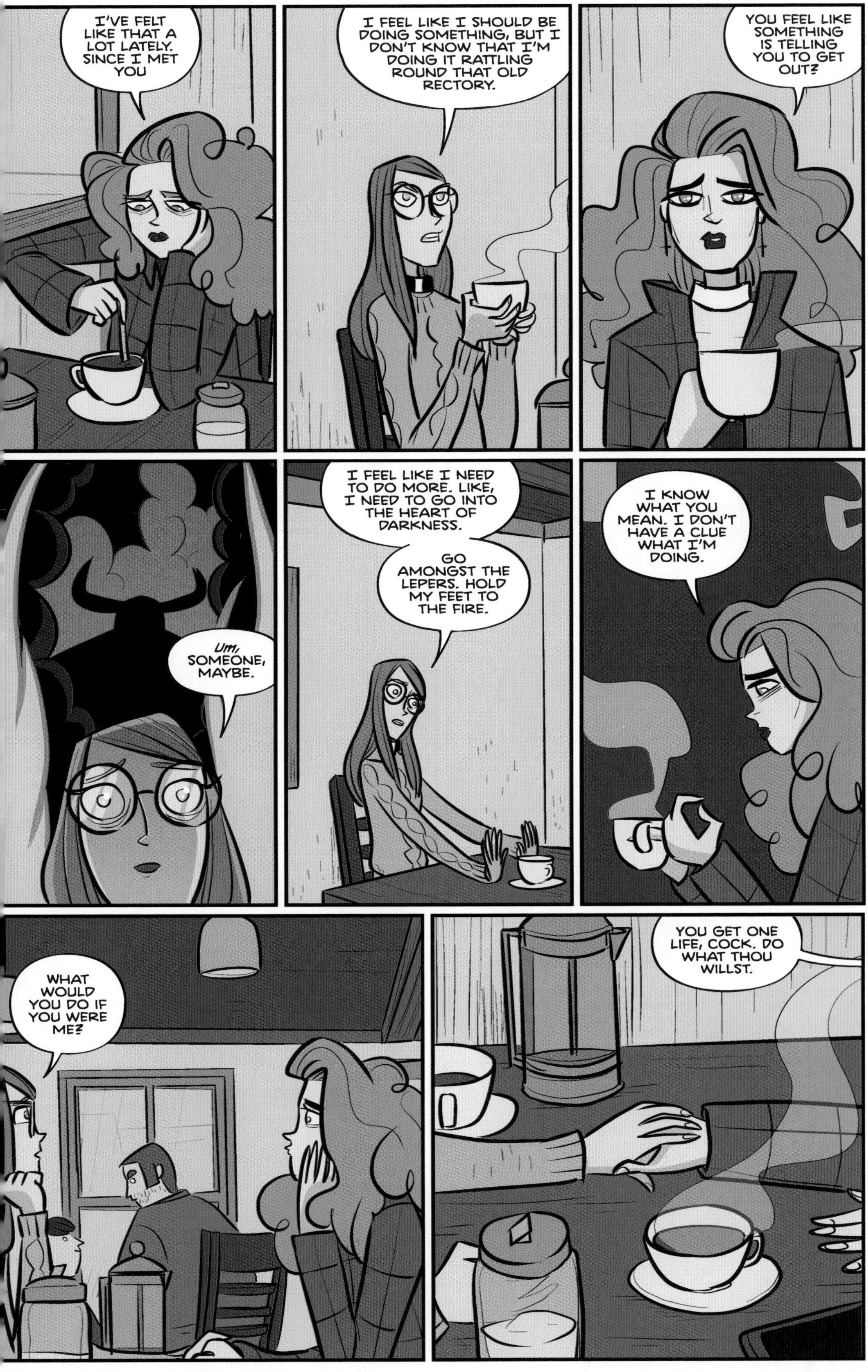
I'VE FELT LIKE THAT A LOT LATELY. SINCE I MET YOU
I FEEL LIKE I SHOULD BE DOING SOMETHING, BUT I DON'T KNOW THAT I'M DOING IT RATTLING ROUND THAT OLD RECTORY.
YOU FEEL LIKE SOMETHING IS TELLING YOU TO GET OUT?
UM, SOMEONE, MAYBE.
I FEEL LIKE I NEED TO DO MORE. LIKE, I NEED TO GO INTO THE HEART OF DARKNESS.
GO AMONGST THE LEPERS. HOLD MY FEET TO THE FIRE.
I KNOW WHAT YOU MEAN. I DON'T HAVE A CLUE WHAT I'M DOING.
WHAT WOULD YOU DO IF YOU WERE ME?
YOU GET ONE LIFE, COCK. DO WHAT THOU WILLST.

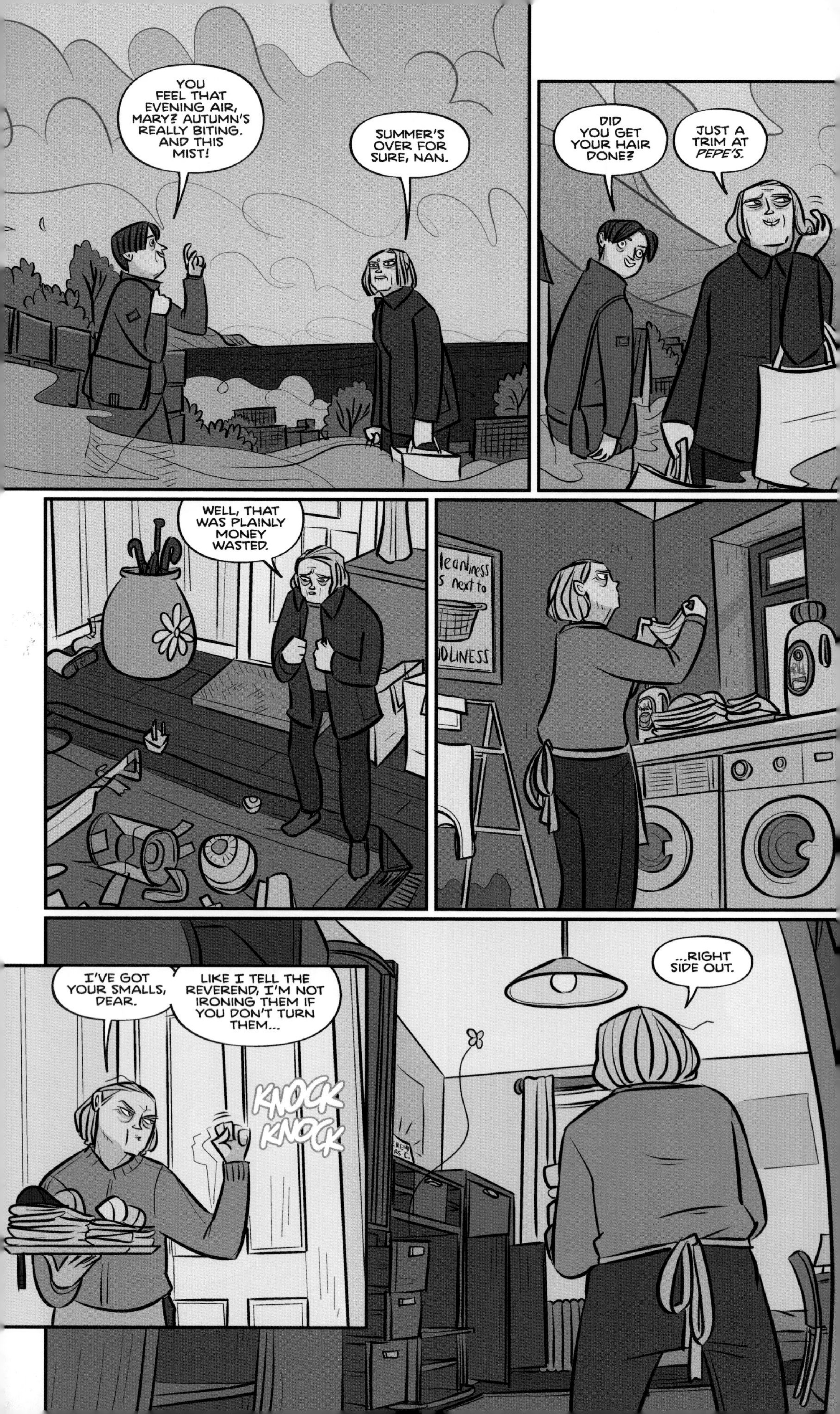
YOU FEEL THAT EVENING AIR, MARY? AUTUMN'S REALLY BITING. AND THIS MIST!
SUMMER'S OVER FOR SURE, NAN.
DID YOU GET YOUR HAIR DONE?
JUST A TRIM AT *PEPE'S.*
WELL, THAT WAS PLAINLY MONEY WASTED.
I'VE GOT YOUR SMALLS, DEAR.
LIKE I TELL THE REVEREND, I'M NOT IRONING THEM IF YOU DON'T TURN THEM...
KNOCK KNOCK
...RIGHT SIDE OUT.

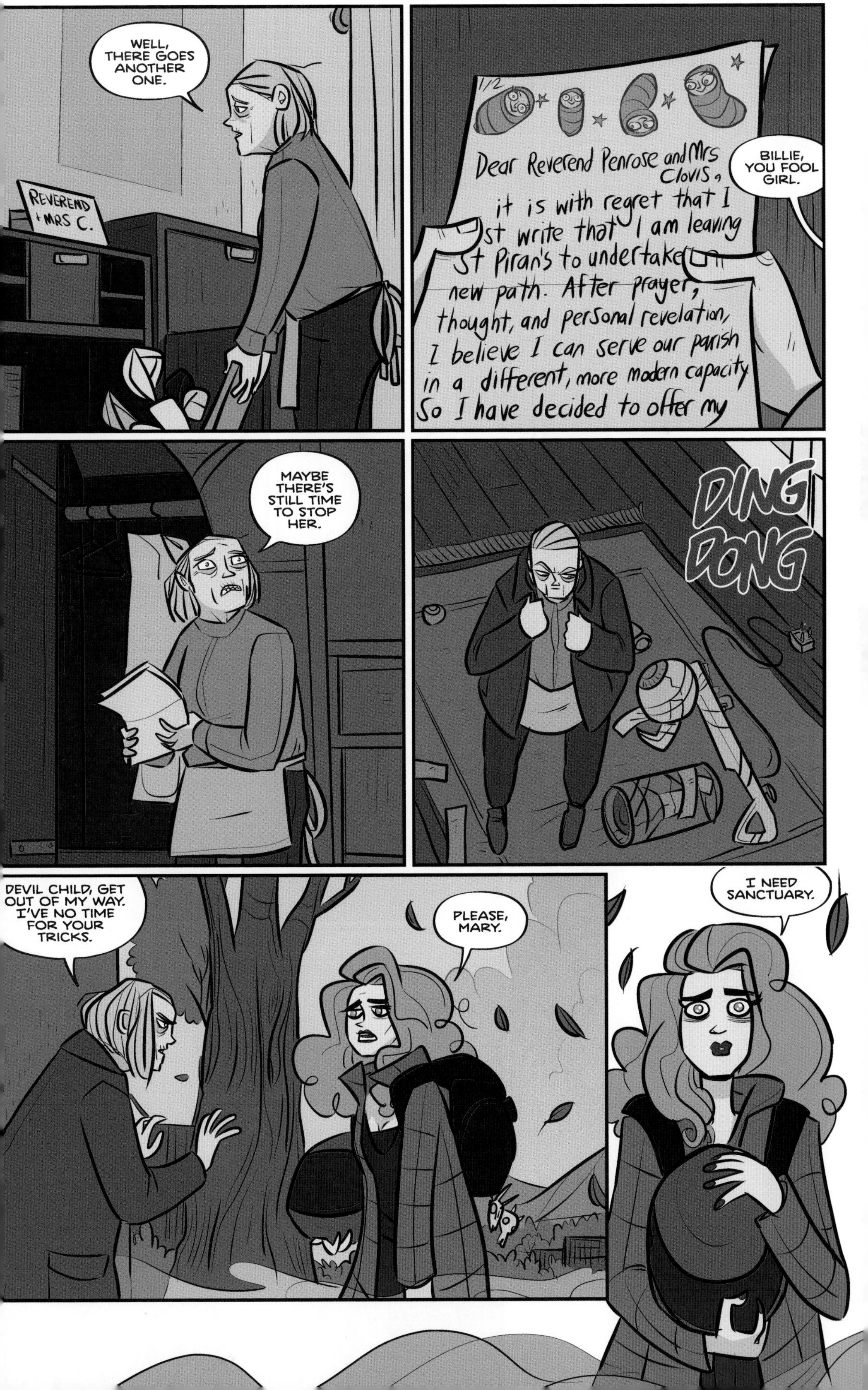
WELL, THERE GOES ANOTHER ONE.
REVEREND + MRS C.
1/2
Dear Reverend Penrose and Mrs Clovis,
it is with regret that I must write that I am leaving St Piran's to undertake a new path. After prayer, thought, and personal revelation, I believe I can serve our parish in a different, more modern capacity. So I have decided to offer my
BILLIE, YOU FOOL GIRL.
MAYBE THERE'S STILL TIME TO STOP HER.
DING DONG
DEVIL CHILD, GET OUT OF MY WAY. I'VE NO TIME FOR YOUR TRICKS.
PLEASE, MARY.
I NEED SANCTUARY.

SANCTUARY FROM **WHAT?**

FROM TARTING IT AROUND TOWN ON YOUR BIKE WITH YOUR BOOBS AND HAIR ALL OVER THE PLACE?

THIS ISN'T ME! YOU REMEMBER ME, MRS. CLOVIS! **NAGGY MAGGIE!**

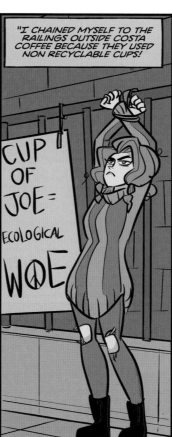

"I CHAINED MYSELF TO THE RAILINGS OUTSIDE COSTA COFFEE BECAUSE THEY USED NON RECYCLABLE CUPS!

CUP OF JOE = ECOLOGICAL WOE

"I LAY IN THE ROAD FOR A WEEK TO PROTECT A WATER VOLE HABITAT...

WATER VOLES NOT DIGGING HOLES

"...AND IT TURNED OUT WATER VOLES WERE ALREADY EXTINCT IN CORNWALL!"

YOU WERE... A REAL NUISANCE.

I COULDN'T TURN MY CONSCIENCE OFF, IT WAS TERRIBLE!

"BUT MAGUS TOM FREED ME FROM IT. THERE WAS A RITUAL. THE CHURCH OF SATAN HELPED ME."

A **RITUAL?**

FINALLY I COULD JUST **LIVE** WITHOUT THINKING ABOUT **MICRO-PLASTICS!**

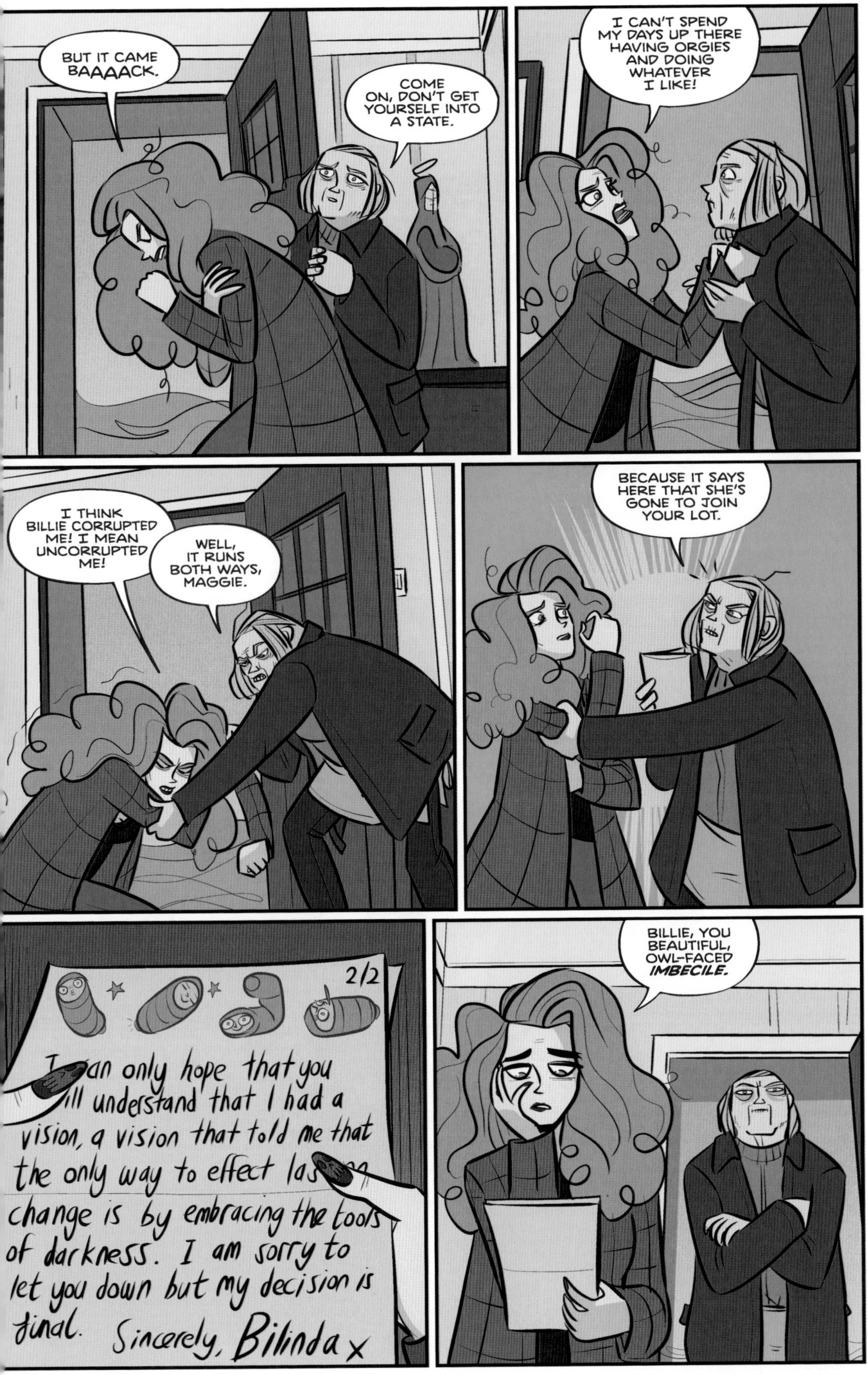
BUT IT CAME BAAAACK.
COME ON, DON'T GET YOURSELF INTO A STATE.
I CAN'T SPEND MY DAYS UP THERE HAVING ORGIES AND DOING WHATEVER I LIKE!
I THINK BILLIE CORRUPTED ME! I MEAN UNCORRUPTED ME!
WELL, IT RUNS BOTH WAYS, MAGGIE.
BECAUSE IT SAYS HERE THAT SHE'S GONE TO JOIN YOUR LOT.
2/2
I can only hope that you will understand that I had a vision, a vision that told me that the only way to effect lasting change is by embracing the tools of darkness. I am sorry to let you down but my decision is final. Sincerely, Bilinda x
BILLIE, YOU BEAUTIFUL, OWL-FACED *IMBECILE.*

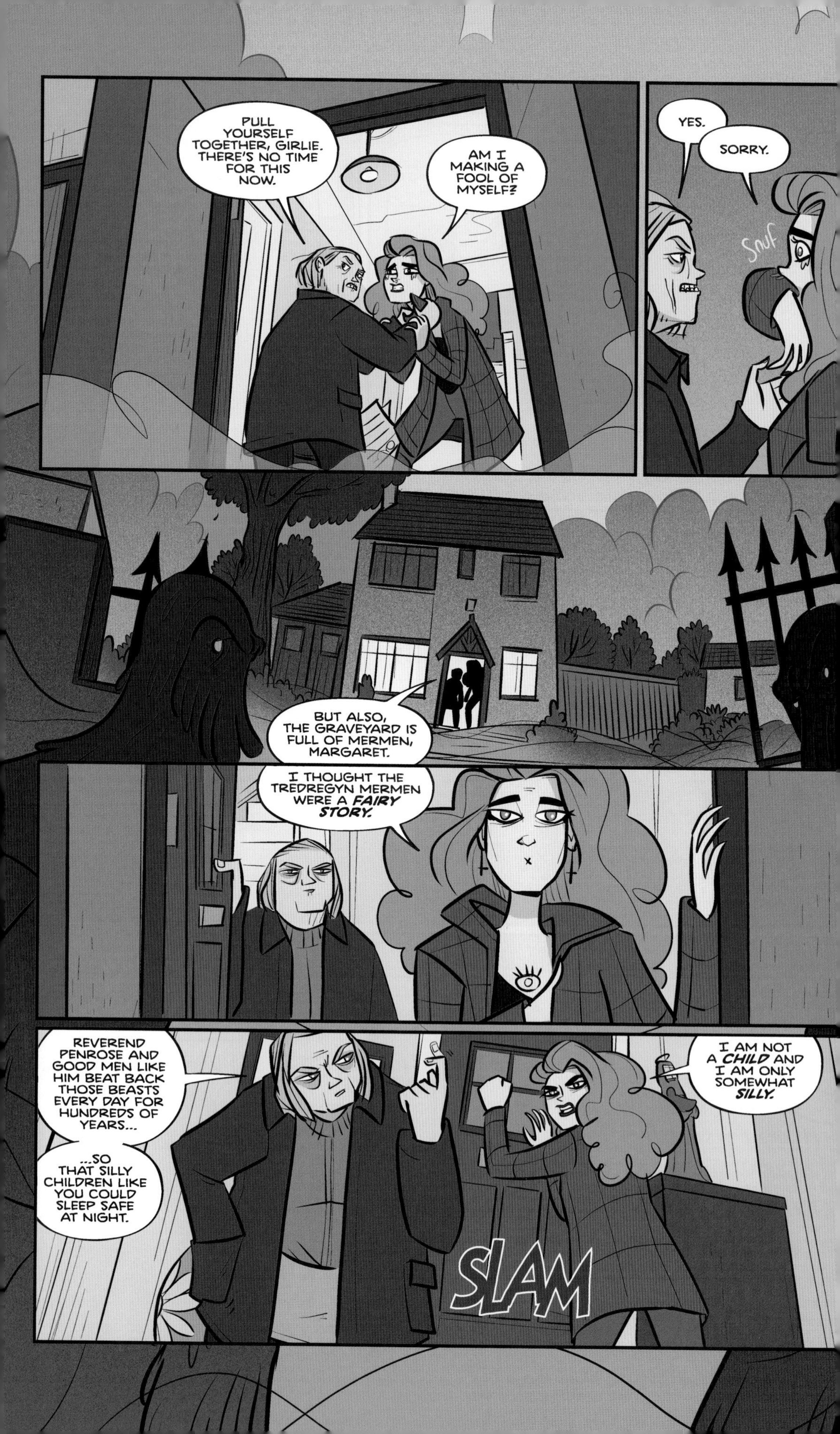
PULL YOURSELF TOGETHER, GIRLIE. THERE'S NO TIME FOR THIS NOW.
AM I MAKING A FOOL OF MYSELF?
YES.
SORRY.
Snuf
BUT ALSO, THE GRAVEYARD IS FULL OF MERMEN, MARGARET.
I THOUGHT THE TREDREGYN MERMEN WERE A FAIRY STORY.
REVEREND PENROSE AND GOOD MEN LIKE HIM BEAT BACK THOSE BEASTS EVERY DAY FOR HUNDREDS OF YEARS...
...SO THAT SILLY CHILDREN LIKE YOU COULD SLEEP SAFE AT NIGHT.
I AM NOT A CHILD AND I AM ONLY SOMEWHAT SILLY.
SLAM

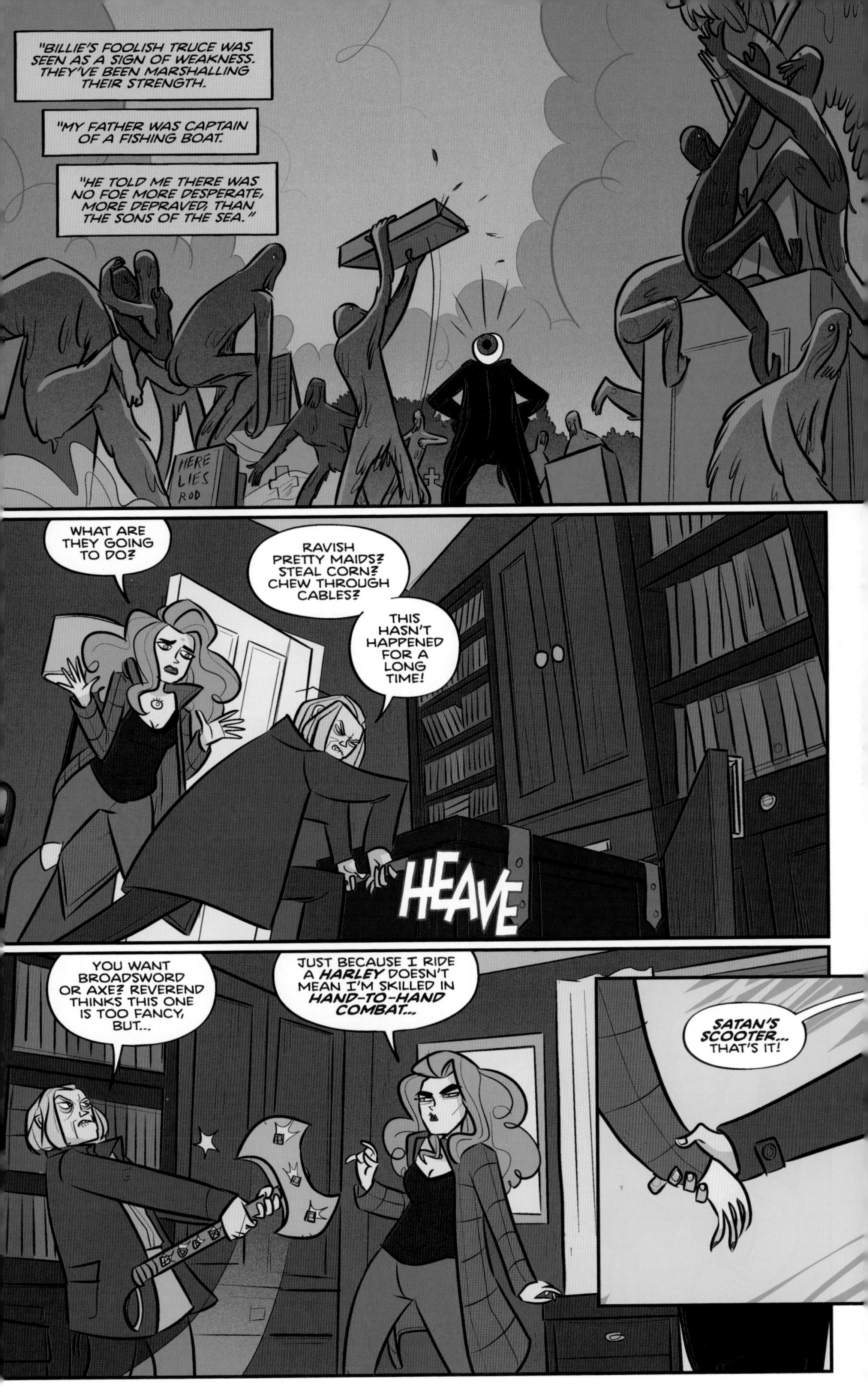
"BILLIE'S FOOLISH TRUCE WAS SEEN AS A SIGN OF WEAKNESS. THEY'VE BEEN MARSHALLING THEIR STRENGTH.
"MY FATHER WAS CAPTAIN OF A FISHING BOAT.
"HE TOLD ME THERE WAS NO FOE MORE DESPERATE, MORE DEPRAVED, THAN THE SONS OF THE SEA."
HERE LIES ROD
WHAT ARE THEY GOING TO DO?
RAVISH PRETTY MAIDS? STEAL CORN? CHEW THROUGH CABLES?
THIS HASN'T HAPPENED FOR A LONG TIME!
HEAVE
YOU WANT BROADSWORD OR AXE? REVEREND THINKS THIS ONE IS TOO FANCY, BUT...
JUST BECAUSE I RIDE A HARLEY DOESN'T MEAN I'M SKILLED IN HAND-TO-HAND COMBAT...
SATAN'S SCOOTER... THAT'S IT!

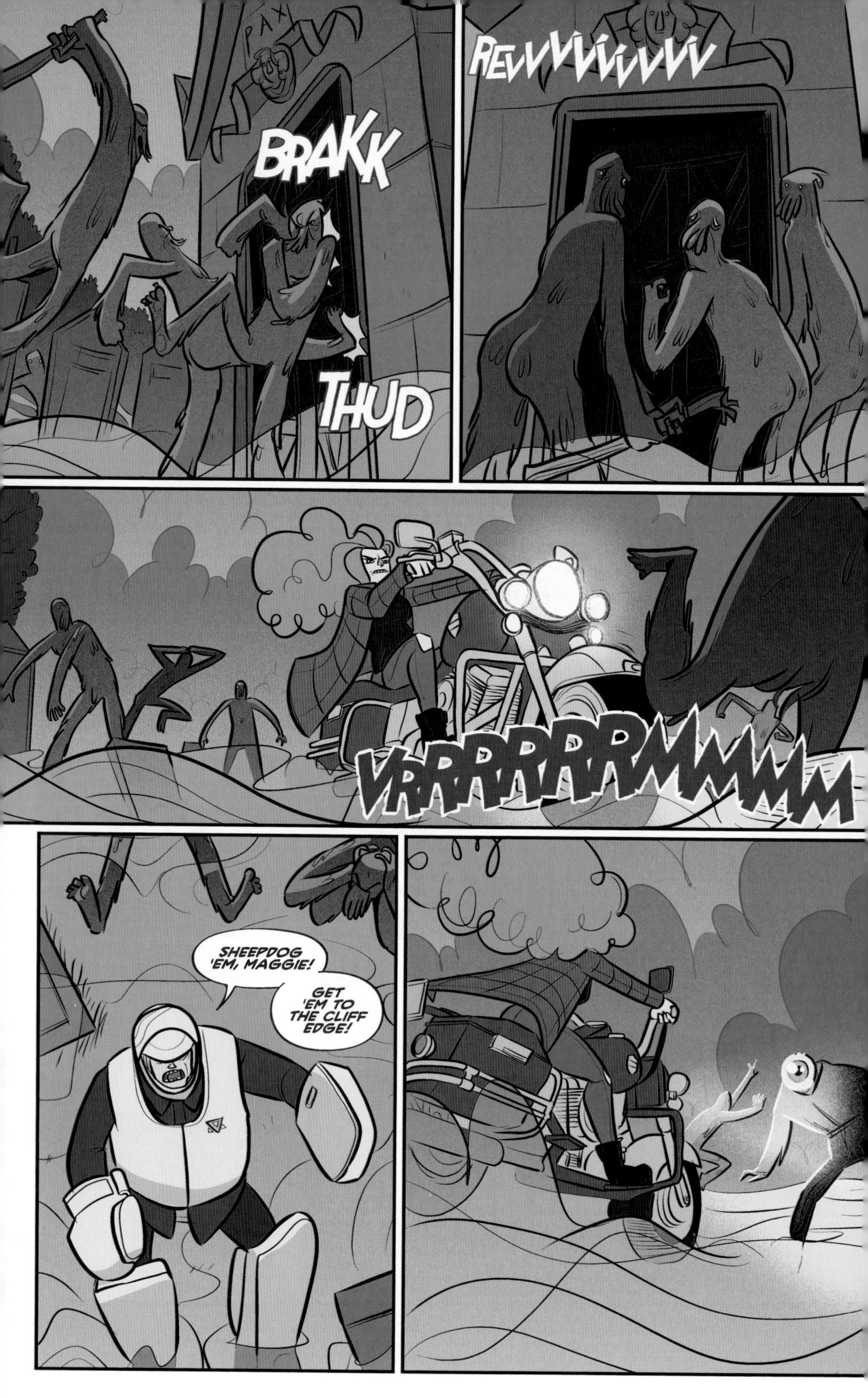
PAX
BRAKK
THUD
REVVVVVVVVVV
VRRRRRRRMMMMM
SHEEPDOG 'EM, MAGGIE!
GET 'EM TO THE CLIFF EDGE!

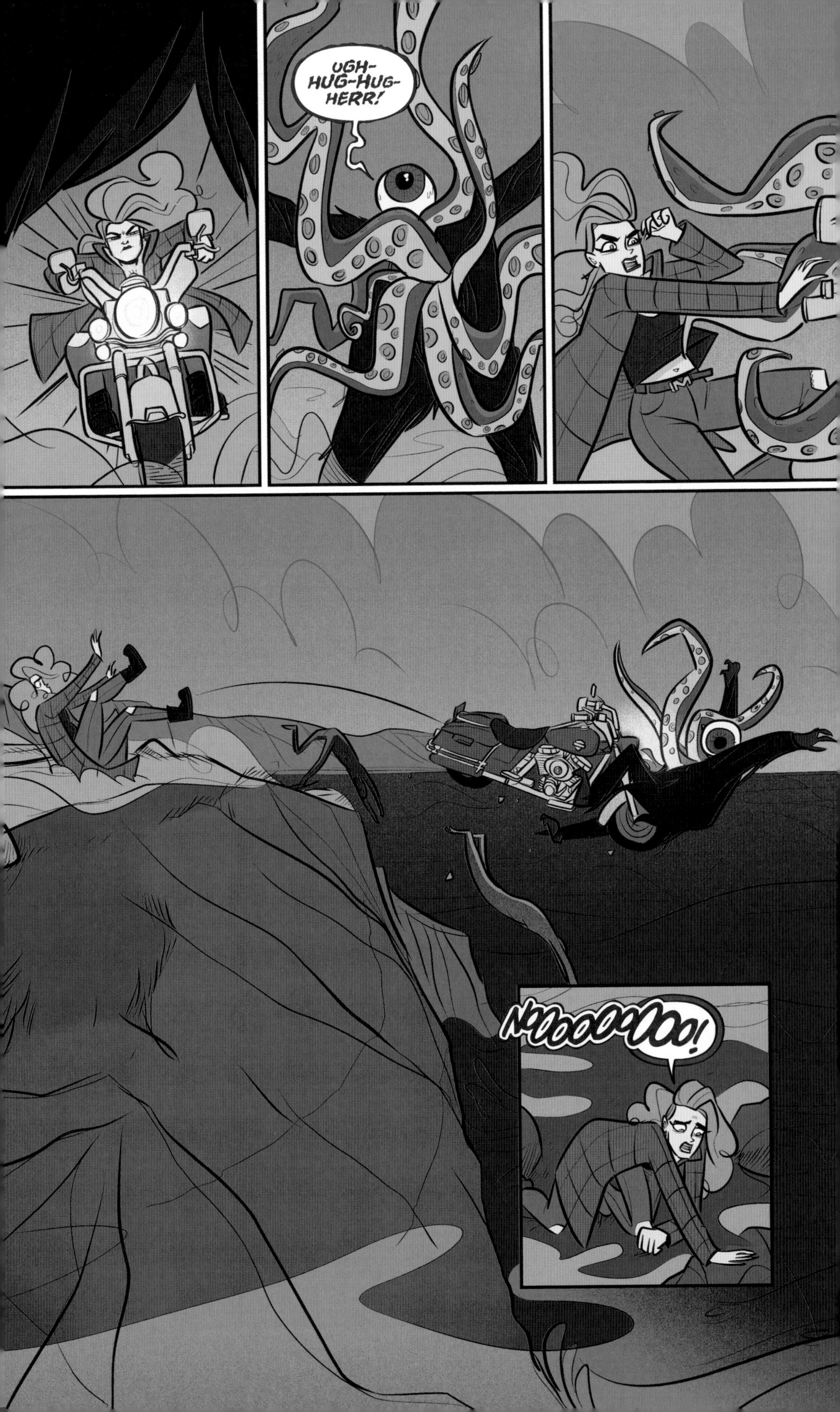
UGH-HUG-HUG-HERR!
NOOOOOOOOO!

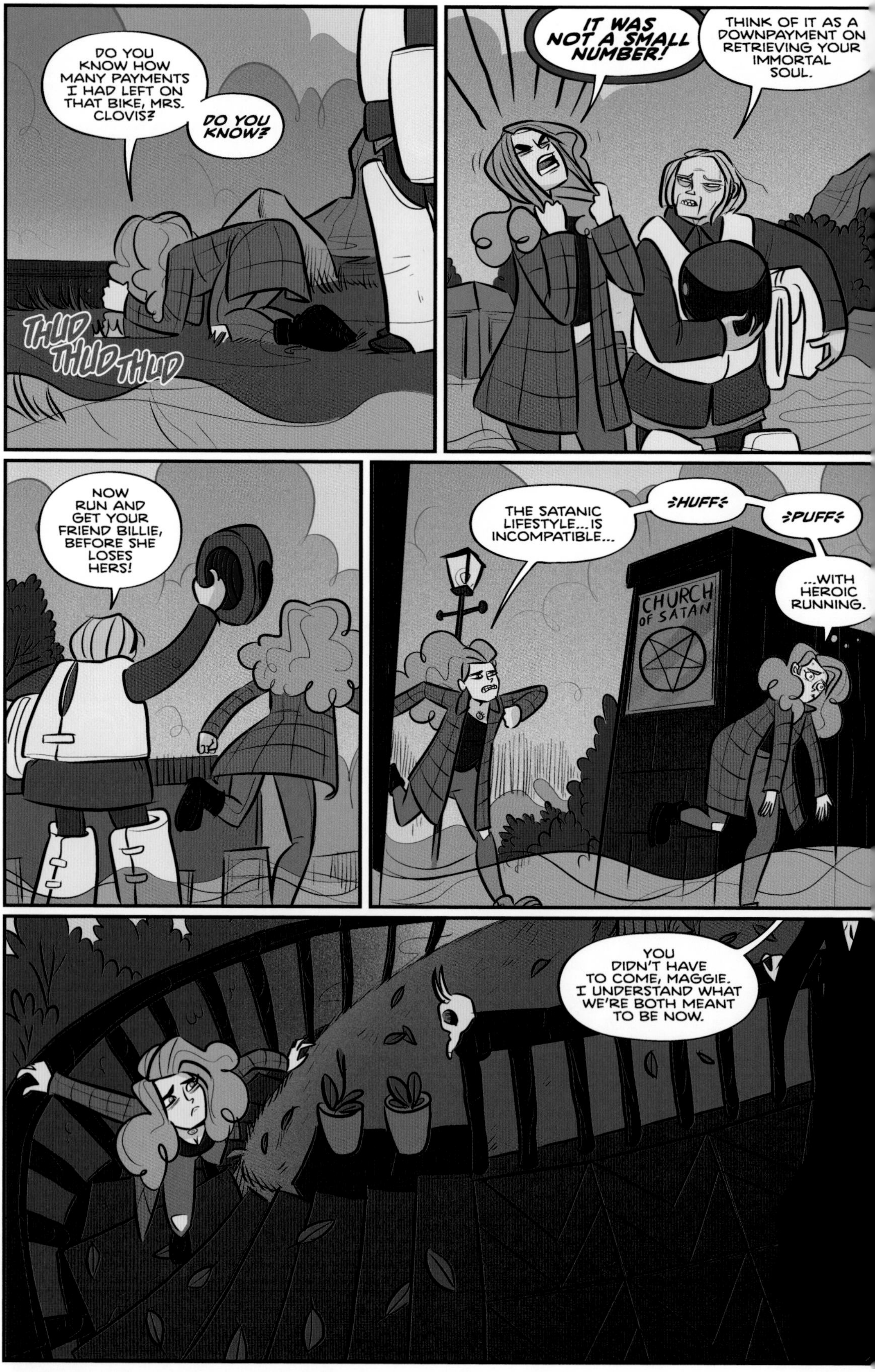
DO YOU KNOW HOW MANY PAYMENTS I HAD LEFT ON THAT BIKE, MRS. CLOVIS?
DO YOU KNOW?
THUD THUD THUD
IT WAS NOT A SMALL NUMBER!
THINK OF IT AS A DOWNPAYMENT ON RETRIEVING YOUR IMMORTAL SOUL.
NOW RUN AND GET YOUR FRIEND BILLIE, BEFORE SHE LOSES HERS!
THE SATANIC LIFESTYLE... IS INCOMPATIBLE...
HUFF
PUFF
...WITH HEROIC RUNNING.
CHURCH OF SATAN
YOU DIDN'T HAVE TO COME, MAGGIE. I UNDERSTAND WHAT WE'RE BOTH MEANT TO BE NOW.

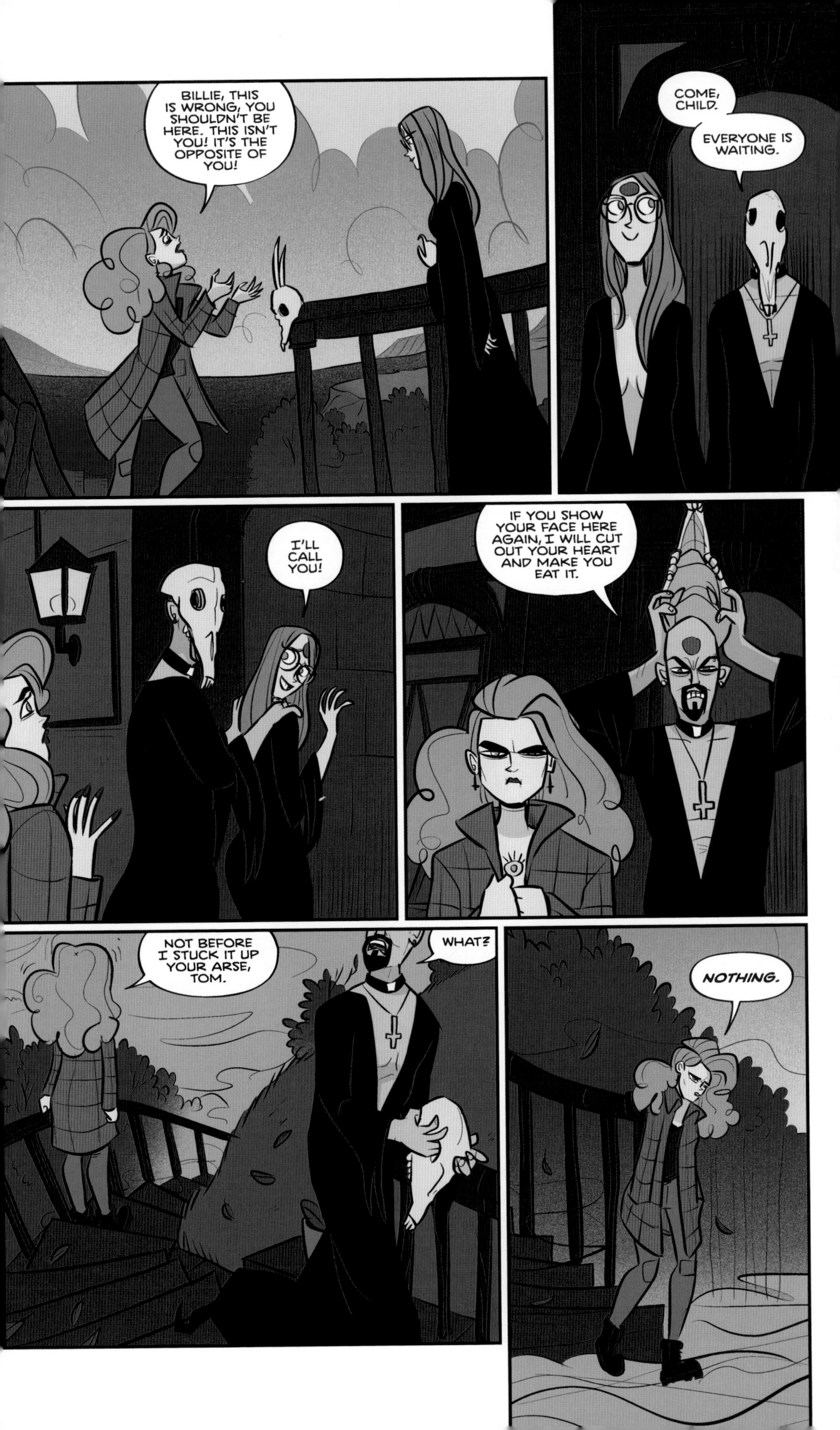
BILLIE, THIS IS WRONG, YOU SHOULDN'T BE HERE. THIS ISN'T YOU! IT'S THE OPPOSITE OF YOU!
COME, CHILD.
EVERYONE IS WAITING.
I'LL CALL YOU!
IF YOU SHOW YOUR FACE HERE AGAIN, I WILL CUT OUT YOUR HEART AND MAKE YOU EAT IT.
NOT BEFORE I STUCK IT UP YOUR ARSE, TOM.
WHAT?
NOTHING.

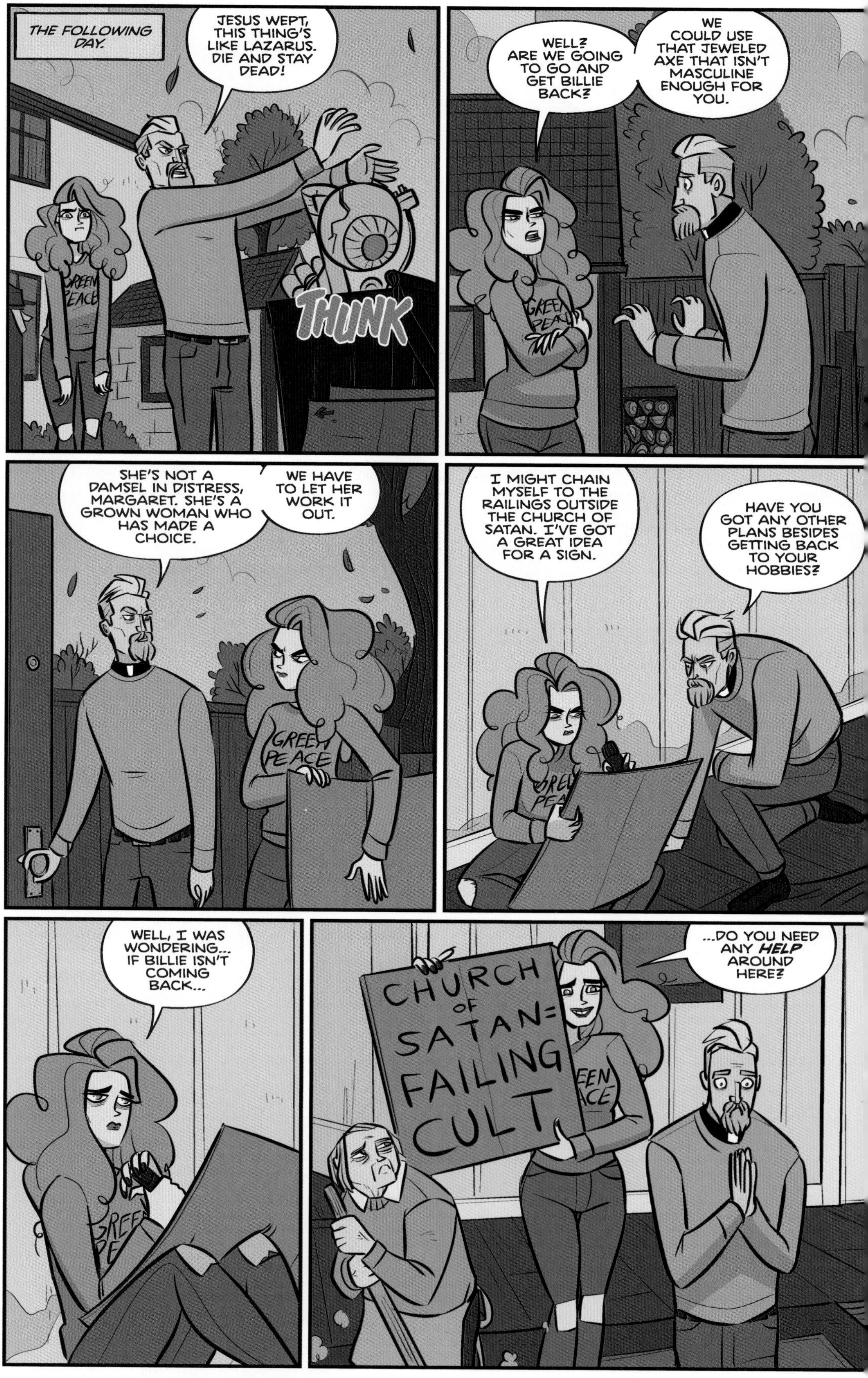

THE FOLLOWING DAY.
JESUS WEPT, THIS THING'S LIKE LAZARUS. DIE AND STAY DEAD!
THUNK
WELL? ARE WE GOING TO GO AND GET BILLIE BACK?
WE COULD USE THAT JEWELED AXE THAT ISN'T MASCULINE ENOUGH FOR YOU.
SHE'S NOT A DAMSEL IN DISTRESS, MARGARET. SHE'S A GROWN WOMAN WHO HAS MADE A CHOICE.
WE HAVE TO LET HER WORK IT OUT.
I MIGHT CHAIN MYSELF TO THE RAILINGS OUTSIDE THE CHURCH OF SATAN. I'VE GOT A GREAT IDEA FOR A SIGN.
HAVE YOU GOT ANY OTHER PLANS BESIDES GETTING BACK TO YOUR HOBBIES?
WELL, I WAS WONDERING... IF BILLIE ISN'T COMING BACK...
CHURCH of SATAN = FAILING CULT
...DO YOU NEED ANY HELP AROUND HERE?

EPILOGUE

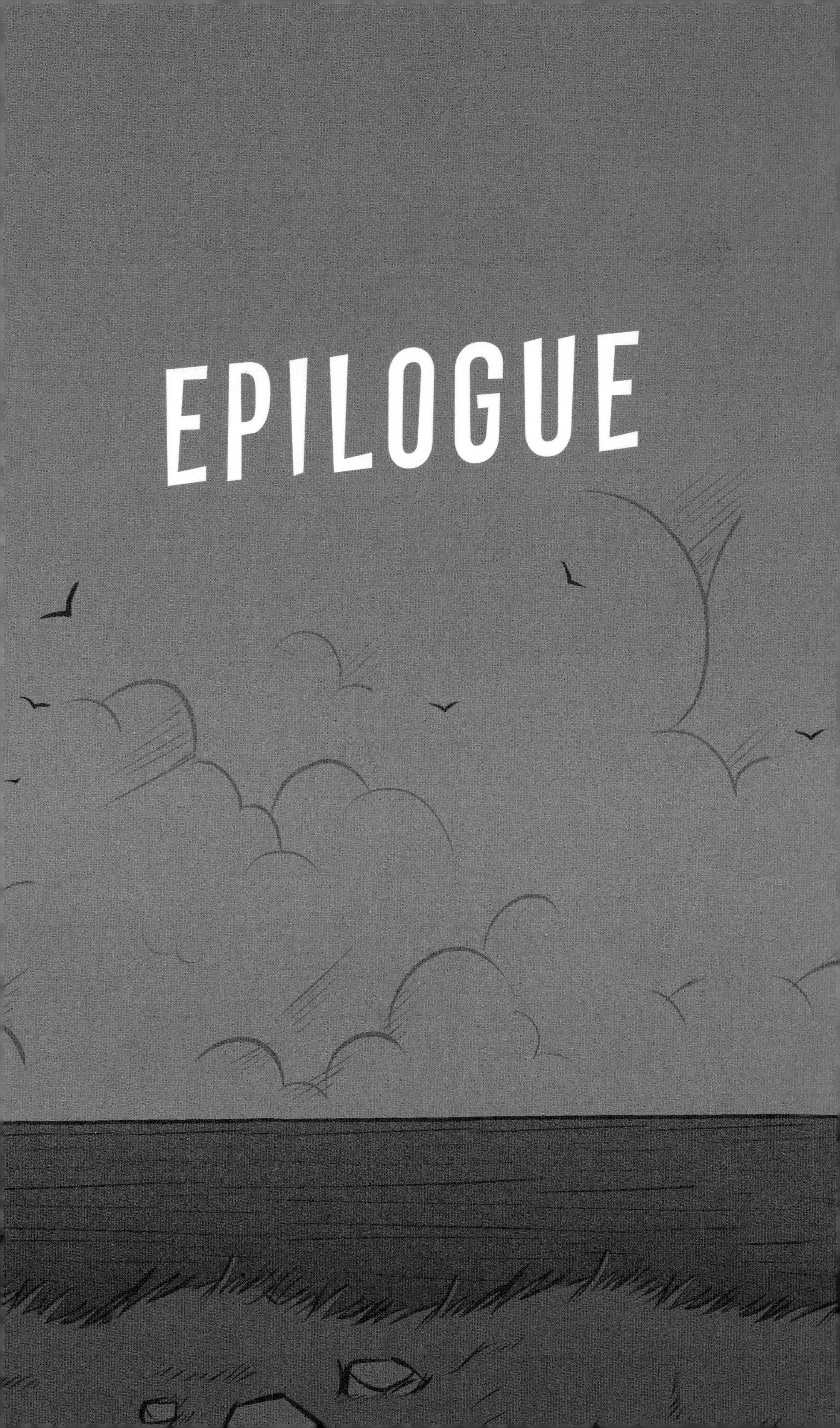

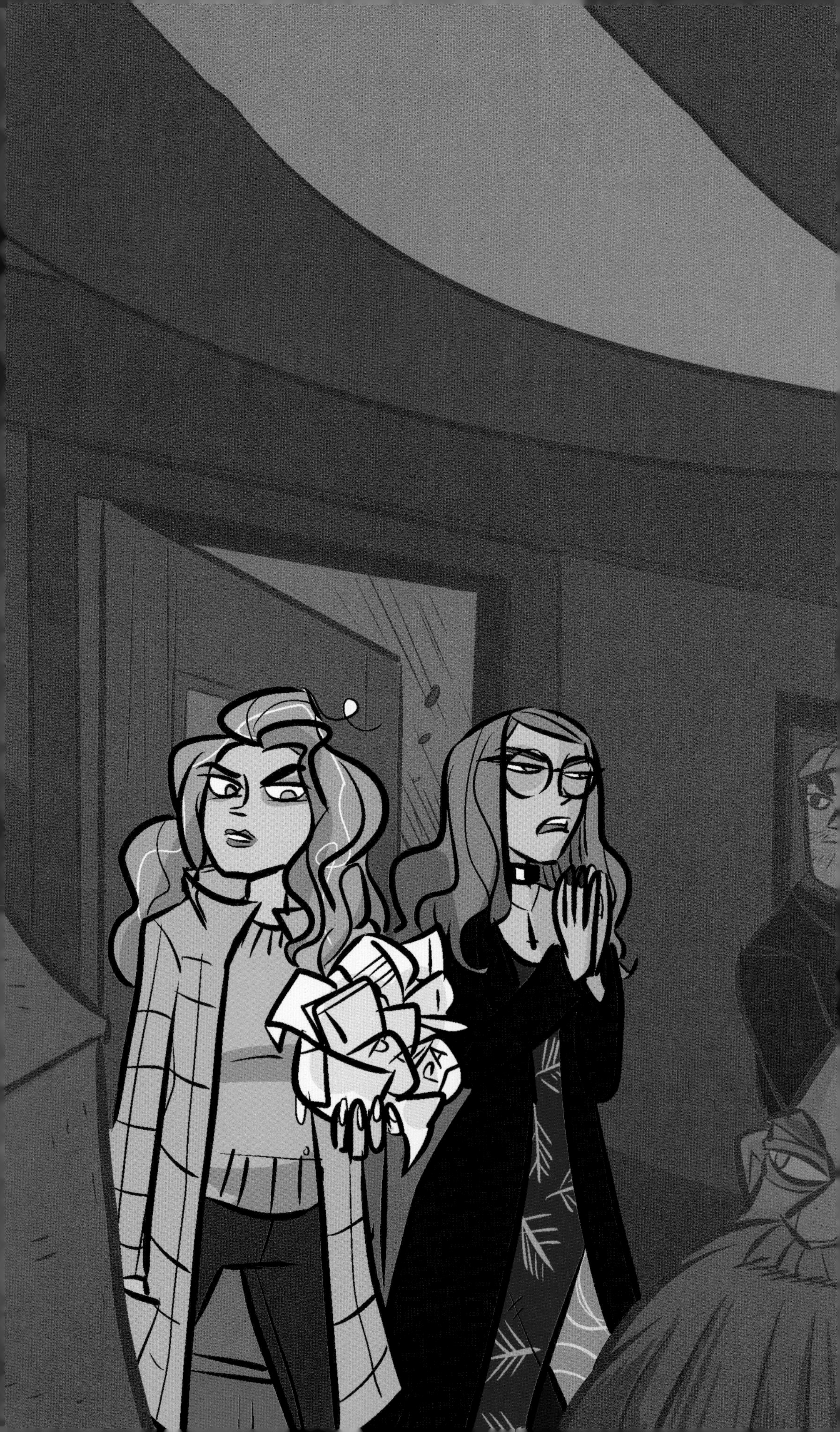

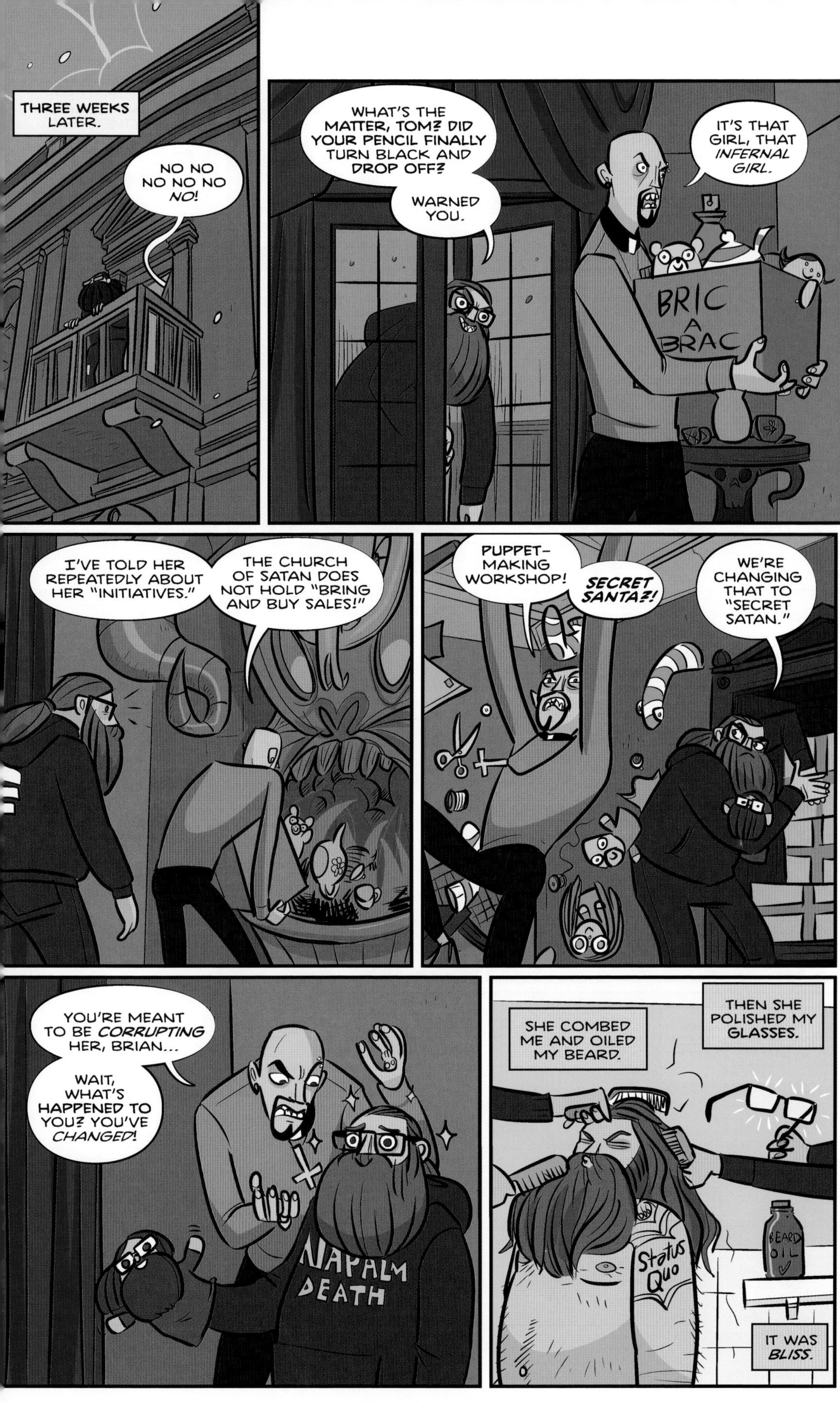
THREE WEEKS LATER.
NO NO NO NO NO NO!
WHAT'S THE MATTER, TOM? DID YOUR PENCIL FINALLY TURN BLACK AND DROP OFF?
WARNED YOU.
IT'S THAT GIRL, THAT INFERNAL GIRL.
BRIC A BRAC
I'VE TOLD HER REPEATEDLY ABOUT HER "INITIATIVES."
THE CHURCH OF SATAN DOES NOT HOLD "BRING AND BUY SALES!"
PUPPET-MAKING WORKSHOP!
SECRET SANTA?!
WE'RE CHANGING THAT TO "SECRET SATAN."
YOU'RE MEANT TO BE CORRUPTING HER, BRIAN...
WAIT, WHAT'S HAPPENED TO YOU? YOU'VE CHANGED!
NAPALM DEATH
SHE COMBED ME AND OILED MY BEARD.
THEN SHE POLISHED MY GLASSES.
Status Quo
BEARD OIL
IT WAS BLISS.

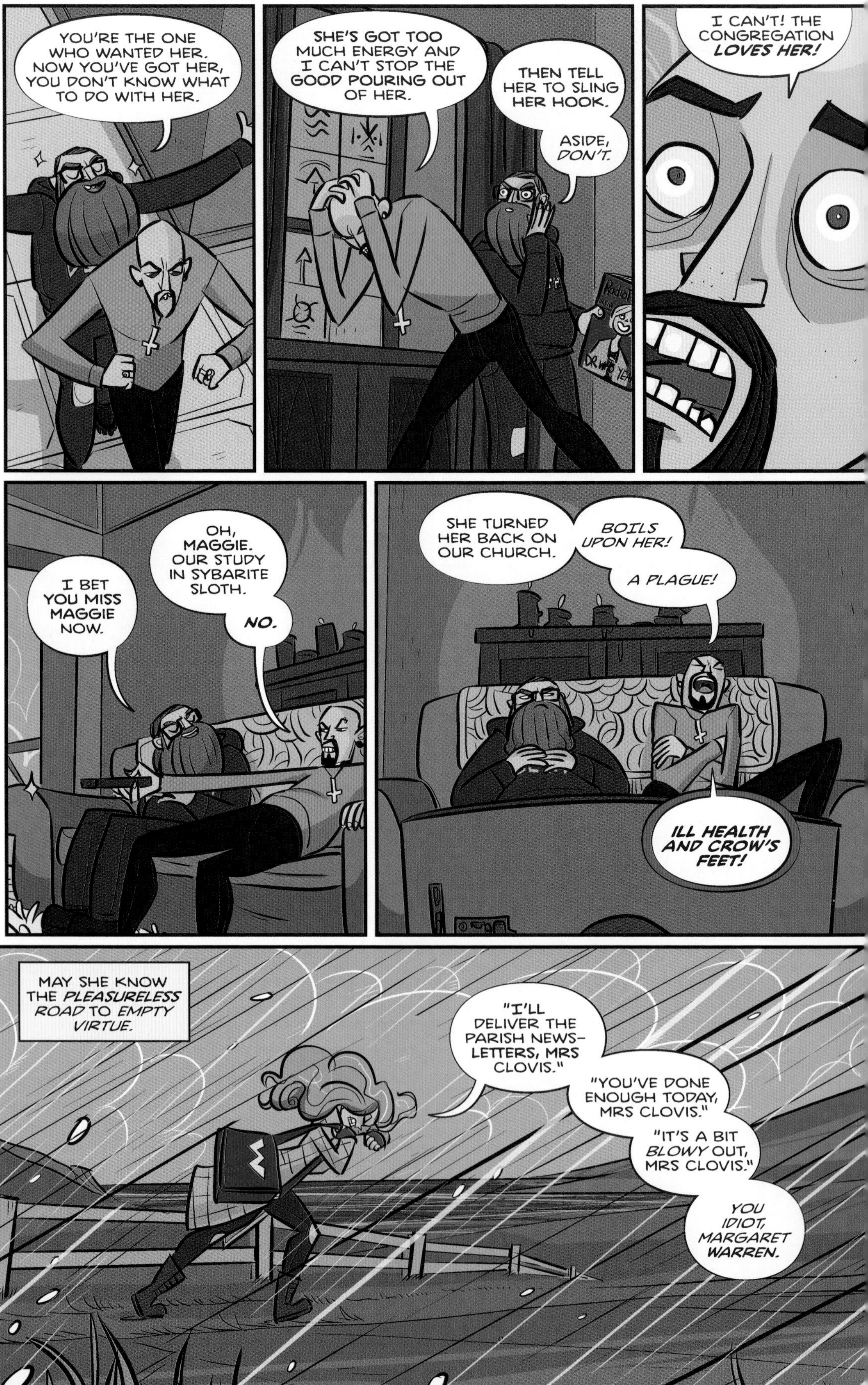
YOU'RE THE ONE WHO WANTED HER. NOW YOU'VE GOT HER, YOU DON'T KNOW WHAT TO DO WITH HER.
SHE'S GOT TOO MUCH ENERGY AND I CAN'T STOP THE GOOD POURING OUT OF HER.
THEN TELL HER TO SLING HER HOOK.
ASIDE, DON'T.
I CAN'T! THE CONGREGATION LOVES HER!
I BET YOU MISS MAGGIE NOW.
OH, MAGGIE. OUR STUDY IN SYBARITE SLOTH.
NO.
SHE TURNED HER BACK ON OUR CHURCH.
BOILS UPON HER!
A PLAGUE!
ILL HEALTH AND CROW'S FEET!
MAY SHE KNOW THE PLEASURELESS ROAD TO EMPTY VIRTUE.
"I'LL DELIVER THE PARISH NEWS-LETTERS, MRS CLOVIS."
"YOU'VE DONE ENOUGH TODAY, MRS CLOVIS."
"IT'S A BIT BLOWY OUT, MRS CLOVIS."
YOU IDIOT, MARGARET WARREN.

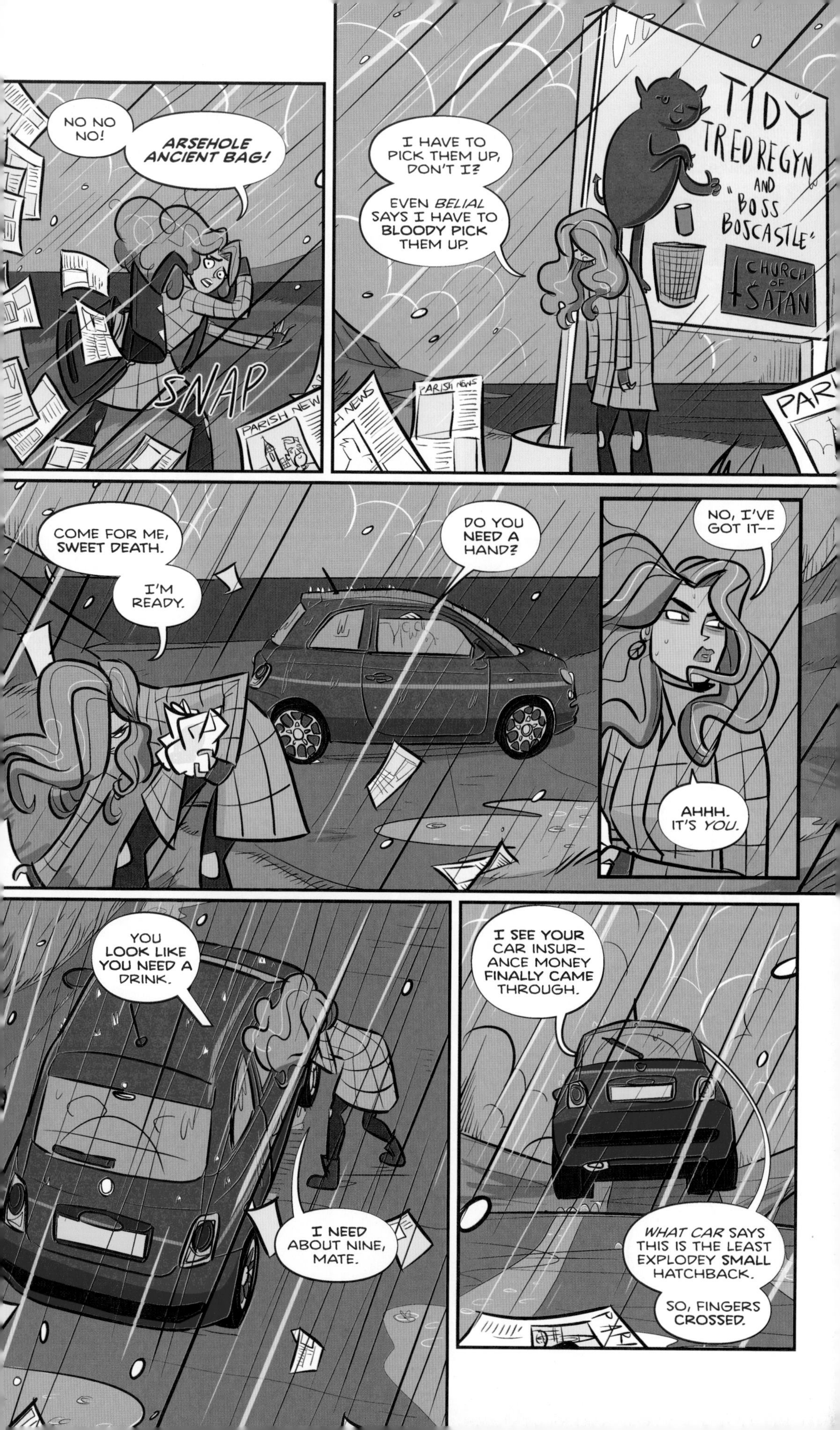
NO NO NO!
ARSEHOLE ANCIENT BAG!
SNAP
PARISH NEWS
I HAVE TO PICK THEM UP, DON'T I?
EVEN *BELIAL* SAYS I HAVE TO **BLOODY PICK** THEM UP.
TIDY TREDREGYN AND "BOSS BOSCASTLE"
CHURCH OF SATAN
PARISH NEWS
COME FOR ME, **SWEET DEATH.**
I'M READY.
DO YOU NEED A HAND?
NO, I'VE GOT IT--
AHHH. IT'S *YOU.*
YOU LOOK LIKE YOU NEED A DRINK.
I NEED ABOUT NINE, MATE.
I SEE YOUR CAR INSURANCE MONEY **FINALLY CAME** THROUGH.
WHAT CAR SAYS THIS IS THE LEAST EXPLODEY **SMALL** HATCHBACK.
SO, FINGERS **CROSSED.**

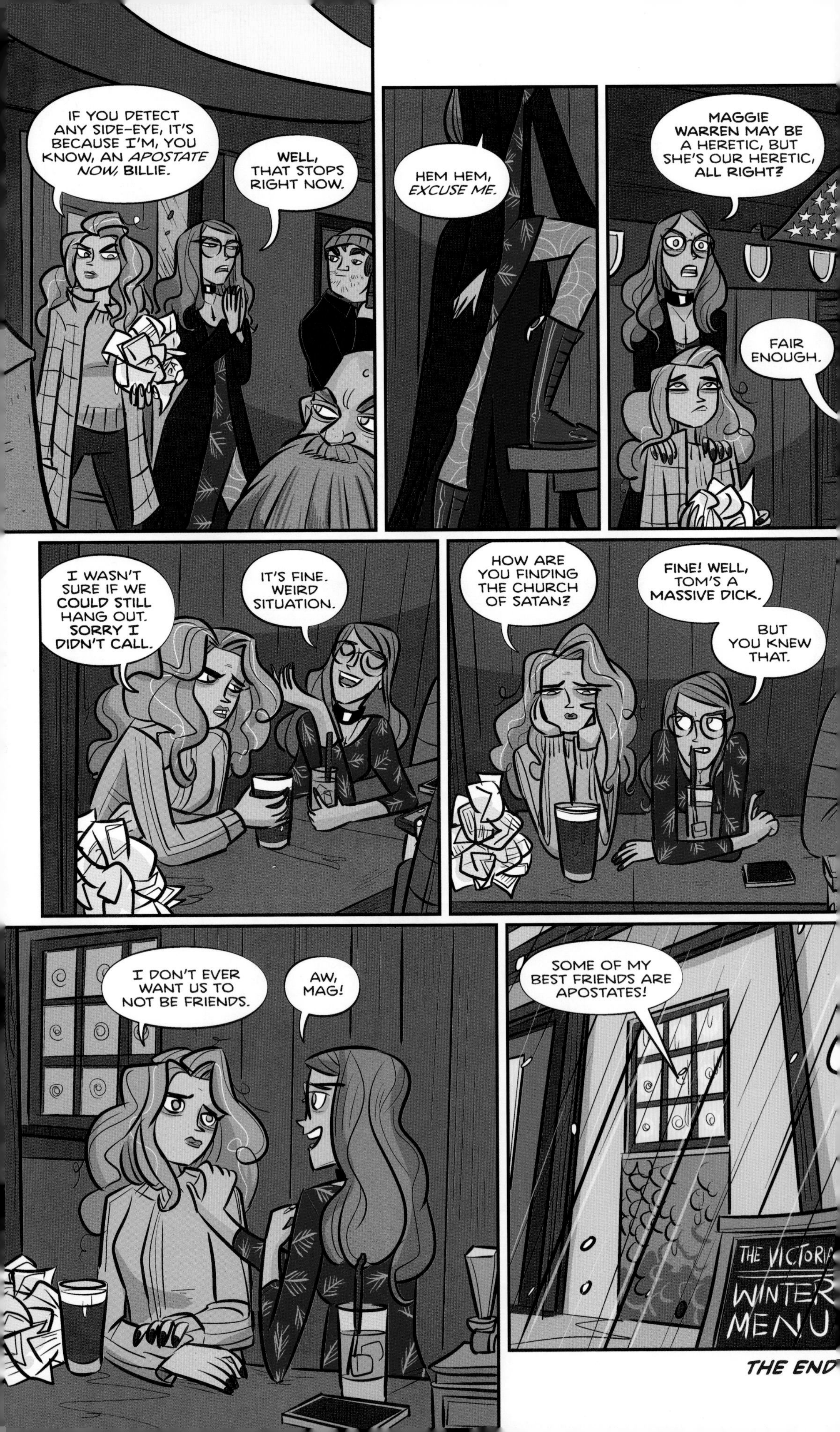
IF YOU DETECT ANY SIDE-EYE, IT'S BECAUSE I'M, YOU KNOW, AN *APOSTATE NOW,* BILLIE.
WELL, THAT STOPS RIGHT NOW.
HEM HEM, *EXCUSE ME.*
MAGGIE WARREN MAY BE A HERETIC, BUT SHE'S OUR HERETIC, ALL RIGHT?
FAIR ENOUGH.
I WASN'T SURE IF WE COULD STILL HANG OUT. SORRY I DIDN'T CALL.
IT'S FINE. WEIRD SITUATION.
HOW ARE YOU FINDING THE CHURCH OF SATAN?
FINE! WELL, TOM'S A MASSIVE DICK.
BUT YOU KNEW THAT.
I DON'T EVER WANT US TO NOT BE FRIENDS.
AW, MAG!
SOME OF MY BEST FRIENDS ARE APOSTATES!
THE VICTORI
WINTER MENU
THE END

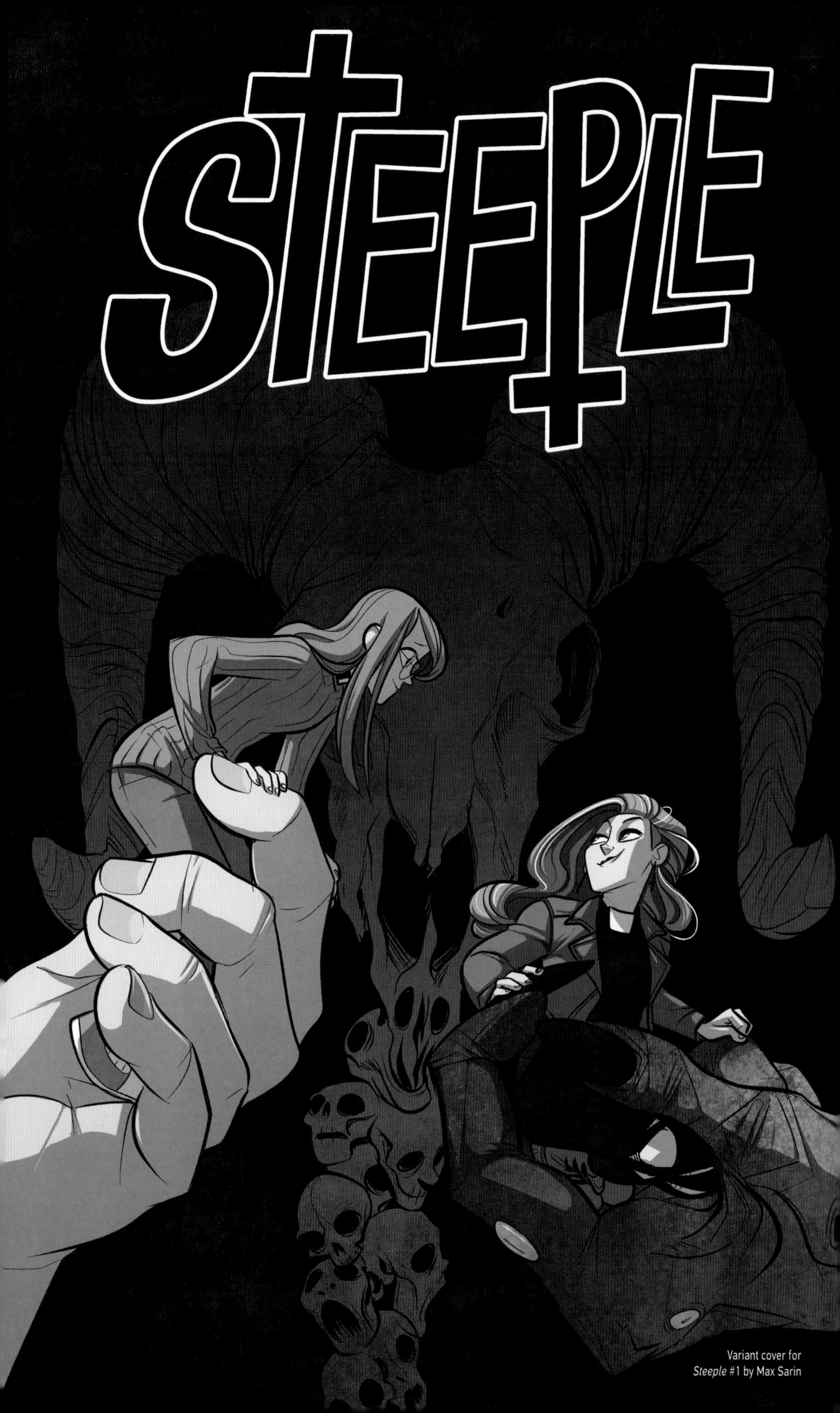
STEEPLE

Variant cover for
Steeple #1 by Max Sarin

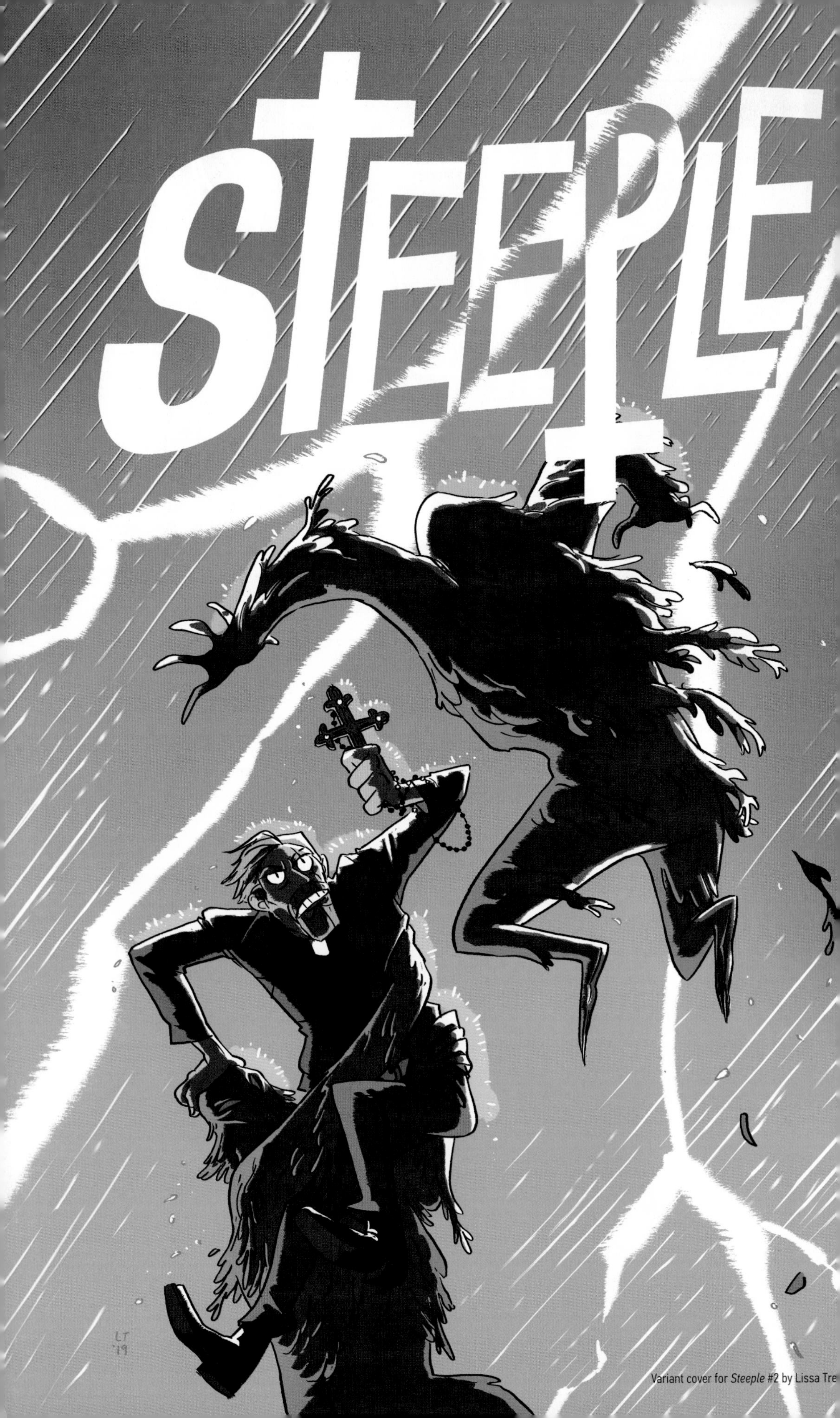
STEEPLE
LT '19
Variant cover for *Steeple* #2 by Lissa Tre

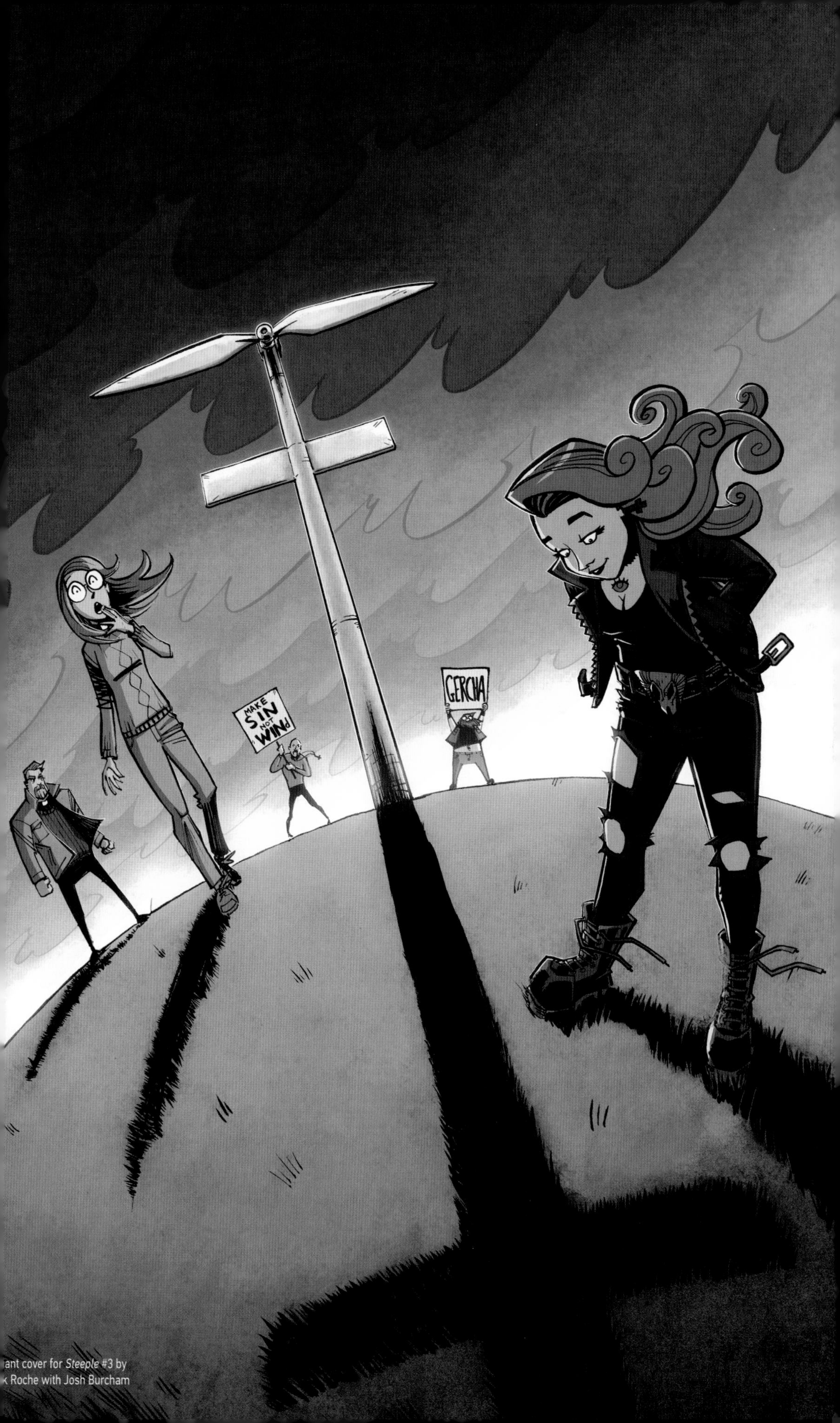
MAKE
SIN
NOT
WIND
GERCHA
ant cover for *Steeple* #3 by
k Roche with Josh Burcham

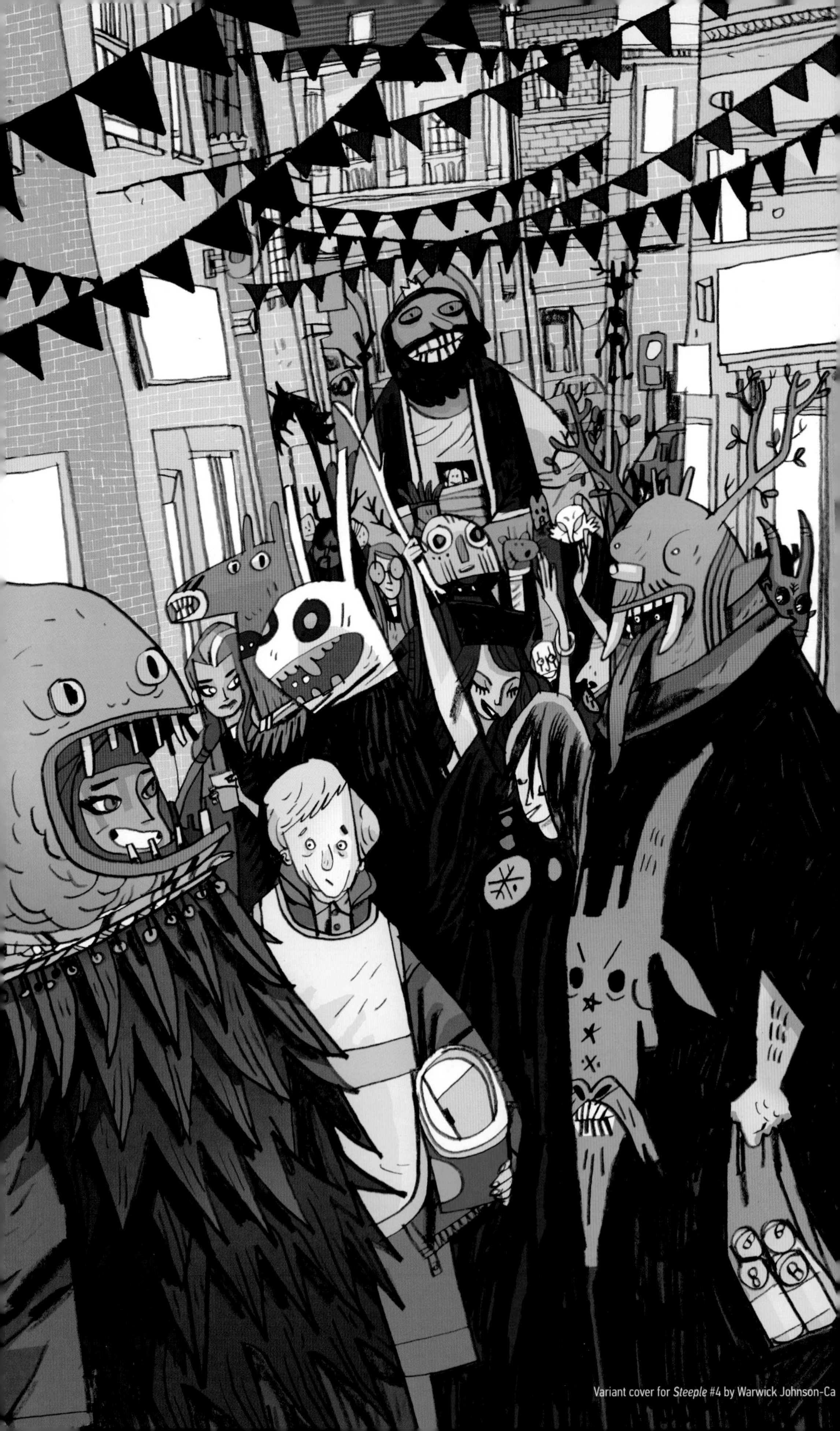

Variant cover for *Steeple* #4 by Warwick Johnson-Ca

ant cover for *Steeple* #5 by Robert Ball

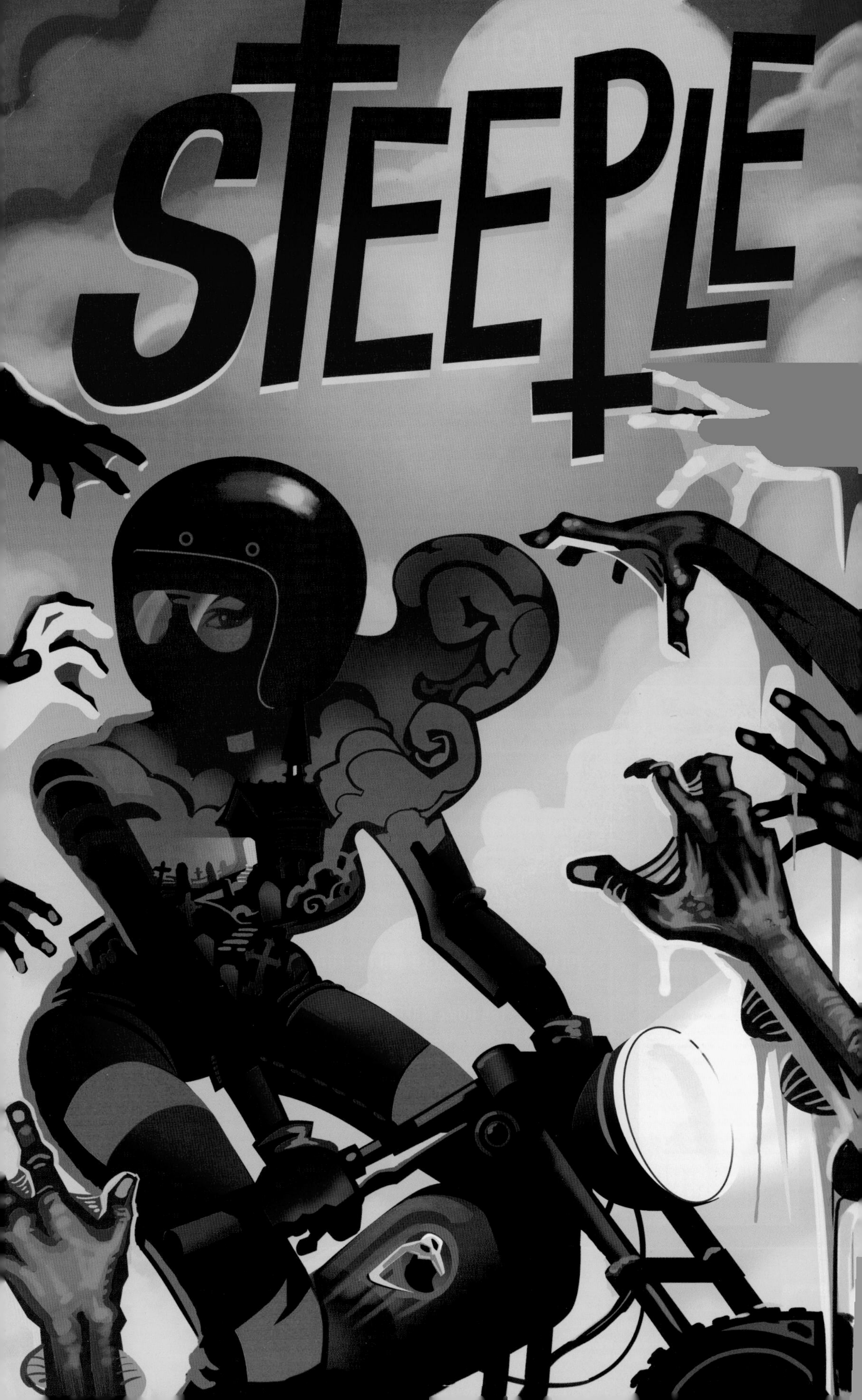
STEEPLE

SPECULATIVE FICTION FROM

darkhorse originals

'Unique creators with unique visions."—MIKE RICHARDSON, PUBLISHER

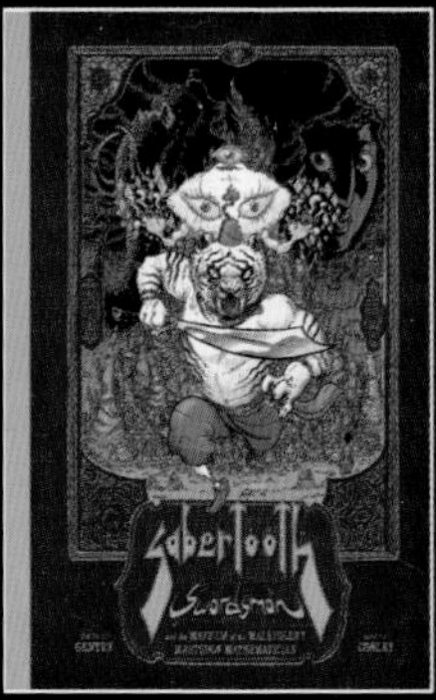

SABERTOOTH SWORDSMAN

Damon Gentry and Aaron Conley

Granted the form of the Sabertooth Swordsman by the Cloud God of Sasquatch Mountain, a simple farmer embarks on a treacherous journey to the Mastodon's fortress!

ISBN 978-1-61655-176-6 | $17.99

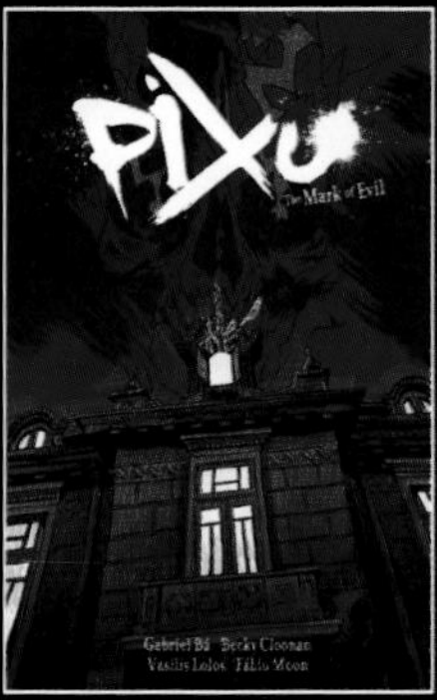
Pixu
The Mark of Evil
Gabriel Bá Becky Cloonan
Vasilis Lolos Fábio Moon

PIXU: THE MARK OF EVIL

Gabriel Bá, Becky Cloonan, Vasilis Lolos, and Fábio Moon

This gripping tale of urban horror follows the lives of five lonely strangers who discover a dark mark scrawled on the walls of their building. As the walls come alive, everyone is slowly driven mad, stripped of free will, leaving only confusion, chaos, and eventual death.

ISBN 978-1-61655-813-0 | $14.99

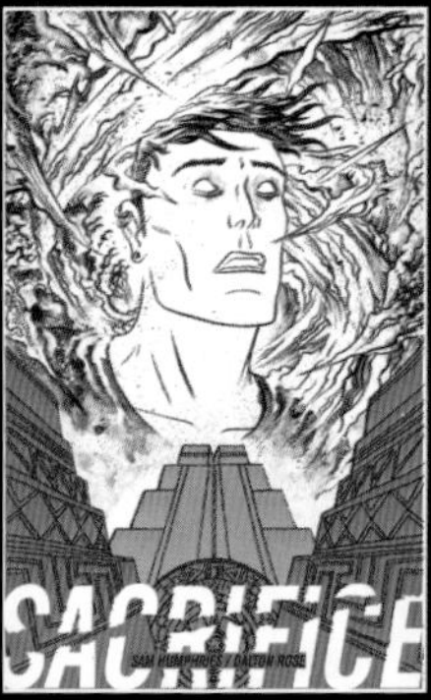
SACRIFICE
SAM HUMPHRIES / DALTON ROSE

SACRIFICE

Sam Humphries, Dalton Rose, Bryan Lee O'Malley, and others

What happens when a troubled youth is plucked from modern society and sent on a psychedelic journey into the heart of the Aztec civilization—one of the greatest and most bloodthirsty times in human history?

ISBN 978-1-59582-985-6 | $19.99

DE:TALES

Fábio Moon and Gabriel Bá

Brimming with all the details of human life, Moon and Bá's charming stories move from the urban reality of their home in São Paulo to the magical realism of their Latin American background. Named by *Booklist* as one of the 10 Best Graphic Novels of 2010.

ISBN 978-1-59582-557-5 | $19.99

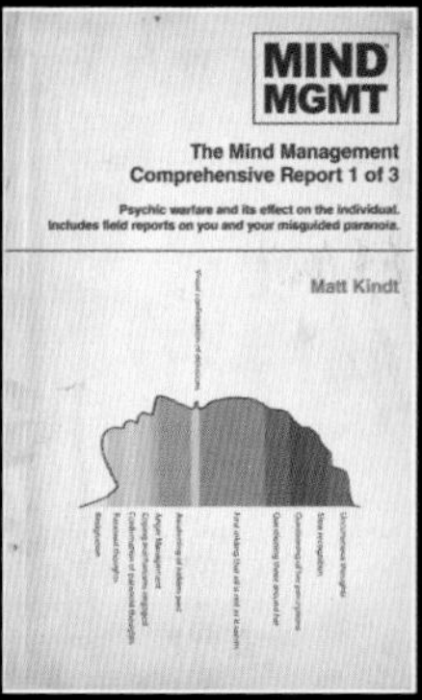
MIND MGMT
The Mind Management
Comprehensive Report 1 of 3
Psychic warfare and its effect on the individual.
Includes field reports on you and your misguided paranoia.
Matt Kindt

MIND MGMT OMNIBUS

Matt Kindt

This globe-spanning tale of espionage explores the adventures of a journalist investigating the mystery of a commercial flight where everyone aboard loses their memories. Each omnibus volume collects two volumes of the Eisner Award–winning series!

VOLUME 1: THE MANAGER AND THE FUTURIST
ISBN 978-1-50670-460-9 | $24.99

VOLUME 2: THE HOME MAKER AND THE MAGICIAN
ISBN 978-1-50670-461-6 | $24.99

VOLUME 3: THE ERASER AND THE IMMORTALS
ISBN 978-1-50670-462-3 | $24.99